Communist Political Systems

Communist Political Systems
An Introduction

Second Edition

Stephen White
University of Glasgow

John Gardner
University of Manchester

George Schöpflin
London School of Economics and Political Science

St. Martin's Press   New York

First published in the United States of America in 1987

Printed in Hong Kong

ISBN 0–312–00722–1
ISBN 0–0312–00723–X (pbk.)

Library of Congress Cataloging-in-Publication Data
White, Stephen, 1945–
Communist political systems.
Bibliography: p.
Includes index.
1. Communist state. 2. Communist countries—
Politics and government. I. Gardner, John, 1939–
II. Schöpflin, George. III. Title.
JC474.W48 1987 321.9′2 87–4262
ISBN 0–312–00722–1
ISBN 0–312–00723–X (pbk.)

Contents

List of Tables and Figures

Tables

Figures

Preface to the Second Edition

Communist states account for about a third of the world's population, for up to 40 per cent of its industrial production, and for a large proportion of its military might. Above all, from the point of view of the political scientist, they represent one of the world's most important and distinctive types of political system, one that is not only different from but profoundly antagonistic towards the liberal-democratic systems of the capitalist West. In the second edition of this book, as in its predecessor, we have sought to provide a reliable and up-to-date introduction to political systems of this type, combining both a reasonably full account of their institutional features with, we hope, some indication of the problems of analysis and interpretation that arise in this connection. We begin with a discussion of the development of the communist states and of some of the major 'models' that have been applied to them by political scientists. We then move on to consider the distinctive political cultures of these states, their governmental structures, and the organisation and roles of their ruling communist parties. Further chapters deal with the policy process in these states and with the question of democracy and human rights, and a final chapter considers the performance of the communist states in a number of respects with that of some of the major states of the non-communist world. Each chapter concludes with a list of items of recommended further reading, full details of which are given in the bibliography at the end of the book. This second edition, like the first, reflects the experience of teaching and lecturing on communist politics at Glasgow, Manchester, London and elsewhere over the past decade or so; we hope that future generations of students will gain as much from it as its authors have gained from the questions and comments of their predecessors over this period.

STEPHEN WHITE
JOHN GARDNER
GEORGE SCHÖPFLIN

Abbreviations

ASSR	autonomous soviet socialist republic
CCP	Chinese Communist Party
CMEA/Comecon	Council for Mutual Economic Assistance
Cominform	Communist Information Bureau
Comintern	Communist Third International
CPSU	Communist Party of the Soviet Union
GDR	German Democratic Republic
GNP	gross national product
LCY	League of Communists in Yugoslavia
NEM	New Economic Mechanism (Hungary)
NEP	New Economic Policy (USSR)
NKVD	People's Commissariat of Internal Affairs (security police in USSR, later KGB)
NPC	National People's Congress (China)
OECD	Organisation for Economic Co-operation and Development
PLA	People's Liberation Army (China)
PPF	People's Patriotic Front (Hungary)
PRC	People's Republic of China
RSFSR	Russian Republic
USSR	Union of Soviet Socialist Republics
WTO	Warsaw Treaty Organisation

Abbreviations

1

The Comparative Study of Communist States

Communist states are a relatively recent phenomenon. When the First World War broke out in 1914 there were none at all; for many years after the Russian Revolution of 1917 there were only three, the USSR itself and two Asian outposts, Mongolia and Tuva; and as late as the end of the Second World War there were only five such states, located for the most part in Eastern Europe (Albania and Yugoslavia as well as the USSR) as well as in Asia (North Vietnam and Mongolia, Tuva having in the meantime been absorbed by the USSR). Since then communist regimes have come into existence elsewhere in Eastern Europe (Bulgaria, Romania, Poland, Czechoslovakia, Hungary and the German Democratic Republic), in Latin America (Cuba), and also in Asia (China, North Korea and most recently Laos and Kampuchea). As a result of these changes there were sixteen states which, in the late 1980s, could reasonably be classified as communist (Table 1.1). In addition a number of other states, particularly in the developing countries, have adopted some of the institutional features of the communist states such as a single ruling party or a centrally planned economy, and communist or workers' parties have come into existence in virtually every country of the world, some of them claiming independence of any of the existing ruling parties but all of them accepting the authority of Marxism–Leninism. The ruling and non-ruling parties make up what is known as the

TABLE 1.1

The communist states in the late 1980s

Name of state	Date established	Area (thousands of sq. kilometres)	Population mid-1986 (millions)	Level of development
Union of Soviet Socialist Republics	1917	22 402	280.1	(Non-market economy)
Mongolian People's Republic	1924	1 565	1.9	Lower middle-income
People's Republic of Albania	1944	29	2.9	(Non-market economy)
Socialist Federal Republic of Yugoslavia	1945	256	23.0	Upper middle-income
Socialist Republic of Vietnam	1945/76	330	60.1	Low income
People's Republic of Bulgaria	1946	111	9.0	(Non-market economy)
Socialist Republic of Romania	1947	238	22.7	(Non-market economy)
Polish People's Republic	1947	313	36.9	(Non-market economy)
Democratic People's Republic of Korea	1948	121	19.9	Lower middle-income
Czechoslovak Socialist Republic	1948	128	15.5	(Non-market economy)
Hungarian People's Republic	1949	93	10.7	(Non-market economy)
German Democratic Republic	1949	108	16.7	(Non-market economy)
People's Republic of China	1949	9 561	1 109.1	Low income
Republic of Cuba	1959	115	9.9	Lower middle-income
People's Democratic Republic of Laos	1975	237	3.7	Low income
People's Republic of Kampuchea	1975	181	6.9	Low income

Source: Based upon the World Bank, *World Development Report 1986* (New York, 1986).

world communist movement; the sixteen communist states together constitute what is officially described as the world socialist system.

Communist states are thus a small minority of the 150 or so states that are members of the United Nations. Their importance, however, is much greater than these limited numbers might suggest. The communist states, for instance, account for about a third of the world's population, and for more than 40 per cent of the world's industrial production. The communist states include the world's largest state, the USSR; the world's most populous state, China; one of the world's two main trading blocs, the Council for Mutual Economic Assistance or Comecon; and one of the world's two major military alliances, the Warsaw Treaty Organisation. Above all, from the point of view of the political scientist, the communist states collectively constitute one of the world's two major models or types of political system, one which is not simply different from but fundamentally opposed to the Western liberal-democratic or capitalist type of system. To official spokesmen in the communist countries the difference is that between the 'socialist democracy' of the East, representing the interests of the vast majority of the working people, and the 'bourgeois democracy' of the capitalist West, representing the interests of a small minority of exploiters. In the Western countries, on the other hand, the difference is seen as one between the 'democracy' of the West, based upon the freely expressed will of the people, and the 'dictatorship' or 'totalitarianism' of the communist East, based upon the power of a self-appointed minority of party functionaries. In both cases, however, the difference is seen as the most fundamental of all those that presently exist in world politics, and the onset of a period of 'detente' between the two sides in place of 'cold war' has not meant that these differences have become less important; it has simply meant that they should so far as possible be resolved by peaceful rather than by military means.

Most political scientists would consider four main differences between communist and Western liberal–democratic states to be of particular importance, and together these features may be regarded as the defining characteristics of a communist state. In the first place, all the communist states in existence at present base themselves upon an official ideology, Marxism–Leninism, which is derived from the theories of Marx, Engels, Lenin and (in China) Mao Zedong, and which provides the vocabulary of politics in these states as well as the basis upon which their rulers claim to exercise authority. (This is not, of course, to say that all the rulers and populations of the communist states are necessarily wholly committed to Marxist values, which is a separate and empirical question.) The economy in the communist states, secondly, is largely or almost entirely in public rather than in private ownership, and production is typically organised through a central planning apparatus and conducted by means of national economic plans. The communist states, in other words, have what are normally referred to as 'command' or 'administered economies', rather than the 'market economies' of the capitalist West.

The third distinguishing feature of the communist states is that they are ruled, in all but exceptional circumstances, by a single or at least a dominant communist party, within which power is typically highly centralised. This is ensured by the application of the principle of 'democratic centralism', by which each level in the hierarchy must submit to the decisions of the level immediately above it, and by the 'ban on factions', which forbids any attempt to organise an opposition within these parties (this does not, of course, mean that there are no differences of opinion or even informal groupings within them). And finally, the range of institutions which in Western societies are more or less independent of the political authorities, such as the press, the trade unions and the courts, are in the communist states effectively under the direct control of the party hierarchy. This wide-ranging control over virtually all areas of society is known as the party's 'leading role', and for the communist authorities themselves it is of particular importance; it was, for instance, to recover this 'leading role' for the communist party in Czechoslovakia that the Warsaw Pact powers justified their intervention in that country in 1968.

These features of the political system are all important, and they all apply, at least in principle, to all of the communist states that we shall be considering in this volume. It does not follow, however, that the differences between one communist state and another are thereby reduced to insignificance. On the contrary it has become apparent, particularly over the last decade or two, that the label 'communism' may conceal almost as much as it may reveal, and that there is a greater degree of variety between the communist states in terms of their political processes – influenced as these are by the different histories, cultures and social structures of these countries – than their common institutional framework might at first suggest. Indeed even here the differences between one communist state and another are by no means negligible. In most communist states, for instance, virtually all productive resources are in the hands of the state, but in others, such as Poland, most agricultural land has been left in private ownership, and in some, such as China, there are even a few remaining private capitalists. In most of the communist states, similarly, a single communist party holds power, while in others, such as Poland, Bulgaria, the GDR and North Korea, a variety of nominally independent parties are permitted to exist (though not to challenge the communist party for power). There are also important social and cultural differences between one communist state and another. Some of the communist states, for instance Poland and Cuba, are traditionally Roman Catholic, while others are Eastern Orthodox or Buddhist, and one (Albania) is officially atheist. And there are wide disparities between them in terms of their levels of economic and social development.

Indeed so considerable are the differences between one communist state and another and so great are the similarities between them and some other countries, particularly in the developing world, that some have gone so far as to suggest that the notion of a communist political system is nowadays of little analytical utility. One of the most influential statements of this view is that of John H. Kautsky. The communist states, Kautsky has argued in an article provocatively entitled 'Comparative communism versus comparative politics' (1973), do not have in fact any particular distinguishing characteristics apart from the symbols they employ, and most of the features supposedly distinctive to these systems can in fact be found elsewhere. Like a number of other political scientists Kautsky prefers to emphasise the distinction between developing or 'mobilised' regimes, some of which are communist, on the one hand, and developed or 'adaptation' regimes on the other, a category which includes the economically more developed communist states as well as the Western liberal democracies. This general thesis will be considered more fully later in this chapter in connection with the modernisation or developmental model of communist politics with which it is associated. It may be sufficient at this point to note that most political scientists have continued to argue that communist political systems do in fact have a number of distinguishing features, such as their official ideology, their largely nationalised economies and the leading role that is played within them by their single or dominant ruling parties, and that these features mark out a group of states which it is reasonable to consider as a group and instructive to compare with one another. This, however, in no way precludes their comparison with political systems in other countries, either in the developing or in the developed world, a number of which share some (though not all) of these distinguishing features. Comparative communist politics should be seen as a sub-field within comparative politics, not, as Kautsky appears to imply, as a substitute for it.

The development of the communist state system

The Russian revolution of November 1917 was carried through on the assumption that Russia, though a backward country and not itself 'ready' for a revolution in the Marxist sense, could be used to break the economic links that held together the major capitalist powers and thus to bring about a European and eventually a world-wide communist revolution. At the time these perspectives did not look entirely unrealistic. Immediately after the First World War ended, in 1918–19, there were revolutionary uprisings in many parts of the world, and in Europe Soviet republics were established in Bavaria and Hungary. In 1920 factories were occupied in Italy, and Councils of Action were set up in Great Britain to oppose government policy towards Russia. The following year there was a communist-led rising in central Germany, and in 1923 there were more serious attempts at insurrection in northern Germany and in Bulgaria. In 1926 there was a general strike in Britain, and by about the same date a powerful communist presence had begun to establish itself in China and elsewhere in the colonial world. Soviet influence over this developing movement was exercised through the Communist International, founded in 1919, which was based in Moscow and whose executive committee was largely dominated by Russians. The Comintern, as it was known, saw its task as the provision of revolutionary leadership for the workers and peasants of the developed and colonial countries; these were only held back from more decisive action, it was believed, by the caution and indecision of their reformist leaders.

The Soviet republics in Bavaria and Hungary, however, soon collapsed, the risings in Germany and Bulgaria were ignominiously defeated, and the later 1920s saw authoritarian governments come into power throughout much of Europe which began to repress their domestic communist and trade union movements with a good deal of energy and efficiency. In China, in 1927, what had been the most promising colonial revolutionary movement was bloodily repressed by Chiang Kai-shek, and elsewhere in the colonial world communist parties were enjoying little success. The USSR, as a result, was left almost entirely isolated as the world's first communist state for most of the period up to the Second World War, participating in international conferences and attempting to win popular support in the West while at the same time developing its military and industrial strength and wondering how long it could safely survive in the 'capitalist encirclement' in which it found itself. The only important respect in which Soviet isolation became less during this period was with the establishment of People's Republics in the small Siberian region of Tannu Tuva in 1921 (absorbed into the USSR as an autonomous province in 1944) and in Mongolia in 1924, after Chinese occupying forces had been defeated with substantial Soviet assistance. In all essentials, however, the USSR remained an isolated outpost of communism in international politics, an isolation whose dangers became readily more apparent as the Western powers continued to fail to offer serious resistance to the rise of Hitler, above all at Munich in 1938. A Nazi–Soviet non-aggression pact was signed in 1939, but in 1941 Hitler abruptly broke it off and invaded the western USSR. In the four years that followed the USSR lost over 20 million dead and suffered material damage on an unimaginable scale. There must have seemed every reason, as the end of the war approached, for Soviet negotiators to try to strengthen the security of their frontiers, above all in the west, and to try in this connection so far as possible to retain control over the parts of Eastern and Central Europe that they had liberated from the Nazis.

At the Moscow, Yalta and Potsdam conferences of 1944 and 1945 these objectives were substantially achieved, in large part with the acceptance of the USSR's Western allies, and the establishment of a system of communist states in Eastern Europe under Soviet control is essentially a product of the division of Europe into rival spheres of influence which was the outcome of these agreements. In some cases there was little domestic support for communist policies and the new government was effectively installed by the Red Army (the German Democratic Republic, North Korea, Poland and Romania). In Bulgaria, similarly, the communist party had previously enjoyed a considerable degree of popular support, but the country had supported the Axis Powers during the Second World War and it was occupied by the Red Army in 1944, with whose assistance a communist government came into being a few years later. In Czechoslovakia and Hungary, on the other hand, the communist party did enjoy a substantial degree of popular support and the Red Army, despite occasional excesses, was seen by many as the agency by which these countries had been liberated from the Nazis. In Czechoslovakia the communist party in fact secured 38 per cent of the vote, the largest for any party, in the relatively free elections of 1946, while in Hungary the communists became the largest single party after the rather less freely held elections of 1947. In both cases coalition governments were established within which communists swiftly assumed a dominant position.

In Yugoslavia, Albania, North Vietnam and China a

rather different path was followed. The communist party in these countries rose to power through its leadership of a popular resistance movement against either Axis or (in the case of North Vietnam and China) Japanese occupation, and had little or no Soviet assistance in doing so. This tended to give these regimes a greater degree of at least initial popular support than the other communist regimes possessed, and it may have encouraged them to take a more independent attitude towards Moscow than the communist governments that were simply imported (as the phrase had it) 'in the baggage train of the Red Army'. In the case of China, and to some extent elsewhere, there was even some doubt about whether the local communists had the backing of the Soviet government in attempting to proceed directly to the establishment of a communist state. Soviet representatives urged a truce with the Chinese Nationalists (the Kuomintang) until the last possible moment, and the Soviet ambassador was reportedly the last to leave the Nationalist government immediately before its downfall. The USSR none the less recognised the Chinese People's Republic on 2 October 1949, the day after its foundation, and in February 1950 the two countries concluded a friendship treaty with a thirty-year period of validity.

The next extension of communist rule was in Cuba, where Fidel Castro assumed power in 1959 with the overthrow of the Batista dictatorship. His programme was initially of a broadly democratic character, but in 1961 he publicly declared his allegiance to Marxism–Leninism, and the country moved subsequently into an increasingly close association with the other communist states. Finally in 1975, following the conclusion of the Vietnam war, North and South Vietnam were merged into a single state with the name of the Socialist Republic of Vietnam (its constitution was formally approved after nation-wide elections had taken place the following year); a People's Democratic Republic was established in Laos following the abdication of King Sayang Vatthana and the abolition of the monarchy; and in Cambodia (subsequently known as Kampuchea) the Khmer Rouge defeated the pro-Western regime of Lon Nol and adopted a new constitution of an essentially communist type. The Khmer

Rouge were in turn ousted by a government sympathetic to the Vietnamese military forces which invaded the country at the end of 1978, but this new regime, headed by the People's Revolutionary Party of Kampuchea, has still to win a wide degree of international recognition and is not yet in undisputed control of the entire national territory.

Relations between the communist states have been by no means as stable as a common dedication to working-class interests might ordinarily have suggested. The first split occurred as early as 1948 when Yugoslavia was denounced by the Soviet Union and by Cominform (the Communist Information Bureau, established in 1947) for supposedly giving too much favour to the peasants at the expense of the workers and for exercising the leadership of the communist party (the Yugoslav League of Communists) in an insufficiently decisive manner. In fact there appears no doubt that Stalin simply resented the independence that the Yugoslav leaders were displaying and believed that they could be brought to heel as national communist leaders had been elsewhere in Eastern Europe. If so, he miscalculated badly; the Yugoslavs arrested Soviet supporters within the Yugoslav League of Communists, placed Soviet representatives in Yugoslavia under the surveillance of the secret police and weathered the storm with a largely united people behind them, not least by emphasising the threat to the country from abroad. In 1955 Khrushchev and Bulganin visited Belgrade, and in 1956 a joint Soviet–Yugoslav communiqué was signed in Moscow which effectively brought the dispute to an end. In the same year there were serious disturbances in Poland, where the workers of Poznań revolted and popular pressures led to the election of a new party leadership headed by Władysław Gomułka, and in Hungary, where a more far-reaching experiment in 'liberal communism' was terminated by the intervention of the Red Army. Some years later, in 1968, an attempt to introduce what was described as 'socialism with a human face' in Czechoslovakia under Alexander Dubček was brought to an end by the intervention of five Warsaw Pact powers led by the USSR.

Relations between the Soviet Union and China, meanwhile, were steadily deteriorating. The Chinese leaders appear to have been dissatisfied with a number of aspects of the Sino–Soviet friendship treaty of 1950, and at the 20th Congress of the Communist Party of the Soviet Union (CPSU) in 1956 they were reportedly unhappy about the manner in which the Stalin question had been handled. The Chinese, as late as 1957, still accepted Soviet leadership of the world communist movement (China, Mao conceded, could not be such a leader because it had 'not even a quarter of a sputnik, whereas the Soviet Union has two'). Soviet support for the Chinese atomic programme, however, was withdrawn in 1958, the USSR was neutral during the Sino–Indian war of 1959, and in 1960 the dispute between the USSR and China came into the open. Khrushchev, speaking at the Romanian Communist Party congress in June of that year, attacked the Chinese leadership by name. All Soviet technicians were withdrawn; trade between the two countries dropped off sharply; and a series of hostile open letters were exchanged, the Chinese accusing the Russians of 'revisionism' (or lack of commitment to Marxist principles) while the Russians accused the Chinese of 'dogmatism' and 'splittism' (or of attempting to break up the world communist movement). In 1966 both sides recalled their ambassadors and in 1969 matters reached the point of military hostilities along the Soviet–Chinese border in Siberia. Since then relations have improved somewhat: negotiations upon matters in dispute were opened in 1969; in 1970 the ambassadors returned to their posts; and trade has increased substantially. But the two countries are separated by traditional rivalries extending over several centuries, by differing interpretations of Marxism, by disputed boundaries and by divergent interests in their deal- ings with other states, and it is unlikely that their previous unity will be restored. Indeed it is perhaps surprising that it lasted as long as it did.

The main institutions through which Soviet control is maintained over the other countries of the bloc are the Council for Mutual Economic Assistance (CMEA or Com- econ) a multilateral economic and trading association, and the Warsaw Treaty Organisation, a military pact. Comecon, the first of these, was set up in 1949 by the Soviet Union and the East European states largely as a response to the establishment of the Organisation for Economic Co-operation and Development (OECD) by the major Western countries in 1948. Its membership in 1987 included Cuba, Mongolia and Vietnam as well as Bulgaria, Hungary, the GDR, Poland, Romania, Czechoslovakia, and the USSR. Yugoslavia, though not a member, takes part in the work of Comecon in matters of mutual interest, and North Korea, Laos, Ethiopia and Angola are represented on a number of its institutions. Albania ceased to be a member in 1961. Comecon is regulated by a statute which came into force in 1960, by an agreement on the 'basic principles of the international socialist division of labour' of 1962, and by a 'complex programme for the further deepening and improvement of the co-operation and development of the socialist economic integration of the member countries of Comecon', signed in 1971, whose ulti-mate objective is the complete economic integration of the economies of member countries. The indications are that this programme of integration is regarded with more enthusiasm in Moscow, where Comecon's central institutions are located, than in the countries of Eastern Europe, whose economies are often more advanced than that of the Soviet Union and which have traditionally enjoyed close trading links with the West. This notwithstanding, the economic plans of Com-econ's member countries all make specific provision for the furthering of these programmes, and the existence of Com-econ serves to bind the economics of its member countries more closely together than would otherwise be the case.

The military side of the alliance is the Warsaw Treaty Organisation, founded in 1955 by a treaty between the governments of Bulgaria, Hungary, the GDR, Poland, Romania, the USSR, Czechoslovakia and Albania (which took part in the organisation after 1962 and formally announced its withdrawal in 1968). The main policy-making body of the Warsaw Treaty Organisation is its Political Consultative Committee, composed of the party leaders and principal government ministers of member countries, but a number of other institutions work within its framework, such as a Committee of Defence Ministers (established in 1969), a Committee of Foreign Ministers (established in 1976) and a Joint Secretariat (established in 1956 and reorganised in

1976). There is also a Joint High Command, invariably headed by a senior member of the Soviet armed forces, which is responsible for the direction of operational military matters. Efforts have been made in recent years to increase the level of activities and the integration of member countries, though this has not prevented the Romanian government, since about 1964, from playing a somewhat independent role (Romanian forces, for instance, did not take part in the intervention of Czechoslovakia in 1968, and no Soviet forces are presently stationed in that country). The Treaty provides for consultation and mutual assistance in the event of an armed attack upon any of its members; most of the states concerned have also concluded bilateral defence treaties with other members of the pact.

Soviet efforts to retain control over the world communist movement have been less successful, if only because most of the communist parties concerned are in countries militarily beyond their reach. Since the dissolution of the Communist International in 1943 and of Cominform in 1956 the main organised form the movement has assumed has been international conferences of communist and workers' parties, three of which have so far been held in 1957, 1960 and 1969. One indication of the declining measure of Soviet control is the fact that at the last of these conferences in 1969 several ruling parties (the Yugoslav, Albanian, Chinese, Vietnamese and North Korean) did not attend; and of the 75 parties that were present only 61 could be persuaded to sign the final communiqué without conditions (five refused to do so altogether), although it made no reference to Soviet leadership of the movement and contained no specific criticism of the Chinese. Since then there have been a number of regional gatherings of communist parties, such as the meeting of Latin American communist parties in Havana in 1975 and of European communist parties in East Berlin in 1976; but many parties have refused to attend these meetings, basically because they refuse to accept even the appearance of external intervention in their domestic policy-making. A number of parties, the so-called 'Eurocommunist' parties, have gone further; they have repudiated many accepted communist doctrines, such as the dictatorship of the proletariat and the need for a single-party system, and have freely criticised what they regard as undemocratic features of the political systems of the communist countries. Although some parties have been persuaded to reconsider their views in recent years a number of others, such as the Spanish and Italian parties, have persisted in their criticisms, and there is some evidence that their arguments have not been without influence upon dissident opinion in Eastern Europe as well as within their own countries.

Models of communist politics

There has been no shortage of models or interpretations seeking to categorise the communist states in a single all-inclusive phrase or label. If the study of comparative communist politics has taught us anything over the years, it is perhaps that the search for labels of this kind is likely to be a vain one and that there is no single model or theory which can adequately accommodate all important aspects of a changing and often contradictory social reality. But an imperfect guide is better than no guide at all, and if we are to make sense of a political system there is really no alternative to making some attempt to identify its most distinctive features and to classify it on that basis. Provided it is understood that models and interpretations of this kind are neither 'right' nor 'wrong', but simply more or less helpful or illuminating in highlighting key features of a political system while necessarily neglecting others, there is no reason why we should not employ them. At least four approaches to the study of communist political systems have enjoyed a particular degree of popularity over the years (a number of others, such as the political culture and group politics approaches, will be considered in subsequent chapters).

The first, the *totalitarian model*, came into widespread use at the time of the cold war, when it was customary to make an extremely sharp distinction between the virtues of democracy, exemplified by the countries of Western Europe and North America, and the evils of communism, which was equated with the tyranny and dictatorship of Eastern Europe. The key feature of the communist systems to which the totalitarian model drew attention was the broad extent of state power, in contrast to the liberal–democratic states of the West in which the power of the state was limited and the rights and liberties of the individual were carefully protected. The leading version of the totalitarian model was put forward by Carl Friedrich and Zbigniew Brzezinski in the mid-1950s. It consisted of six essential traits or features: an official ideology, binding upon all members of the society; a single mass party typically led by one man; a system of terroristic police control; a near-monopoly of control by the state of all means of mass communications; a near-monopoly by the state of all means of effective armed combat; and central control and direction of the entire economy. Some years later Friedrich added two more features to this list: territorial expansion and administrative control of the courts. These features were held to characterise not only all existing communist systems but also the political systems of Nazi Germany and Fascist Italy, and for many years this model was widely accepted as perhaps the single most useful categorisation of the communist states, particularly by those who were impressed by their more illiberal or authoritarian features.

The totalitarian model has subsequently come under criticism for at least two kinds of shortcomings. It has been argued, in the first place, that many of Friedrich and Brzezinski's six or eight points apply not only to the communist states but to many others as well, particularly in the developing countries (whose numbers have of course increased considerably since Friedrich and Brzezinski first put forward their theory). Central control and direction of the economy, for instance, is a common feature of many third world states, few of which could readily be classified as totalitarian, and so also is a single-party system, although this does not necessarily mean that no legal opposition is permitted. A near monopoly of the means of effective armed combat in the hands of the state is indeed a characteristic of virtually all modern states. Conversely, many of Friedrich and Brzezinski's list of characteristics can hardly be said any longer to apply to the communist states, not, at least, without a great deal of qualification. A system of terroristic police control, for instance, typically directed 'not only against demonstrable "enemies" of the regime, but against more or less arbitrarily selected classes of the population', has not been a normal feature of political life in the major communist states since at least the early 1950s. The role of the official ideology has arguably become less restrictive, and the parties tend now to be ruled by groups of oligarchs rather than the 'dictators' specified in Friedrich and Brzezinski's definition. Some have suggested, in the light of these criticisms, that totalitarianism should no longer be regarded as a model but as an ideal type, that is to say a system logically conceivable in theory but most unlikely to be encountered in real life; others have suggested more limited modifications to the model, such as re-designating it 'partialitarianism' or 'totalitarianism without terror'. Few, however, now find the totalitarian model in its original form a useful framework for analysing the communist systems, though some communist states (as well as others) may exemplify a number of its features at different times.

A further and more general objection has been made to the totalitarian model, that it is 'static' or in other words that it fails to allow sufficiently for the possibility of political development and change beyond a somewhat nebulously conceptualised process of 'maturing'. This shortcoming has been regarded as particularly important by those who have been attempting in more recent years to develop an alternative model of the political system, one that emphasises the impact of socio-economic change upon the polity both in the communist states and elsewhere. What may be called the *modernisation or developmental model* has been the result of such activities, though its roots go back to the evolutionary theories that were popular in the nineteenth century and earlier which assumed a single and beneficent line of development from backward and agrarian societies to the more 'modern' and 'rational' societies of the developed West. Modernisation theories assume, broadly speaking, that there is a link between socio-economic change and the political system; that a high level of socio-economic development and a competitive or 'polyarchical' political system are significantly associated; and that the higher the level of socio-economic development the higher the level of competition or polyarchy within the political system, in the communist states or elsewhere. The greater the degree of social and economic development, it is argued, the more complex are the decisions that have to be taken by government, the wider is the range of specialist expertise that has to be taken into account, the greater is the amount of decision-making that has to be devolved from the centre, and the less appropriate become the instruments of coercion and command that may have been effective at an earlier stage of social development. The mass population, at the same time, becomes more urbanised and educated, increasingly sceptical of official dogmas, and increasingly able to protect their interests through professional groups and associations. The logic of economic and social development thus leads, as Alexander Eckstein has put it, to the 'modification, and ultimately the transformation, of the communist systems and their political superstructures'.

Most writers in the political modernisation school point out that there need be no one-to-one correspondence between socio-economic change and the political system: external influences, cultural traditions and so forth will intervene and thus modify the impact of one upon the other. But there is a wide measure of agreement that in the long run communist states must acquire the competitive, pluralistic political system that corresponds to their relatively high level of social and economic development. Roy Medvedev, for instance, has described the democratisation of political life in the USSR as an 'inevitable tendency' that follows from the social and economic changes the USSR has been experiencing; Ghiţa Ionescu has written of 'pluralisation and institutionalisation' as an 'inevitable trend' that 'accompanies the process of economic, social and political development'; and Karl Deutsch has identified an 'automatic trend towards pluralisation and disintegration'. The American political scientist Gabriel Almond, in perhaps the most far-reaching of these prognostications, has spoken of the 'pluralistic pressures of a modern economy and society' and a 'secular trend in the direction of decentralisation and pluralism'. As their societies and economies evolve, Almond has written, communist political systems will face the 'inevitable demands of a healthy,

educated, affluent society' for both more material goods and
what Almond calls 'spiritual consumer goods', such as opportunities for participation and a share in the decision-making
process. Already, Almond has written, 'Russian success in
science, education, technology, economic productivity and
national security has produced some decentralisation of the
political process. I fail to see how these decentralising, pluralistic tendencies can be reversed, or how their spread can be
prevented.'

Empirical inquiries have in fact found little evidence to
support these deterministic assumptions. A study by Nelson
(1977), for instance, examined the relationship between social
and economic development (defined in terms of energy consumption per capita, changes in infant mortality and so forth)
and political change in nine European countries over a period
of more than twenty years (1949–72). None of the political
variables considered – the educational level of the leadership,
the proportion of party members drawn from the intelligentsia, instability or executive change – showed a strong positive
correlation with either the level of socio-economic development or the rate of social and economic change; in some cases,
indeed, there was a moderately strong negative correlation.
Overall 'no strong support was found for the hypothesis that
relationships exist between political variables and socio-
economic levels and/or rates of socio-economic change in
communist states'. Another study (White, 1978a) found that
there was no increase in political pluralism, measured in terms
of participation in sessions of the national legislature and of
the party central committee, in the USSR over the post-Stalin
period (1954–75), despite the major social and economic
changes that had occurred over the same period. In most
respects, indeed, the relationship was if anything the reverse
of that which had been postulated. Empirical tests such as
these are obviously open to criticism in terms of the indicators
that have been selected for consideration; but no studies have
so far satisfactorily demonstrated a strong positive relationship between socio-economic change and political liberalisation in the communist states, nor, considering the trend of
policy in the communist states in recent years in such matters
as economic reform and the treatment of political dissidents,

would such a relationship seem very plausible even if it had been discovered.

Indeed, though clearly some kinds of connection between socio-economic change and the political system cannot be excluded (there may, for instance, be a link between the increased education of the Polish working class and the development of an independent trade union movement in that country in the 1980s), there are theoretical as well as empirical grounds for doubting that the relationship must necessarily be as the writers in the political modernisation school have generally presented it. A number of the more developed communist states, for instance, have relatively high levels of social and economic development but low levels of political pluralism; while there are other states, such as the United States in the nineteenth century and India in the twentieth, which have successfully combined a liberal–democratic political system with relatively low levels of urbanisation, industrialisation and per capita national income. In these and some other cases it may in fact be possible to argue that a causal link exists but that it operates in the reverse direction, from competitive politics to social and economic development and not vice versa. Even where political liberalisation and socio-economic development have occurred together, moreover, it does not necessarily follow that they are causally related. A greater degree of political pluralism may be the result of the imitation or implantation of the political systems of other countries – the USSR, for instance, has arguably been influenced by some of the more pluralist practices of its Eastern European neighbours – or it may derive at least in part from the cultural and political traditions of the country concerned before it came under communist rule, as for instance in Poland and Czechoslovakia. Theorists of political modernisation generally overlook the fact that it is ultimately people who must bring about the political changes they regard as inevitable, and that people may be influenced by perceptions, aspirations and levels of political knowledge which may bear very little relation to the level of social and economic development of the state in which they find themselves.

The shortcomings of modernisation theory have led during

the last decade or so to a renewed interest in what may be called the *'bureaucratic politics' model*. Those who adopt this approach focus upon three key features of politics in the communist states: first, the dominant position within them of the communist party, and within the party of its top leadership; secondly, the absence of competitive elections or of other effective instruments of democratic control, leaving the party, in effect, in a position of permanent government; and thirdly, the wide scope of the powers that are exercised by the communist parties in these states, as a sort of 'super bureaucracy' superior to and intertwined with the government and social institutions such as the trade unions, the press, industry and the courts. Unlike the theorists of totalitarianism, who also emphasise these points, writers in the bureaucratic politics school do not argue that this means there can be virtually no politics, or competition for influence, within these states (they also place less emphasis upon the role of ideology and coercion). Politics, however, takes place not between the communist party and other contenders for power, as in a Western pluralist system, but within the party and the other bureaucratic organisations that collectively administer the state. The system is conceived as a 'mono-hierarchical' or 'mono-organisational' one, with the top political leadership standing in relation to other parts of the political system much as the board of directors of a large Western corporation stand in relation to their administrative subordinates, and politics takes the form that the struggle for resources and influence typically assumes in a large bureaucratic organisation of this kind.

Perhaps the best-known exponent of this approach is Alfred Meyer. Meyer's views were first set out in an article entitled 'USSR, Incorporated', published in 1961, and were then elaborated in a volume entitled *The Soviet Political System: An Interpretation*, which was published in 1965. Meyer summed up his thesis as follows:

> The USSR is best understood as a large, complex bureaucracy comparable in its structure and functioning to giant corporations, armies, government agencies, and similar institutions – some people might wish to add various churches

– of the West. It shares with such bureaucracies many principles of organisation and patterns of management. It is similar to them also in its typical successes and inefficiencies, in the gratifications and frustrations it offers its constituents, in its socialisation and recruitment policies, communications problems, and many other features. The Soviet Union shares with giant corporations everywhere the urge to organise all human activities rationally, from professional life to consumption patterns and leisure activities. It has in common with them a thoroughly authoritarian political structure, in which the élite is independent of control by the lower-ranking member of the organisation, even though all or most giant bureaucracies in the modern world insist that their rank-and-file constituents participate in the organisation's public life.

Like modern bureaucracy, Meyer suggested, communist rule was 'essentially an attempt to impose rational management over social life by means of complex organisations', and the Soviet Union, the largest such state, could 'best be understood as a giant bureaucracy, something like a modern corporation extended over the entire society'. The political system in the communist states was in effect 'bureaucracy writ large'.

Meyer himself devoted relatively little attention to the manner in which policies were formulated and implemented in political systems of this kind. Other writers, however, have identified some of the forms of what T. H. Rigby has called the 'crypto-politics' that are involved. Major institutional interests, for instance, bargain informally for scarce resources; local party officials and ministries press the claims of 'their' area or of 'their' industry in their dealings with the central political authorities; ministries attempt to become as large and as self-sufficient as possible ('empire-building' or 'narrow departmentalism'); and little attention is paid to external opinion on matters that impose no cost upon the organisation itself, such as traffic and environmental pollution. Writers such as Jerry Hough and Darrell Hammer have been so impressed by the autonomy in practice enjoyed by the major interests in communist societies that they have proposed terms such as 'bureaucratic' or 'institutional pluralism' to characterise their political systems as a whole. More recently, writers such as Valerie Bunce have pointed to the analogies between Soviet-type polities and 'corporatist' systems in other developed and developing countries, in which the central authorities enjoy a close and mutually advantageous relationship with the major functional interests that are represented within the society. Interests of this kind (such as business and labour) are typically granted an institutionalised role in central decision-making and a 'representational monopoly' in return for accepting some controls upon their selection of leaders and their articulation of demands.

Valuable though such perspectives are, it must be said that many studies have tended to assume too readily that bureaucratic behaviour in the West and in the communist states must necessarily be comparable, and relatively few studies have been able to demonstrate empirically the similarities in bureaucratic functioning and motivation in the East and West or that the heads of leading institutions do indeed represent and promote the interests of 'their' institutions against those of other bodies in the policy-making process. John Armstrong, for instance, in a comparative study of the sources of administration behaviour in the Soviet Union and the West, found many similarities: hierarchical command principles were frequently ignored, informal relationships were important, and motivation tended to be performance rather than ideologically oriented. There were more differences than similarities between the two systems, however, particularly where matters such as welfare, communications and career contacts were concerned. Dmitri K. Simes, who worked as a research associate at the Institute of the World Economy and International Relations of the USSR Academy of Sciences between 1967 and 1972 and in that capacity prepared a number of informational bulletins on foreign policy issues for the top political leaders, found similarly that 'in the Soviet political system, bureaucratic loyalties and . . . affiliations, as a rule, play only a marginal role'. The supreme loyalty of the Politburo members was to the Politburo itself, and members usually considered themselves Politburo representatives in their respective bureaucracies rather than representatives of these bureaucracies in the Politburo.

More generally, a closer examination of major institutional interests has found them by no means so united in defence of a supposed common interest as the bureaucratic politics approach assumes. Institutions like the military, for instance, contain rivalries between the various services, and personal links, such as those between the 'Stalingrad group' (who took part in the battle of Stalingrad in 1942), frequently cut across more functional or sectoral divisions. The party apparatus, similarly, contains internal differences based upon age, ethnic background and career patterns, and is not necessarily united behind a conservative political position, particularly when departures from official guidelines are necessary to improve the economic performance of the area or industry for which they are responsible. Writers, to take another example, are not necessarily united in favour of an extension of the boundaries of literary self-expression; many would not survive without them, particularly the less talented writers typically associated with the literary bureaucracies, and bodies such as these may often take a more conservative political position than the party authorities themselves.

Parallels in administrative behaviour, moreover, do not in themselves justify conceptualising the political system as a whole as a giant bureaucracy. This neglects, for instance, the distinctive role of the communist parties, particularly their monopoly over appointments to key positions in the hierarchies that are subordinate to them, and also the role of ideology. And even if the bureaucratic politics model is taken to represent a reasonable approximation of the political system as a whole, it may still be open to criticism in terms of its relative neglect of the sources of development and change within such systems. It has been the party bureaucracies, after all, that have initiated the rapid and often coercive transformation of their societies, scarcely the policy to expect from bodies that are supposed to respond passively to institutional pressures and to respect established legal and bureaucratic procedures. The bureaucratic politics model also makes little attempt to specify the various and perhaps conflicting social interests of the different groups with which it deals. Party and state officials, generals and trade union officials differ not simply in their bureaucratic roles that they perform; they differ also in their social backgrounds, status, earnings and relationships with their constituents, and their behaviour may often make little sense abstracted from a broader political sociology of Soviet-type systems and of the relationship between rulers and ruled in the society as a whole. A concern of this kind, to specify the social rather than bureaucratic origins of political development and change, has lain behind the renewed interest in *Marxist or critical Marxist approaches* to communist politics in recent years.

At least two major variants of a Marxist approach to communist politics may be identified. In the first place there is what may be called the official Marxist approach, that favoured by the regimes themselves, in terms of which the expropriation of the capitalist class in these countries has led to the inauguration of a period of socialist development which will lead ultimately to full communism. An approach of this kind is exemplified, for instance, in the revised Programme of the Communist Party of the Soviet Union which was adopted in 1986. The 1917 Russian revolution, according to the Programme, brought into being the first workers' and peasants' state and began a new era in world history, an era of the transition from capitalism to socialism and ultimately to full communism. A socialist society, such as that constructed in the USSR and the countries with which it is associated, is held to put an end forever to the exploitation of man by man based upon the private ownership of the means of production. It provides, rather, for the planned and dynamic growth of productive forces for the benefit of all citizens, for the widest possible access to social benefits and cultural resources, and for a genuine rather than spurious democracy based upon the broad and equal participation of all citizens in the management of public affairs. A society of this kind is expected to extend itself internationally as more and more peoples seek to take advantage of 'general laws of socialist development' such as the dominant role of the working class and its party, social ownership of the means of production in the interests of the people as a whole, socialist democracy and the friendship of all nations and nationalities on a basis of peace, equality and social progress.

An approach of this kind, its rhetoric apart, does at least

serve to identify some of the principal features of the communist systems presently in existence. Within such countries it is indeed the case that private ownership of the means of production has (with minor exceptions) been abolished. There is (again with minor exceptions) no unemployment, and the basic necessities of life such as transport and housing are available at very modest cost to all citizens. Educational and cultural resources are widely accessible, and ordinary working people are well represented in institutions of government at all levels. There is admittedly only one party, or at least one ruling party, but workers and peasants form a very large proportion (usually more than half) of its members, and for them it serves as an instrument of rule, a means of ensuring that the policies promoted by the state are those that they themselves favour. According to this view there can be no 'democracy' in the abstract but only 'bourgeois' or 'proletarian democracy', depending upon which class owns the productive wealth of the society and thereby holds political power. In capitalist societies, it is argued, a small minority of exploiters own this productive wealth and political power is exercised in their narrow class interests; in socialist societies, on the other hand, the means of production are nationalised and the policies followed are those that reflect the interests of the working people as a whole.

Official Marxist perspectives of this kind have not been very influential outside the communist countries themselves, and for good and obvious reasons. In the first place, while it is indeed true that productive wealth is owned by the population as a whole and that working people are well represented in party and state institutions, it has widely been noticed that ordinary workers and peasants become steadily less well represented the closer one comes to bodies of real executive or decision-making power. Among the parties' mass memberships and in local institutions of government, for instance, workers and peasants, as well as women, young people and members of minority nationalities, are indeed represented in proportions that correspond closely to their proportions in the population as a whole. In parliaments and central committees, however, their numbers drop sharply, and in governments and politburos the representation of these less favoured groups drops almost to zero. The communist countries, in other words, are 'workers' states' in a purely formal sense: ordinary working people are indeed well represented within the parties' mass memberships and in local institutions of government, but they do not predominate in higher-level bodies where national policies are actually formulated.

This would matter less if executive and decision-making bodies were genuinely and not just formally accountable to the institutions which elect them, and in which ordinary workers and peasants are typically well represented. A second major reservation about official Marxist theory, however, concerns the reality of 'socialist democracy' in the countries that claim to practise it. Despite recent reforms in some of these countries, for instance, elections do not provide for a genuine exercise of popular choice, and both party and state institutions are centrally dominated and based upon principles such as democratic centralism and the ban on factions which effectively insulate their leaderships from any challenge from below. Associational groups such as trade unions, sports clubs and women's organisations are permitted to come into legal existence only if they agree to support official policies, and their activities are closely regulated and their leading personnel selected by the party and state authorities. The central authorities also control the mass media through the censorship system and in other ways, and there are no independent courts which here as elsewhere might serve as an ultimate guarantee of individual liberties (all of these points are considered more fully in Chapter 6). An authoritarian system of this kind diverges not simply from the official communist self-image; it diverges also, in the view of many scholars, from the democratic traditions of the socialist movement and of classical Marxism itself.

A third objection to official Marxist theory is that it takes no serious account of the substantial material privileges, not simply political powers, which are in practice available to party, state and other officials. In communist countries, which are generally characterised by shortages of various kinds, administered benefits have a greater degree of importance than they would have elsewhere. The existence of such benefits, on a broad and sometimes extravagant scale, has by now been extensively documented in almost all of the countries concerned. Privileges of this kind typically embrace, for instance, an official car and more spacious housing. They also include special shops where a wider range of goods is stocked at lower prices than those that obtain in the state retail network, special hospitals, special sporting and recreational facilities and a variety of other benefits. Well-placed officials can make further use of their connections to secure, for instance, tickets to pop concerts given by visiting Western musicians or access for their children to the most prestigious educational institutions. In some cases official privilege has extended even further. A villa occupied by the former Polish party first secretary Edward Gierek, for instance, was reported by Solidarity to be situated in 4000 acres of parkland, with a dining-room to seat forty, a billiard-room and a private cinema. One of Gierek's closest associates, the former head of Polish television Maciej Szczepański, was reported to have possessed a fleet of luxury yachts and villas, a private harem of prostitutes, and a foreign bank account which he made use of when taking safari holidays in Africa. Soviet, Chinese and other leading communist officials have been reported to enjoy comparable if less spectacular advantages.

The degree of privilege enjoyed by ruling circles in the communist countries is indeed such that a number of scholars have been persuaded they may best be analysed within a 'critical Marxist' framework, in terms of which the ruling group in these countries is conceptualised as an equivalent to the exploitative ruling class of capitalist societies. The most influential statement of this approach is still that of Leon Trotsky, particularly in his book *The Revolution Betrayed* (1937). In this work Trotsky argued that the USSR was still a proletarian or socialist state because it was one in which land, industry and the other means of production had been taken into public ownership. The productive resources of the society, however, were not being used for the benefit of all its members because the bureaucracy, the 'sole privileged and commanding stratum in Soviet society', had taken control over the state machinery and was using that control to further its own selfish interests. The means of the production belonged to the state; the state, however, 'belonged' to the bureaucracy, who had 'expropriated the proletariat politically'. If the bureaucracy succeeded in making its position a more permanent and legally-based one, particularly through the creation of special forms of private property, the gains of the October revolution would eventually be liquidated. The revolution, however, had been betrayed but not yet overthrown, and it might still be redeemed by a 'supplementary revolution' in which the working class would seize political power back from the bureaucracy. More contemporary critical Marxists have developed this into a model of 'transitional society', midway between capitalism and socialism, which is capable of reverting to its capitalist origins but which may also be restored to a state of authentic socialism by a political revolution supported by the working class of other countries.

Critical Marxist theories of this kind have little difficulty in accommodating the existence of privilege such as that enjoyed by ruling circles in the communist countries (which they typically define as 'deformed workers' states'). They are also more willing to confront issues such as political and social inequalities in the communist countries, on which official theory is notably reticent. Critical Marxist interpretations are none the less themselves open to a number of serious objections. In the first place, they are generally rather vague about the nature and composition of the 'bureaucracy' which is so central to their accounts. Should it be defined, for instance, in terms of income (but then many writers, musicians, ballerinas and others should be included), or in terms of position (but many who enjoy a substantial degree of political power may not necessarily enjoy a comparable degree of material advantage)? How large is it, and how does it cohere as a social group in the absence of special 'ruling class' educational and other institutions? Secondly, and perhaps more important, how does 'the bureaucracy' reproduce itself? Given the absence of private ownership of productive wealth, a ruling group in the communist countries, however defined, cannot transfer a position of guaranteed material advantage to its descendants, as a ruling group can do in capitalist countries. Certainly, something may be achieved through personal connections, and particularly through privileged access to higher education. It is none the less striking how few senior members of this 'sole privileged and commanding stratum' have been succeeded to their positions of political power as well as social advantage by their children or close relatives.

Material inequalities, such as special shops and hospital facilities, are in any case not in themselves evidence of exploitation in a properly Marxist sense. For this to apply, it would be necessary to show that one class regularly appropriated the surplus value produced by another, the exploited or subordinate class. Marx, however, defined classes in terms of their relationship to the means of production, and there is no private ownership of such resources in the communist countries which could provide a basis for the appropriation of surplus value in the manner he had indicated. Nor is it appropriate to speak of a working class producing 'surplus value' when individual workers have security of employment and guaranteed wages and do not trade their labour upon the market. The fact that workers may produce more than they directly consume is in itself no evidence of exploitation, given the need for reinvestment and defence and for the redistribution of resources towards the old, the sick and the very young. Nor are even substantial differences in earnings. Indeed it is by no means clear that Marxist terms of any kind provide an adequate basis for the analysis of a form of society that Marx himself did not experience and which he refused to discuss in detail. Some writers in the Marxist tradition, such as Fehér, Heller and Márkus (1983), have argued that Soviet-type societies are in fact best conceptualised in a manner which employs the vocabulary of neither capitalism nor socialism but instead accepts that these are historically unprecedented social formations which require analysis in their own quite specific terms. In such a 'dictatorship over needs' it is political power which confers economic advantage, not vice versa as orthodox Marxism would suggest, and it is forms of political control rather than economic ownership which must be central to any adequate analysis.

If this examination of models of communist politics has served any useful purpose it is perhaps to suggest the inadequacy of any single explanatory formula and the need to employ a more variegated, multi-mode form of analysis. Models, by their very nature, tend to oversimplify and ignore many aspects of a political system in order to call attention to other features which are regarded as of primary importance. The totalitarian model, for instance, rightly emphasises the wide-ranging nature of state power in the communist states but exaggerates the extent to which they are nowadays sustained by terror; the modernisation or developmental model properly draws attention to the importance of social and economic change and its impact on the political system but tends to assume too readily that this must lead to liberalisation or democratisation on Western lines; while the bureaucratic politics model gives due weight to the centrality of the party-state bureaucracy in such systems but tends to ignore important respects in which a communist system is not simply 'bureaucracy writ large'. Official and critical Marxist approaches, for their part, rightly focus attention upon forms of property and the different interests of the various social groups concerned, but neither provides an entirely convincing account of the politics of such societies and critical Marxism in particular tends to counterpose 'actually existing' communist societies to alternative forms of genuine socialism which have never existed and which (for some) are hardly likely to be achieved in the real world. It is perhaps safest to conclude, with Archie Brown, that a 'discriminating methodological eclecticism' is the best policy in present circumstances. All of the models of communist politics we have considered have their merits and their shortcomings, the areas they illuminate and the areas they neglect; it would be premature to abandon the variety of insights that they provide in favour of a single all-embracing formula.

Further reading

A reliable introduction to the development of the communist states system is available in Seton-Watson (1960). This may be supplemented, in most cases for particular periods, by Hammond (1975), Fetjö (1974), Brzezinski (1967), McCauley (1977), Deakin, Shukman and Willetts (1975), Seton-Watson (1985), Narkiewicz (1981), Szajkowski (1983) and Westoby (1983). Developments over the past couple of decades are reviewed in Seton-Watson (1980). Recent events may be followed in the *Annual Register* (London) and the *Yearbook on International Communist Affairs* (Stanford, Calif.) A selection of relevant documentary sources is presented in Bogdan Szajkowski (ed.), *Documents in Communist Affairs*, which has been published annually since 1977 (for the period 1982–4 it appeared in the form of a journal, *Communist Affairs* (Guildford, Surrey, quarterly)). The vexed question of the definition of a communist system is considered further in Kautsky (1973), Waller and Szajkowski (1981), White (1983a), and Furtak (1986, ch. 1). Von Beyme (1982), Wiles (1983) and Holmes (1986) are also helpful.

A number of important older articles on the interpretation of communist politics are collected in Fleron (1969) and Kanet (1971). These may be supplemented by Johnson (1970), Ionescu (1972), Brown (1974), Cohen and Shapiro (1974), Tarschys (1977), Hough (1977), Solomon (1983) and most recently White and Nelson (1986). The standard treatment of totalitarianism is still Friedrich and Brzezinski (1965). See also Friedrich (1969), Schapiro (1972), and Curtis (1979). On modernisation theory, see Kautsky (1973), Nelson (1977) and (1978), and White (1978a) and (1979, ch. 8), from which the quotations in this section are taken. On the bureaucratic model, see Meyer (1961) and (1965), and for further discussion Armstrong (1965), Simes (1975), Dawisha (1980), which is followed by a useful discussion, Bunce and Echols (1980) and Solomon (1983), the last two of which review more recent corporatist approaches. On Marxist approaches, see the general accounts in Kolakowski (1978) and McLellan (1979) and (1983), and more specifically Bellis (1979), Nove (1975) and (1983), Nuti (1979) and Fehér, Heller and Márkus (1983).

Basic details about all Marxist–Leninist regimes presently in existence may be found in Szajkowski (1981) and Furtak (1986) and in a 36-volume series of studies under the general title 'Marxist Regimes' (Szajkowski, 1985ff). The Soviet Union and Eastern Europe more particularly are fully covered in Shoup (1981) and Schöpflin (1986). These may be updated by reference to annual publications such as the *Statesman's Yearbook* (London), *Whitaker's Almanack* (London) and the *Europa Yearbook* (London). Periodicals of particular interest to the student of comparative communist politics include *Soviet Studies* (Glasgow, quarterly), *Slavic Review* (Stanford, Calif., quarterly), *Survey* (London, quarterly), *Soviet Union* (Irvine, Calif., quarterly), *China Quarterly* (London, quarterly), *Problems of Communism* (Washington, DC, bimonthly), *Studies in Comparative Communism* (Guildford, Surrey quarterly), and the newly-established *Journal of Communist Studies* (London, quarterly).

2

The Political Cultures

Political culture may be defined as the 'attitudinal and behavioural matrix within which the political system is located', or in other words as the way in which a social group behaves politically and the nature of the political beliefs and values of its members. Political scientists have usually employed the term as a means of identifying what is unique or distinctive about the politics of a country's population and likely to be of continuing significance in the evolution of their political beliefs and behaviour patterns. This is not, of course, to imply that a country's previous political experience is the only factor that needs to be taken into account in explaining how its political system operates at the present time, or that it will necessarily be the decisive factor in determining its future political development. A country's political culture, for instance, will certainly be affected by its level of social and economic development, by changes in the nature of its political institutions, and perhaps also by the programme of political socialisation which communist governments in particular have sponsored since they have come to power. Most scholars, none the less, take the view that a nation's political experience over the centuries is likely to impart at least a certain bias to the manner in which its political system will subsequently evolve, and students of the communist states in particular have usually been agreed upon the continuing importance of the distinctive national heritages of these countries despite the great similarities between them in terms of institutions, economy and ideology. In this chapter we shall look in turn at the political cultures of the Soviet Union, Eastern Europe and China, identifying in each case a number of aspects of their distinctive historical experience and assessing the extent to which they have exerted an influence upon subsequent political developments.

The USSR: the heritage of autocracy

Both the dangers as well as the opportunities of a political cultural approach are evident in the study of the largest of the communist states, the USSR. In such an enormous territorial expanse, for instance, extending over one-sixth of the world's land surface, there will always be a danger of neglecting local variations as well as the difficulties of the central authorities in making their rule effective in the face of poor communications and the corruption and apathy of their local officials. (Nikolai Gogol's *The Government Inspector* (1836) is an amusing illustration of this phenomenon.) It is also important to be aware of variations over time, particularly over the last decade or so of Tsarist rule when a limited kind of constitutional government was temporarily established; and of the complex and many-sided nature of popular political beliefs and behaviour patterns, in which, for instance, a naive faith in the Tsar could coexist quite happily with the belief that if the Tsar's instructions did not coincide with the people's own immediate interests, particularly in relation to the land, this meant that the Tsar must have been misled or misinformed and need not necessarily be obeyed. Yet for all the reservations and qualifications, one central tendency is clear: 'If there is one single factor which dominates the course of Russian history, at any rate since the Tatar conquest', as Professor Hugh Seton-Watson has put it, 'it is the principle of autocracy'.

A central element in this autocratic inheritance was the weakness of representative institutions in pre-revolutionary Russia. There were, it is true, a number of bodies in medieval times with which the Tsar periodically took counsel upon various matters of state. But these bodies – the Boyar Duma and the Zemskii Sobor (Assembly of the Land) – had little independent authority and established no permanent existence, and the first institution of an even remotely parliamentary character to make its appearance in Russia was the State

Duma, established in the aftermath of the revolutionary events of 1905–6. Formally speaking the powers of the new State Duma were very extensive. It had the right, for instance, to enact and amend legislation; it could put questions to government ministers; and it had the right to consider the national and ministerial budgets. Without the Duma's consent, the Tsar's manifesto of 17 October 1905 promised, 'no law can come into force'. Ministers, however, remained responsible to the Tsar not to the Duma, and subsequent legislation made it clear that all expenditure connected with the armed forces and the imperial household (amounting to some two-thirds of state spending) would be outside the Duma's control. The Tsar, moreover, appointed more than half of the members of the upper house, the State Council, which could veto any proposals that the Duma might submit to it, and he could promulgate decrees on his own authority which had the force of law. Under the terms of the Basic Laws of the Russian Empire, which he alone could modify, the Tsar remained an 'autocratic and unlimited monarch' whose powers were conferred by 'God Himself'.

It has sometimes been suggested that the Duma's powers, however limited, were gradually increasing, and that if the First World War and then the revolution had not occurred they would gradually have developed into the forms of constitutional government familiar elsewhere in Europe. The Duma, certainly, acquired an increasing amount of authority as time went by, and in 1915 Duma pressure led to the resignation of four government ministers, the most considerable success that it had yet achieved. The experience of countries such as Germany and Japan, and more recently of Spain and Portugal, suggests that there is little to prevent autocracy from being transformed into a more limited form of constitutional government if suitable circumstances are present. Yet there were many observers at the time who thought that such a development was unlikely, and certainly in comparative perspective it is the weaknesses and limitations rather than the strengths and potentialities of representative institutions in Russia that are more immediately apparent (see Table 2.1). The representative institutions which had been established had very limited powers, they developed at a

TABLE 2.1

Patterns of political development in selected countries

	First constitutional regime	First parliamentary regime	First extension of suffrage	% of population enfranchised c. 1910
Russia	1905	1917	1905	2.4
Great Britain	1689	1741	1832	17.9
USA	1787	1789	c. 1840	26.3
France	1789	1792	1789	28.9
Prussia/Germany	1848	1918	1824	22.2
Italy	1848	1876	1848	23.4

Sources: Peter Gerlich, 'The Institutionalization of European Parliaments', in Allan Kornberg (ed.), *Legislatures in Comparative Perspective* (New York, 1973), pp. 100 and 106; Dieter Nohlen, *Wahlsysteme der Welt* (Munich, 1978), p. 37; and standard reference works.

very late stage by the standards of the time, and in some respects they were actually losing rather than gaining powers over the period we have been considering, particularly at the local level. So far as the facts are concerned, at any rate, it is clear that Russia was still governed, as late as the early twentieth century, by a scarcely modified autocracy, and it was the only major European country of which this could still be said (even Turkey had established a form of constitutional government a generation earlier).

The weaknesses of representative institutions in Russia were not simply those of formal powers. Perhaps more crucially, they drew upon a very restricted range of public acceptance and support. This was partly a matter of the franchise, which was extremely limited in comparison with other European nations at this time (see Table 2.1). Only about $3\frac{1}{2}$ million citizens had the right to vote in the years before the First World War, a proportion of the total population about the same as had been admitted to the franchise in Great Britain a century earlier, and the system of elections was indirect and heavily biased in favour of landowners and the urban classes at the expense of workers and peasants, who constituted the overwhelming majority of the population. There were further restrictions upon the activities of political parties, upon the reporting of Duma proceedings and upon the holding of public meetings, which could be closed by the police at any time if they appeared likely to 'incite hostility between one section of the population and another'. Patterns of representation in the Duma were also heavily weighted in favour of the landowning classes, and Russia's merchants and manufacturers, a smaller and less influential section of the population than in other European countries at this time, were particularly poorly represented.

Not surprisingly perhaps, the new institutions of representative government appear to have been regarded with no great interest or commitment by the population in whose name they operated. For instance, when the First Duma was arbitrarily dissolved by the Tsar in 1906, after it had met for less than three months, there was no serious attempt to defend it despite an appeal from a number of deputies to that effect, and there was scarcely any greater resistance to the dissolution of the Constituent Assembly by the Bolsheviks in January 1918. Many citizens appear to have been unaware of the existence of the Duma, or at least uninterested in its proceedings, and a knowledge of the relevant democratic procedures seems to have been rather imperfectly founded. Peasants, for instance, appear often to have deliberated together and then cast their votes as a group, and even in the towns electors asked to be told for whom to vote and put letters, petitions, bad verse and insurance policies into the ballot boxes rather than the voting slips they were supposed to have brought with them. Indeed there appear to have been few members of the Russian public at this time who conceived of their political objectives in terms of gaining influence through institutions of this kind. 'The people have a need for potatoes, but not in the least for a constitution', as the radical literary critic Vissarion Belinsky put it, and even liberals were often doubtful of the wisdom of strengthening the Duma and other representative bodies, believing that this would simply transfer power from the hands of the Tsar to those of the landowning nobility where it might not necessarily be exercised more equitably.

One consequence of the weak development of representative institutions in pre-revolutionary Russia was the tendency to conceive of political authority in highly personalised terms, as a link between Tsar and people unmediated by parties, the rule of law or elected bodies of any kind. This 'naïve monarchism', as it has been called, may have been discreetly encouraged by the Tsars themselves, and it was certainly in decline by the late nineteenth century and particularly after 'Bloody Sunday', 22 January 1905, when the St Petersburg police fired upon a crowd of unarmed demonstrators who were approaching the Winter Palace with icons and the Tsar's portrait to beg for help and the redress of grievances. Yet it is still a remarkable fact that in Russia, unlike Western Europe, the large-scale peasant revolts which swept across the country in the seventeenth and eighteenth centuries were generally directed not against the Tsar himself but against the aristocracy, who were typically supposed to have removed the Tsar from effective control of the nation's destinies and to which the rebels generally proposed to restore him. The same centuries also saw a large number of imposters who claimed to be the rightful Tsar and who appear to have been able to secure substantial popular support upon this basis, even when (as in the case of the peasant leader Emel'yan Pugachev) they were illiterate. The popular image of the Tsar as recorded in folk-song, literature and proverb provides further evidence of these attitudes. 'Without the Tsar, the land is widowed'; 'God in the sky, the Tsar on earth'; 'No one is against God or against the Tsar'; these were some of the proverbs collected by the lexicographer Dahl in the mid-nineteenth century, for instance, and folk-songs spoke similarly of rulers such as Ivan the Terrible and Peter the Great as friends of the people but ruthless enemies of aristocratic or ecclesiastical intrigue. If popular wishes were not respected it must be because the Tsar was an impostor or because he was being opposed by the nobility ('the Tsar is willing but the boyars resist'); between the real Tsar and his people no such conflict of interest appears to have been conceivable.

These patterns of thought and behaviour, admittedly, were more typical of central Russia than of the outlying parts of the Empire, and they appear to have applied more to national and urban politics than to politics at the level of the local village community. In some areas, such as Finland and the Baltic, there was a greater experience of and attachment to the forms of representative democracy, and in Siberia, the north and the Cossack lands of the south-west, where serfdom had been less firmly established and with which communications in any case were often difficult, a different and more independent-minded set of attitudes towards government appears to have prevailed. Even in central Russia the rising incidence of rural unrest in the nineteenth century, and rather later the establishment of soviets, suggests that deference might not be without its limits. The life of the local community, moreover, went on with little reference to national political developments and was based upon an institution that was at least formally self-governing in character, the village commune or *mir*, within which each adult householder had a vote. Robert Tucker has described the disjunction between these two social worlds as the phenomenon of 'dual Russia', consisting of 'official Russia' (the court, the bureaucracy and state affairs in general) on the one hand and 'society' (the mass of ordinary people and their immediate and largely local concerns) on the other. Popular orientations towards government, the first of these, appear to have been highly personalised, largely supportive of the Tsar as the means by which the country was preserved from anarchy and destruction, and little concerned with procedures and institutions by which he might periodically be held to account. They coexisted, however, with a rich and democratic community life with which all but the political elite identified more closely.

One further aspect of the pre-revolutionary political culture requires some emphasis: the unusually broad scope of government, whether at the local or the national level, extending not simply into matters such as the preservation of public order and the raising of taxation but also into religious affairs, the detailed administration of justice and public morals. The state was a major participant in the economic life of the nation, for instance, as the owner of extensive collieries, oilfields, forests, industrial enterprises and railways, and in addition it exercised close control over other sectors of the economy through the provisions of contracts, the regulation of tariffs, the supervision of company affairs and the operation of a factory inspectorate. Independent bodies, such as trade unions or associations of any kind, could not legally be formed until 1905, and even thereafter they functioned under a variety of restrictions of a formal or informal character. Moreover, it was difficult to defend such civil liberties as did exist through the courts: for despite a major legal reform in 1864, involving the introduction of a jury system for criminal cases, the government retained extensive powers of administrative arrest and, if necessary, the power to suspend the operation of most laws. In political cases – which were defined unusually broadly – trial by jury had in any case been suspended in 1878 after a young woman revolutionary had been acquitted of an attempt on the life of the police chief of St Petersburg. There was also an unusually restrictive censorship system under which, as today, it was permissible to criticise the performance of individual bureaucrats but not to challenge the principles of the regime itself.

Perhaps most important of all was the fact that the religious faith of the overwhelming majority of the population, Russian Orthodoxy, was never as independent of the state as was generally the case elsewhere in Europe. Orthodoxy derived from the Eastern branch of Christianity, the Byzantine, under which spiritual and temporal powers were united in the person of the ruler than separated as in the West, and Orthodoxy in Russia functioned similarly as more or less an official state religion. Church affairs were regulated by the Holy Synod, whose members were chosen by the Tsar and which operated effectively as a department of state. The Church was in turn represented within the government and upon local councils in the provinces; it received financial support from the state; and it enjoyed a monopoly of religious propaganda, including the right to carry out religious education within the schools and to conduct missionary work. There was little suggestion in any of this that religious values were different from and perhaps superior to those of the state; on the contrary they seemed so closely related as to be almost identical. The same, admittedly, could not be said of the numerous schismatic groups which rejected the authority of the state and of the Orthodox Church and saw them both as instruments of Antichrist. The most important of these were the 'Old Believers', so called because they opposed a seventeenth-century liturgical reform, and their presence is a reminder that the Russian theological tradition contains a strong element of non-conformity as well as perhaps a greater tendency towards collectivism and support for official doctrines.

From traditional to Soviet political culture

There are obvious parallels between many of these features of the pre-revolutionary political culture and that of modern times, though it is difficult and perhaps impossible to demonstrate the direct continuity between them. What should at least be clear is that ideas such as that the state should concern itself with the morals and wellbeing of the citizen as well as with his behaviour towards others, that it should take a central role in the ownership and management of the economy, and that it should exercise wide-ranging powers for the citizen's benefit with few restrictions imposed upon it by parliament, the press or political parties, were firmly rooted before the October revolution of 1917 and did not necessarily come into existence subsequently because the Bolsheviks were in favour of them. The new Soviet government, however, set itself a series of further tasks which went beyond or conflicted with the political culture it had inherited, such as eliminating the influence of religion, mobilising the population into higher levels of social and political activity, and replacing values based on private property with values based upon Marxism–Leninism, and it has sought to bring about these changes over more than two generations by a deliberate programme of political socialisation. The political culture of the contemporary USSR, accordingly, still bears the marks of its pre-revolutionary origin, passed on through the family, organised religion, literature and social custom, but it also reflects the impact of Soviet rule since 1917 as well as of the socio-economic and other changes that have occurred over the same period, such as industrialisation and urbanisation.

It is probably not very helpful to consider the degree of 'continuity' versus 'change' any further in such general terms; let us therefore look more closely at nationalism, a value which appears to have persisted throughout the pre-revolutionary and Soviet periods, and at the changes in the political culture which appear to have stemmed from the experience of Soviet rule more directly.

Nationalism in the USSR is perhaps most immediately associated with the nationalism of the non-Russian nationalities. It is less often realised that nationalism in various forms has always been and still remains a central element in the political culture of the Russian people themselves. In part this was a matter of official doctrine, summed up in the celebrated formula 'Autocracy, Orthodoxy and Nationality' which was propounded by S. S. Uvarov, later Minister of Education, in 1832, and which was taken as the basis of official political doctrine until the revolution of 1905, if not beyond. The formula was intended to imply support for the principle of autocracy, and thus opposition to liberal reforms; for Orthodoxy, or the teaching and ritual of the Russian Orthodox Church; and devotion to the Russian national heritage, together with a reluctance to take Western European thought and institutions as suitable models for developments in Russia. In fact neither Uvarov himself nor some of the later emperors appear to have adhered entirely faithfully to these precepts, and there is some evidence that official nationalism was used, as in other countries, as a means of bolstering popular political support for the regime. At the same time there is no doubt that a popular identification with the strength and territorial integrity of the Russian nation did not have to be invented by the authorities; it emerged particularly strongly in times of war, such as during the Napoleonic war of 1812 and at the beginning of the First World War, and it was also evident in the amorphous but real belief that Russia, as the only major Orthodox power, had to some extent a special destiny as well as a certain superiority to her perhaps more prosperous European neighbours. The less attractive face of popular and official nationalism was apparent in the policy of Russification, carried out with particular vigour in the later nineteenth century, and anti-Semitism.

The Soviet government in its early years took a hostile attitude towards the capitalist and reactionary past that had preceded it and repudiated these elements of continuity, but from the 1930s onwards a revived form of Russian nationalism (called 'socialist patriotism') began to receive a greater degree of official favour. Peter I became 'the Great' again; military leaders of the past, such as Kutuzov and Suvorov, became models for the Red Army; and the expansion of the Russian Empire began to be regarded as more of a civilising than a colonialising enterprise. To some extent, as before, official doctrines of this kind were used by the party leadership in an attempt to manipulate popular political opinion to their advantage. This was particularly the case during the Second World War, when Russian and Slavic patriotism reached an unusual pitch of intensity in part as a result of the deliberate encouragement of the authorities. 'We shall never rouse the people to war with Marxism–Leninism alone', as Stalin is reported to have remarked at this time. And yet popular nationalism, once again, does not seem to have been simply the creation of the party leadership. Soviet soldiers in the field quite spontaneously took up the cry of 'For the Motherland, for Stalin!', and the Orthodox Church immediately identified itself with the defence of the nation as it had done at crucial periods throughout its history. Even *émigrés* found it possible to support the Soviet government, at this time as at others, since although they were hostile to socialism it was at least defending the national territory and accomplishing many necessary social and economic reforms. Many Russians appear to take a comparable pride today in Soviet achievements in sport, science and outer space as well as in the more prominent role the Soviet Union now occupies in international affairs, and it is a source of support for the authorities that it would be unwise to minimise.

The Soviet government appears to have been less successful in developing a comparable commitment to Marxism–Leninism among the population over whom they rule. Despite a considerable effort over more than two generations there appears to be very little interest in or knowledge of the ideology to which the authorities are officially committed, and certainly not enough to be sufficient in itself to legitimate their rule. The main impact of Soviet government appears rather to have been to reinforce the feelings of remoteness of ordinary people from high-level politics and their belief that it would be unprofitable and probably unwise for them to intervene directly in such matters. This lack of political trust or efficacy had some foundation in the pre-revolutionary period when the government maintained a network of spies and it had a generally deplorable record in relation to civil liberties, but it has increased still further in the Soviet period as a result of the behaviour of the authorities and particularly of the experience of Stalinism. This was a period, still within the memory of older Soviet citizens, when political opponents were executed after show trials, or perhaps after no trial at all; when many millions of people were imprisoned by the secret police on the flimsiest of pretexts; and when an atmosphere of suspicion poisoned relations not only at the workplace but also within the family itself.

'Any adult inhabitant of this country, from a collective farmer up to a member of the Politburo, always knew that it would take only one careless word or gesture and he would fly off irrevocably into the abyss', as Alexander Solzhenitsyn has commented on this period in his *Gulag Archipelago* (1973–75). Perhaps 20 million people lost their lives as a result of the political repression of those years, according to the best Western estimates, and there were still 15 million Soviet citizens in prison camps at the time of Stalin's death in 1953. Many of those who profited from their lack of principle during these years still occupy prominent positions in Soviet life, and it would not be surprising if this period, with the lives and careers it made and unmade, continued to influence Soviet political culture for many years to come. At the same time a number of Soviet citizens, particularly those now in leading positions, may have drawn the rather different conclusion from these years that the substantial achievements they recorded, such as industrialisation, the elimination of illiteracy and the defeat of Hitler, could not have been attained without a high degree of central discipline. And many appear to have believed that Stalin, like the Tsars in pre-revolutionary times, was unaware of the repression that was taking place in his name and that he would put matters right as soon as he was informed of it.

It is perhaps best to end this section by pointing once again to the enormous variety of political attitudes and experiences that are concealed by any generalisations of this kind. There were and still are, for instance, considerable differences of political belief and behaviour between Soviet men and women, between the generations, between the social classes, and between town and country. Perhaps most important of all, there are considerable differences between the political cultures of the various nationalities or ethnic groups of which the Soviet population is composed, the largest fifteen of which have their own union republics with a substantial range of devolved powers. These nationalities are set out schematically in Table 2.2. Russians, it will be seen, account for no more than about half of the total population (a proportion which has been slowly declining over the years). Taken together, Slavs (Russians, Ukrainians and Belorussians) account for nearly three-quarters of the total population, but there are major differences of language, history and culture between them and most other nationalities in the USSR, as well as

TABLE 2.2

The major Soviet nationalities

	Census population, 1979 (millions)	% of total	Linguistic group	Traditional religion
The Slavs:				
Russians	137.4	52.4	East Slavic	Russian Orthodox
Ukrainians	42.3	16.1	East Slavic	Russian Orthodox*
Belorussians	9.5	3.6	East Slavic	Russian Orthodox
The Balts:				
Latvians	1.4	0.5	Baltic	Protestant
Lithuanians	2.9	1.1	Baltic	Roman Catholic
Estonians	1.0	0.4	Finno-Ugrian	Protestant
The Caucasian Peoples:				
Georgians	3.6	1.4	Kartvelian	Georgian Orthodox
Armenians	4.2	1.6	Indo-European	Armenian Orthodox
Azerbaidzhanis	5.5	2.1	Turkic	Muslim (Shi'ite)
The Central Asians				
Uzbeks	12.5	4.8	Turkic	Muslim (Sunni)
Kazakhs	6.6	2.5	Turkic	Muslim (Sunni)
Tadzhiks	2.9	1.1	Iranian	Muslim (Sunni)
Turkmenis	2.0	0.8	Turkic	Muslim (Sunni)
Kirgiz	1.9	0.7	Turkic	Muslim (Sunni)
Others:				
Moldavians	3.0	1.1	Romance	Romanian Orthodox

*There is a substantial Roman Catholic (Uniate) minority in the Western Ukraine

Source: adapted from *Naselenie SSSR po dannym vsesoyuznoi perepisi naseleniya 1979 goda* (Moscow, 1980), pp. 23–7, and standard reference works.

long-standing animosities among themselves, particularly between Russians and Ukrainians, which the passage of time appears to have done little to alleviate.

Of the major non-Slavic groups, the Baltic nations have a rather different history, having come under strong German, Polish and Swedish influences at different times. They are generally Protestant or Roman Catholic in religion, not Russian Orthodox; they have been under Soviet rule for a rather shorter period of time than most other nationalities, since about 1940 rather than since the revolution; and even today their way of life remains demonstrably more 'Western' than that of most of the other Soviet nations. The Caucasian peoples – Georgians, Armenians and Azerbaidzhanis – have also a very different history, religion and culture to that of the Slavic majority, and they are perhaps even more conscious of these differences than the Baltic nations (for instance, there were mass riots in Tbilisi, the capital of Georgia, in 1978 when it was rumoured that Georgian was about to be dropped as one of the official languages of the republic). The Caucasian nationalities are renowned for their Mediterranean climate, their fruit and wine, their paternalistic attitude towards women, their feuds and their corruption, but also (particularly the Georgians) for their high levels of education and cultural achievement. Both Georgians and Armenians have their own independent churches and have been Christian since about the fourth century, some six centuries earlier than the Russians (a difference to which they are generally not slow to draw attention).

The greatest cultural division of all, however, is between the Slavs and other European peoples and the predominantly Muslim nationalities of Central Asia. The peoples of these republics are the descendants of the great Mongol empire of medieval times, and they have generally been under Russian rule for no more than the last hundred years or so. The peoples of these republics – Uzbeks, Kazakhs, Kirgiz, Tadzhiks and Turkmenis – speak languages that are generally of Turkic origin; they are predominantly Muslim in religion; and their traditional culture and values, with which their religion is inextricably bound up, appear to have been altered very little by the experience of Russian and now of Soviet rule. The Central Asians, for instance, are generally reluctant to permit the employment and education of women, and even today the proportion of women members of the communist party and of local soviets in these republics is a good deal lower than it is elsewhere in the USSR. Fewer pigs are kept in these republics (pork being an unclean meat for Muslims, as it is for Jews), and traditional customs such as the charging of bride money, elaborate wedding feasts and pilgrimages to the graves of local holy men are still practised (very few Soviet Muslims are permitted to make a pilgrimage to Mecca), sometimes with the covert support of local party members and officials. There is generally little intermarriage between the Central Asians and non-Muslim nationalities, particularly Slavs, and a knowledge of Russian is much less common than it is among the other peoples of the USSR. Perhaps most alarming of all from a Russian point of view, the population of these republics has been increasing much more rapidly than the all-union average and on some projections may amount to 25–30 per cent of the total Soviet population by the end of the century.

Official Soviet theory continues to assert that national differences of this kind will eventually disappear as socio-economic conditions become more similar between one part of the USSR and another, as a knowledge of Russian becomes more widespread, and as younger generations brought up under wholly Soviet conditions displace those that acquired their formative experiences under capitalist regimes. There is a certain amount of evidence which supports these assumptions. At the same time most national groups appear to have remained loyal to their native language, at least within the home, and there has been little obvious tendency for the major non-Russian cultures to lose their vigour or their self-confidence. Indeed in some respects present governmental policies may be increasing national differences rather than diminishing them. Better education in the formerly backward parts of the USSR, for instance, has led to the formation of a local intelligentsia who see no reason for responsible positions in the areas to be filled by outsiders, and as the rate of economic growth declines and the competition for resources becomes more intense the authorities in each republic, representing as they generally do a major non-Russian nationality, may increasingly be tempted to resort to 'nationalist' arguments as a means of maximising their leverage upon the central economic authorities in Moscow. At all events it is clear that differences of this kind show no immediate prospect of disappearing, and it may be significant that recent pronouncements by the Soviet leadership have placed more emphasis upon the 'harmonious relations' that exist between the various nationalities of the USSR than upon their ultimate fusion into a single Soviet nation.

Eastern Europe: political traditions old and new

The pre-communist political cultures of Eastern Europe were characterised by backwardness. This backwardness manifested itself in a variety of ways, some of which have survived the communist revolution largely untouched. In other ways, however, the communist revolution has brought about a far-reaching transformation. To understand how the existing political cultures of Eastern Europe may be assessed, one must look at the pre-revolutionary culture, at the communist political culture of the post-revolutionary period and at the state of affairs a generation after the revolution.

The traditional political culture

In the political arena, the most striking aspect of the East European political cultures was the dominance of the state and the weakness of society. The principle of reciprocity of rights between ruler and ruled was much weaker than in the West, if it existed at all. With considerable variations from polity to polity, going roughly from Central Europe to the Balkans, the state was the primary political actor and principal entrepreneur and exercised something close to hegemony *vis-à-vis* society, both in regulation and in initiative. In particular, although nowhere in Eastern Europe did a Russian-type patrimonial state develop, the dominance of the state was guaranteed by the absence of popular control over the money-raising powers of the ruler (taxation) and over the means of coercion (army and police). The position of the ruler, which by the twentieth century had become the bureaucracy, was based on the doctrine of the discretionary power of the state, derived from the royal prerogative, whereby the state had the right to take action untrammelled by constraints from below. In other words, the discretionary power of the state inherently excluded the doctrine of parliamentary sovereignty and resulted in the transformation of legislatures into façades. In the entire pre-communist period there was only one instance of a ruling government losing power through elections (Bulgaria 1931); rather, a new prime minister would be appointed by the managers from the power elite and he would 'make elections' by using the coercive apparatus of the state or other illegal and semi-legal methods. This was the reverse of the order in which governments were changed in genuinely democratic societies, where the concept of popular sovereignty had meaning.

The power elite itself varied in composition, but it was invariably constituted by an alliance of the bureaucracy and other elites. In Poland and Hungary the alliance included the magnates and large landowners, the gentry (*szlachta* in Poland), finance capital and large-scale commerce, the military and the church or churches. The bureaucracy was recruited from these elites and it successfully co-opted the bulk of the intelligentsia (similarly recruited) to carry out the various tasks requiring technical knowledge. The small working class and the peasantry tended to be excluded from this alliance. But consonant with the hegemonial and façade quality of the system, social democratic and peasant parties could and did function – uninfluentially. The bourgeoisie (understood as the entrepreneurial class) was politically weak and deferred to the gentry–bureaucratic alliance. In the Czech lands there was no native aristocracy to speak of and the political elite was more broadly based on the bourgeoisie, finance capital and other sectional interests; peasant and working class interests also secured some representation in this system. Nevertheless in inter-war Czechoslovakia, as in the other Eastern European countries, politics rested on the power of the bureaucracy, which mirrored the permanent coalition of five political parties in power, the *pětka*, and which ruled through a series of interpenetrating elites – the trade unions, the press, the military, to some extent the churches, and the judiciary. In all these states, therefore, there was no full political integration, in which state and society were co-terminous and where all the subjects of the state were genuinely citizens with equal rights. In Poland and Czechoslovakia the fabric of the state was further weakened by an absence of national integration – large national minorities remained in some form or another outside official favour by reason of their nationality. In systems of this kind there could be no single public opinion, because society was divided into several social and/or national fragments with limited or non-existent communication between them.

Much of this was true of the Balkans, but there were also differences. The traditional native aristocracies had been swept away (Bulgaria, Serbia, Greece, Slovenia) or else they had been co-opted into the state (Romania, Croatia, Bosnia, Albania). In the Balkans a merchant–patrician elite and the military were also of importance. The most striking factor, however, was the overwhelmingly peasant character of these societies, up to 90 per cent of the total population. The states were run in the interests of the bureaucracy; the peasantry were excluded and viewed the bureaucracy with hostility as an alien and exploitative agency. The failure of national integration was as much of an issue as in Central Europe, afflicting Yugoslavia and Romania with particular problems.

As far as religion was concerned, Eastern Europe was an area of enormous diversity. Poles and Croats were overwhelmingly Roman Catholic and Czechs, Slovaks, Hungarians, and Slovenes largely so. There were significant Protestant minorities in Hungary (Calvinist and Lutheran) and among the Czechs and Slovaks; and the area that eventually became the German Democratic Republic was four-fifths Lutheran. In the Balkans there was a closer link between religion and nationhood, and Christians belonged to the various Orthodox churches. Islam was represented by the Bosnians, who spoke Serbo-Croat, by the Albanians and by the Turkish minorities, the remnants of the erstwhile Ottoman empire. There were sizeable Jewish communities at various stages of assimilation in Central Europe.

In all these states, the instruments of coercion were freely used to ensure the unchallenged hegemony of the elite, whether these challenges derived from social or national grounds. However, it is worth noting that where there was no conflict of interests the state did not necessarily interfere and did not necessarily seek a monopoly position. The objectives of the elites did not, on the whole, go much beyond securing their own positions; there was a rhetorical commitment to modernisation, which could be jettisoned as soon as conflict arose. At the same time it was noteworthy that during the 1914–45 period (i.e. including the accelerated growth of the two world wars) some development did take place, such as improvements in communications and education. Modernisation was seen primarily as a means of extending the power of the state (by creating a greater tax base and an increase in the size of the armed forces) rather than of increasing the welfare of society; this was a pattern inherited from the military–bureaucratic empires of the nineteenth century.

Thus by 1945, the political cultures of the Eastern European societies included acceptance of the power of the state to regulate society over a wide area of life, a habituation to arbitrary methods and authoritarianism which could be off-set by corruption, hostility towards the state on the part of the majority coupled with a messianic concept of political change, and a feeling among a minority of the intelligentsia that change could only be effected from above through the agency of massive state action. Among both the intelligentsia and the peasantry there were strong elements of messianism, and change was generally viewed as a radical transformation rather than as a series of orderly steps towards reform, albeit in different forms. In general, the radical intelligentsia took various intellectual models as their utopia (Marxism, Fascism, neo-Catholicism or populism), whereas peasant messianism derived from the restricted world-view of the East European peasant (bounded by highly conservative, traditional peasant communities and drawing on religion as the source of the myth values which formed the benchmark of desired change).

The peasant challenge to the established order and the ruling elites, both in 1917–21 and in the 1930s (when it emerged as right-wing radicalism), was defeated throughout Eastern Europe because the peasantry lacked a tradition of sustained, organised action and was weakened by its antagonism towards politics. Both these shortcomings could be traced to the limited political experience of the peasantry, its political illiteracy, in politics where the contact between the peasant and the state was limited to the gendarme, the tax-gatherer and the recruiting sergeant. Not surprisingly, the peasant tended to regard politics and the seat of politics, the city, as alien and parasitical. Finally, the capriciousness and inexperience of peasant leaders likewise contributed to the failure of the first challenge of mass politics in Eastern Europe. The acute economic crisis of the 1930s and the dislocation of the war intensified the frustration and resentments of the peasants and made them susceptible to political sloganeering promising immediate transformation.

On the other hand, it should be stressed that in these polities the elites exercised a hegemony and not a monopoly. Thus some political pluralism – the autonomous functioning of social institutions capable of articulating political alternatives and representing particular interests – could and did coexist with the discretionary power of the state. Institutional and social autonomy was often circumscribed and might be confined to the upper echelons, the privileged sections of society. If the state wished to extend control over them it could do so, although it might have to pay a political price. The areas in which such nascent pluralism did exist included the educational system, the press, the trade unions and some other social organisations. Even the courts were not necessarily under strict control, unless power interests were threatened, and the same applied to local interests. The right to autonomous economic initiative, i.e. private enterprise, likewise existed. This had the important result that national and social minorities could find some protection against discrimination by the agencies of the state controlled by the majority nationality. Overall, the hegemonistic and authoritarian political cultures of pre-war Eastern Europe were moderated to some degree by incipient pluralistic values and practices of this kind.

The cement binding rulers and ruled together in an at least

partially consensual framework was nationalism. In all the states of Eastern Europe, the newly emergent elites of the nineteenth century took power against the ruling empires by the propagation of nationalist ideologies. These ideologies were, of course, received from the West, although they were significantly modified in their reception by the different political context of Eastern Europe. But the mobilising element of nationalism was highly successful, in that it brought to political awareness increasing numbers of individuals who had until then had next to no political self-identity and a largely static one at that.

Nationalism proved effective in creating a new political identity *vis-à-vis* the state and towards other polities, especially when the nation could be presented as being under threat. But it offered no answers whatever to the challenge of mass politics, to the problem of creating social institutions to mediate between the individual and state; indeed, if anything, it promoted an unmediated concept of mass politics, in which the utopian ideal was one where all national awareness was identical and where conflicts of interest did not arise. This was exacerbated by the manipulative qualities inherent in nationalism and the use made of them before 1945, while urgent socio-political problems were neglected. Hence by 1945 the system associated with nationalism was widely discredited and there was something of a revulsion against nationalism as such. Nevertheless, that did not signify that national identity ceased to be of relevance. All or almost all East Europeans when they considered their relationship to the state of which they were subjects identified themselves in national terms, and that identity, based on factors of shared culture and language (and in the Balkans of religion as well), and on a concept of the 'ideal territory' of the nation-state, retained its power of attraction.

The communist tradition

The communist tradition and political culture of East European parties developed against the background. The communists' interpretation of their experience, however, differed from that of the majority, and they learned different lessons from it. Driven by an ideology with a claim to a total transformation of society, the communists had initially had high hopes of achieving objectives during the revolutionary upsurge that gripped Eastern Europe in 1917–21. The upsurge had its origins in war weariness and dislocation, in the radical expectations of massive change promoted by war and the example of the Russian Revolution. On the face of it the communists, who had their antecedents in the left of Social Democracy and were reinforced by prisoners-of-war returning from Russia (where many had taken an active part in the revolution), should have been well placed to profit from the radical upsurge.

Their record, however, was one of failure. In Yugoslavia, the communists emerged as the third largest party in the elections to the Constituent Assembly in 1921, and in Montenegro they polled an absolute majority of votes. In Poland, where the leaders of the reconstituted state were able to draw on massive popular support in the defence of the country against the Soviet Union, a solid core of communists retained their beliefs. In Czechoslovakia, when the socialists split, the communists emerged more numerous and better organised than the social democrats. Yet despite these gains and the radical groundswell that made them possible, the communists were nowhere able to translate their support into long-term political strength. They misunderstood or overestimated the nature of the upsurge, which was based on the discontent of the peasants, who generally distrusted and despised the urban intellectuals and workers who led the communist parties. The experience and ability of the established political elites, moreover, proved more than a match for the messianic radicals, who had expected that the 'bourgeois state' would collapse after one determined push; and the communists' messianism and radicalism alienated many potential supporters who might have wanted change but not in the direction insisted on by the communists. Thus the lesson drawn by communist leaders from the 1917–21 experience was to distrust mass politics as unreliable, to seek no allies except for tactical ends and to opt for conspiratorial methods of organisation. In this they were assisted by the ruling elites which banned the communist parties (except in Czechoslovakia) and helped to drive them into a political ghetto.

The second formative process undergone by East European parties was Sovietisation. This might be seen as a kind of intellectual, ideological, political and organisational colonisation of East European institutions by Soviet ones. Whatever autonomous traditions, aims, concepts, experience or roots these parties might have had, they were forced to abandon them and to subordinate themselves absolutely to Soviet experience (this applied to West European parties as well, of course). Those who refused to submit were expelled or liquidated. The imposition of this Soviet-type political system may have weakened or eliminated local Marxist traditions, but it had the result of welding together disparate, often disputatious individuals into an effective political force. By the 1930s obedience to Moscow was unconditional and Soviet instructions were carried out even when these clearly ran counter to a party's local interests. The Romanian Communist Party, for instance, was obliged to proclaim a policy of self-determination for Romania's national minorities 'up to and including secession'; this ensured that the party would be shunned by ethnic Romanians and would attract support almost exclusively from the country's ethnic minorities.

The membership of all the East European parties was therefore seriously depleted by their own actions, by Soviet colonisation and by police persecution, but those who remained or were recruited in the 1930s were steeled in a tough school of 'conspiratorial politics' and ruthlessness, the underground, infiltration of other legal bodies (like trade unions), and obedience to Moscow. This experience bred contempt for other political forces, especially the social democrats (which was reciprocated), for the established institutions of the state and the political system generally, and an attitude which regarded one's political opponents as enemies to be liquidated. Political change was not to be the result of debate and compromise, the aggregation of competing interests, but of ruthlessness and force; and criticism was not legitimate comment but hostile attack. All in all, the communists brought a rather simple, black-and-white view of the world with them into the post-war era.

The third formative experience was to some extent the practice of the first two lessons, the application of the conspiratorial principle and organisational efficiency in the resistance during the war. The resistance role and the prestige of the Soviet Union as liberator proved to be the factor that brought the communists out of the political ghetto. Non-communist parties or groups co-operated with the communists against the enemy, found that collaboration in some areas was possible (although not without problems) and assumed that wartime co-operation could be extended into a post-war era of radical reform. For the communists, on the other hand, the equation had not really changed – they had been too deeply marked by their local and Soviet experiences. Imbued by an intransigent sense of their own infallibility, they acted decisively and with the assumption that 'history was on their side'. Above all, in the initial post-war period, they persuaded or bludgeoned non-communist reformers (social democrats or peasant parties) into co-operation by raising the spectre of 'reaction' and by insisting that only two positions were possible in the political constellation of the time – whole-hearted co-operation (i.e. subordination) or wholehearted opposition. This black-and-white worldview and the dynamism that accompanied it – a certainty that the communists had all the answers – carried the communists into the early post-war era.

The contemporary synthesis

The political cultures that evolved from a conflation of the communist, revolutionary value system and the original pre-communist tradition have all the marks of the difficulties of combining two such disparate elements, despite the points of similarity between them. On the one hand, the communists were clearly able to make use of much of the pre-existing tradition of deference to authoritarianism and acceptance of the dominance of the state over society. The wartime radical-isation and, for that matter, actual radical change, like the sweeping away of the old order, coupled with a widespread expectation of change (if not necessarily in the direction taken by the communists) were likewise put to good use by the new communist administrations.

Their historic achievement of concentrating energies to begin the initial push towards industrialisation, which had eluded their predecessors, at the same time resolved the most acute socio-economic problem besetting Eastern Europe: the peasant question. (In Czechoslovakia and the GDR an industrial base had already been created and the agrarian question lacked the same degree of urgency.) With industrialisation came an end to rural over-population, hunger in the countryside, limited opportunities, and the exclusion of the majority of the population from the ambit of the state. The communist revolutions also brought improved health and welfare, education, transport and communications, and administrative techniques. For the first time ever the whole of Eastern Europe was exposed to equal standards of administration, whether in towns or in the countryside. The promotion of a generation of individuals of working-class and peasant origins, who came to form the new class, brought untapped talents into politics and the intelligentsia. The concentration of power in the hands of the state, broadly speaking, was not as such out of line with East European political traditions and has continued to receive conditional backing from the bulk of the population throughout both periods.

On the whole, the populations of Eastern Europe appear to accept the nationalisation of large-scale industry, finance and the state control of planning; and seem likewise to accept the welfare benefits and job security that are provided by the state. Where collectivisation has taken place, it has become accepted – in Czechoslovakia in 1968, for instance, there were no calls for decollectivisation. And they probably support at least the principle of egalitarianism preached by the party. In general, it is a tenable proposition that in Eastern Europe there is an acceptance of a wider and more encompassing role accorded to the state by society, both in terms of regulation and of initiative, than in the West. On the other hand, in so far as it can be estimated, few East Europeans would care for the much more far-reaching role claimed over its subjects by the Soviet state.

Where disharmonies have arisen and where a clash between the communist political culture and the traditional or dominant political culture does exist is in the continued exclusion of the mass of the population from political power. The initial concentration of energies was of necessity accompanied by a concentration of power; it was not followed by any significant deconcentration, such as would have permitted wider and increasing social representation in the political arena. The communist tradition of monopoly of power, as practised in the Stalinist era, has indeed been modified to a claim of a monopoly of political initiative, but the weight of the communist tradition, the privilege of power and the Soviet constraint have made it impossible for East European parties to meet the challenge of mass politics in any institutionalised form. Every major East European crisis since 1945 has raised some aspect of this issue – Hungary and Poland in 1956, Czechoslovakia in 1968, Yugoslavia in 1971 and Poland in 1980 and after. In each case, the automatic communist response has been negative, to reaffirm the doctrine of the leading role of the party (i.e. monopoly) and to offer concessions on an informal basis, rather than political rights. As far as possible, concessions have been restricted to economics, and welfare benefits have been traded off against depoliticisation.

At the popular level, on the other hand, the continuity of pre-war traditions was never completely broken. Informal agencies of transmission, like the family, ensured not only that non-communist values would survive, but even that they would appear more attractive than they were at the time. National identity has proved to be the most enduring of these. However much communist ideologists may have striven to eradicate 'Polishness' or 'Hungarianness' as political categories and to have them replaced by 'socialist internationalism', the attempt has failed. Secondly, despite the weakness of the pluralistic elements in the traditional political culture, they did exist and distance has lent them retrospective glamour (e.g. the cult of Masaryk in Czechoslovakia). Furthermore, the very process of modernisation initiated by the communists has contributed to creating demands for wider participation among some sections of the population. As the role of the state increases in society as a corollary of economic development and as greater provision is made for collective consumption, countervailing pressures arise in the form of a growing desire for control over one's immediate environment and then over other areas. The communist tradition, rooted in the claim to a monopoly of truth and power, has shown itself singularly ill-fitted to cope with pressures of this kind.

This is not to suggest that the values of the *ruling elites* have not changed since the assumption of power. There have, indeed, been serious modifications in their attitudes to society and the use of power, but none of this has been sufficiently thoroughgoing to allow the mass of the population a greater role in the political process. The pivot of the change was the abandonment of the monolithic concept of power. This had asserted that in a communist society there could be no conflicts of interest, and that where such conflicts did arise they were the consequences of a hostile conspiracy. Monolithism of this kind involved the use of a high level of coercion – the terror. With the second phase of de-Stalinisation from about 1961 onwards, East European polities – Albania excepted – came to recognise that conflicts of interest could occur in a socialist society and that they were not necessarily antagonistic or criminal. This constituted a major transformation in the elites' attitude to power, because it meant a diminution of coercion, an acceptance of interest aggregation and some competition of interests (e.g. between workers and managers). The change held out prospects for an eventual general political democratisation – the adaptation of the institutional framework to correspond to popular aspirations – which in fact was what the Czechoslovak reformers of 1968 sought to achieve. More generally it shifted the elites' view of their own legitimacy from one of political monopoly by virtue of 'the revolution' and 'the class struggle' to one of rationality and efficiency, even if the rhetoric of revolution was retained.

This shift allowed for a greater measure of depoliticisation of decision-making and reliance on apolitical expertise, known colloquially as the 'switch from red to expert', and a privatisation of individual life. In practical terms this meant that enterprise managers could be appointed on the basis of their technical skills rather than their political reliability, and that constant reaffirmation of loyalty to the party through compulsory rituals was no longer required. Greater scope was also provided for private, mainly economic activity. At the same time the elites were forced to take stock of the enduring national qualities of the East European polities, and with greater or lesser enthusiasm they came to accept that communist leaderships were also national leaderships. In the event, the identification of communism with nationalism, despite the theoretical irreconcilability of the two, permitted a greater degree of consent to enter the political equation, in as much as nationalism provided a stronger social cement then socialist internationalism. Inevitably this also resulted in a rise in the degree and intensity of the expression of nationalism, although with marked differences from polity to polity.

Parallel with the decline in revolutionary fervour and purely Marxist–Leninist ideological considerations in the management of power, there arose a new climate in which the exercise of power in itself became to some extent the new ideology and, as might have been predicted, the uncontrolled use of power was accompanied by a growth of corruption, abuse of power and distortions in the functioning of the system. Thus as the East European political elites entered the 1980s, their value systems (with differences from country to country) could be defined as consisting of a claim to the monopoly of political initiative, of the allocation of resources, of rule making as among different competing interests and of rationality. The elites recognised that attempts to exclude society from power totally would fail and that there was a margin beyond which the elites ventured at their peril (as happened in Poland in 1970, when the leadership unilaterally introduced higher food prices). The room for manoeuvre within this margin, however, appeared to be shrinking in the 1980s, especially as the means of economic co-operation were diminishing.

This concentrated the attention of the elites on the problem of their power and on how they should sustain it. As the longer term ideological goals of the system faded, the legitimation of the system tended to be reduced to power itself, as if to say, 'We are in power and we stay in power; there are no alternatives; challenges are pointless.' But this had the consequence that if a challenge did develop, the resources and self-confidence of the elite could rapidly decline, as happened in Poland in 1980. Equally, the weakening of ideological determined goals and the gap between proclaimed and real ideology tended to raise a question-mark over the purposiveness and goal-rationality of elite strategies. There was growing evidence in the 1980s that elite horizons had contracted and that concerns were largely focused on remaining in power and little else.

The *intelligentsia* has to some extent been successfully co-opted by the elite by being given access to the outer fringes of power and privileges. This has had the effect of creating a potential partnership between elite and intelligentsia (defined here to include the scientific, technical, cultural, artistic and literary intelligentsia). The intelligentsia drew clear benefits from this partnership and was in return expected to offer its loyalty to the system, whether it subscribed fully to Marxism–Leninism or not. This co-option was achieved basically because the intelligentsia had a concept of its role as being that section of society which possessed a monopoly of technical knowledge, and it argued that this knowledge was ideologically neutral – that there was not, for instance, a Marxist–Leninist way of building a bridge. The intelligentsia was prepared, by and large, to settle for a political system within which it could exercise technical functions of this kind, having been prevented from doing so during the Stalinist period. The impulse towards the creation of a 'better society' inherent in the application of technical knowledge could be reconciled with the modified definition of the leading role adopted by the party which had, in turn, recognised that a modern society could not adequately be ruled by the criterion of political reliability alone – that experiment had resulted in gross irrationality and waste. Thus a tacit compromise between the elites and the intelligentsia, reached in the early 1960s, provided for at least a limited degree of participation in the political process by the intelligentsia. A minority of intellectuals questioned the compact, the nature of the political order and its ideological justification, and sought to express criticism which went beyond the limits acceptable to the elite. This minority was then subjected to a variety of sanctions and tended to be excluded from public life. The minority, in which Marxist and non-Marxist intellectual currents existed, provided the roots from which the opposition movements of the 1970s and 1980s grew and from which some of the concepts of political innovation arose.

The device of co-option through material benefits has been the principal means of excluding the *working class* from effective political participation. But other factors, some of them deriving from the political cultures have also been at play. With the exception of the GDR and the Czech lands (Bohemia and Moravia), the East European working class is overwhelmingly a new class. Workers are very largely first generation off the land and have brought memories of rural privation and subsistence-level farming with them, together with traditional peasant hostility to the state. By meeting working-class aspirations in the field of consumption and seeking to confine them to this area, the elites have so far pre-empted widespread demands for mass participation. In the GDR a similar result has been achieved through high levels of individual and collective consumption thanks to high levels of economic development, relatively high levels of coercion in politics, a traditional deference to the state even in the mobilised urban population and the emigration of about 3 million people to West Germany after 1945. In the Czech lands workers have been similarly assured of a high standard of living and have had their political aspirations artificially depressed by the traumatic experience of the failure of the 1968 reform programme and the 'normalisation' that followed. The Polish crisis of 1980, on the other hand, erupted essentially because the party was not able to keep its side of the bargain and guarantee a high standard of living to the workers in return for their political passivity.

There are indications, however, from Poland and from some other East European countries, that the second generation of workers now coming to maturity is less accommodating than its parents and has higher political aspirations. Furthermore, with the decline of social mobility there has not been the creaming off of talented individuals into the elite as happened in the previous generation, so that potential leaders are much less likely to have been promoted out of the working class. For this second generation the communist order has been the norm – it was born and brought up in it – so that it takes its achievements for granted and is more ready to criticise shortcomings. So pressure for increased worker participation, for control over the immediate environment and for greater local investment in matters such as working conditions or transport seems likely to increase and to become a stronger component of working-class attitudes. For the time being, however, some of the energy that might have been devoted to political ends has been siphoned off into the 'second' or unofficial economy; this helps to satisfy aspirations for wider choice by providing for a degree of leeway in personal economic initiatives.

The *peasantry* has generally been quiescent since collectivisation was completed and tolerable conditions in the countryside were established. Collectivisation or the extension of state power over the land, a necessary concomitant of economic development, was a major trauma for the peasantry, which has been moving slowly from patrimonial to commodity production. Traditional peasant values tended to be apolitical and to concentrate on the single goal of acquisition of land; since this last cannot be fulfilled it has been transmuted into the acquisition of a higher standard of living, better housing and the possession of consumer durables both as indicators of status and for actual consumption. For the rest, the traditional rural attitude of deference and suspicion towards the state has persisted and has helped to ensure that agrarian populations have given a passive loyalty to the state, thereby forming one of the pillars of the consensus of the post-Stalinist system. A further factor in this complex has been the rapid decline in the numbers of the peasantry, from about 50 per cent of the population of these countries after the war to perhaps 25 per cent in the 1980s.

The political culture of China

The dangers of generalisation inherent in the political culture approach, noted earlier in this chapter, apply with special force to China. Although less than half the size of the USSR, China's land area is vast and is criss-crossed with mountain ranges. Communications are relatively poor and regional differences are therefore fairly marked. Moreover, while most of the country lies in the temperate zone, there are wide variations of climate. The forces of nature have not been tamed as fully as in more advanced countries, and these impose different sets of problems in different provinces. The severity and diversity of these problems may be illustrated by the fact that in 1981 millions of people in north-central China faced quite severe food shortages because of extensive drought; in the western province of Sichuan, 1.5 million people lost their homes because of floods.

There is also the sheer size of the population. At the time of the Roman Empire the Han dynasty was already ruling over a state of 60 million people. The population today exceeds 1100 million. Some 94 per cent of the population is Han (as the Chinese call themselves) and the ethnic question does not loom so large as in the USSR. Nevertheless the minority nationalities, which are ethnically, culturally, religiously and/or linguistically distinct from the Han, exceed the total population of the United Kingdom.

Above all there is the richness of the Chinese past. A Chinese state has existed for over two millennia, except for relatively brief periods of disintegration. Chinese civilisation as such is considerably older. To attempt to encapsulate this history in the space of a few pages involves making some sweeping statements with which Sinologists might well take issue. Nevertheless it is essential that the attempt be made as distinctive features of the political culture can only be understood in terms of its sheer continuity.

The origins of Chinese political culture

When a bronze culture and a writing system developed in north China in the second millennium BC the civilisations of Mesopotamia and Egypt were already old. Unlike them, however, Chinese civilisation was never 'lost', but has continued to develop and expand up to the present day. The

characters used in *People's Daily* and *Red Flag* derive from
inscriptions used for divination over 3000 years ago and a few
of the archaic forms are still recognisable to any literate
Chinese. The weight of the Chinese tradition was already
apparent in the days of Confucius (551–479 BC). Far from
claiming to innovate, the sage and his disciples merely
claimed to look back to an earlier Golden Age and urged
rulers to revert to 'the ways of antiquity'. Confucius's teach-
ings provided the ideological cement for imperial China,
although subject to reinterpretation to produce a doctrine
appropriate to the interests of the state. Until the collapse of
the Qing dynasty in 1911 Confucius was revered as the
greatest teacher and philosopher that had ever lived, and no
man was considered educated unless he was steeped in the
classics.

This easy familiarity with their own history which Chinese
enjoy persisted into the communist era, although of course
radically different lessons were then drawn from the 'feudal'
past. Thus in the 1970s rival leaders cloaked their disagreement over politics and personalities under a mass campaign to
'criticise Confucius' in general and Confucians in particular.
They did so on the reasonable assumption that 'the masses'
would not be unduly surprised to find their newspapers filled
with discussion of events which had occurred perhaps 2000
years previously, but which were deemed to be relevant to
contemporary affairs. There is simply no exact parallel to this
in the European tradition. To invent one it would be necessary to imagine that Graeco-Roman civilisation had flourished
without a break from Homer onwards. One would also have
to assume that the Roman Empire, despite occasional difficulties, had continued to regenerate itself in its full glory until
in the twentieth century it had been destroyed by a revolt of
the Roman *plebs*. For Chinese civilisation contributed to, and
was in turn preserved by, political unification.

The word 'China' derives from the state of Qin whose ruler
hammered rival states into submission and so became the
'first emperor' in 220 BC. His tyrannical reign was marked by
the building of the Great Wall, although his dynasty was
short-lived. For more than 2000 years thereafter, however,
the norm was for China to be unified into a large and

powerful state, the eras of imperial greatness being identified by the names of the major dynasties: Han, Tang, Song, Yuan, Ming and Qing. Two of these were alien in origin, having been imposed by conquest from the north. The Yuan dynasty was established by the Mongols in the thirteenth century. China's last dynasty, the Qing, was set up by the Manchus in 1644. But in neither case did the fundamental nature of the Chinese state change significantly. China was vast, its population numerous, its economy rich and its political institutions highly developed. The conquerors were 'barbarians' whose temporary superiority rested mainly on military prowess. They found it easier to govern along traditional Chinese lines, and very quickly succumbed to sinification.

The physical and cultural superiority which China generally enjoyed in East Asia had major consequences for China's view of her place in the world. Whereas western states co-existed with others of roughly comparable strength and a similar level of economic and cultural development, China enjoyed a splendid isolation. To the north there were nomads, to the east the Koreans and Japanese and to the south the peoples of what is now Vietnam. Where relations existed these 'lesser' peoples were regarded as 'barbarians' who, in return for accepting tributary status, were permitted to enjoy the benefits of Confucian civilisation. But China considered that they had little to offer in return. Only India, separated by the Himalayan ranges, provided a major cultural input in the form of Buddhism.

Nor was China greatly interested in the wider world, although a certain amount of long-distance trade had always taken place. This was dramatically revealed in the early fifteenth century when the Ming dynasty sent armadas on seven great voyages which ventured as far as Aden and the coast of Africa. Despite this demonstration of an incredible capacity for sea-power, there was no follow-up. In marked contrast to the Portuguese at the end of the century, the Ming concluded that distant lands held little of interest or value and the voyages ceased. China remained inward-looking, the 'middle kingdom'.

This remarkable lack of awareness persisted even at the end of the eighteenth century when, in 1793, George III sent Lord

Macartney to Peking to press for greater trade links and the establishment of diplomatic relations. Macartney took as gifts for the emperor a number of examples of the products of industrialising Britain, including a hot-air balloon, clocks and watches, and scientific instruments. On arrival he was expected to kowtow like any other 'barbarian' and considerable time elapsed before a satisfactory compromise was eventually reached. Even then, the mission was unsuccessful. The emperor presented Macartney with a letter to George III which illustrated vividly China's ignorance of what was happening elsewhere. This informed the king that 'we have never valued ingenious articles, nor do we have the slightest need of your country's manufactures'. The monarch was also instructed to 'simply act in conformity with our wishes by strengthening your loyalty and swearing perpetual obedience so as to ensure that your country may share the blessings of peace'. Such an attitude was to cost China dear, and was to make her eventual exposure to modernisation a particularly traumatic experience.

Turning to internal arrangements, state, society and family were organised on strictly hierarchical principles. Confucianism stressed the importance of maintaining harmony and, in its official version, this meant that the lower orders were taught to 'know their place' and to subordinate themselves to their superiors. At the pinnacle of the system stood the emperor, an awesome figure with divine attributes. He was an absolute ruler entrusted with power through the 'Mandate of Heaven'. Some emperors were great scholars, warriors and active in state affairs, carrying out tours of their domains. Others rarely left their palaces and were heavily dependent on information given to them by the most senior imperial advisers.

The state was actually governed by a sophisticated salaried bureaucracy which, as early as the first century BC is said to have been composed of 130000 officials. At the centre the bureaucracy was divided into a number of specialised departments, but at lower levels imperial 'magistrates' exercised a wide range of administrative and judicial functions. Although large in absolute terms, China was not 'overgoverned'. The imperial administration stopped at the seats of government of approximately 2000 countries into which China was divided.

The official elite was unusual in that from Han times it was recruited primarily from men of education. This practice became institutionalised in the famous 'examination system'. With the exception of a few 'dishonourable' groups, males of all classes of society were free to compete, and only rarely was it possible to buy success or to acquire an official post by means of 'connections'. The belief that this method of selection was both fair and rational contributed enormously to the legitimacy of the elite, and the manifest link between educational achievement and political power encouraged a reverence for the former. It also resulted in a reasonable degree of social mobility in that families blessed with a succession of bright offspring could achieve a degree of eminence while the latter held official positions but tended to revert to their original obscurity as soon as nature showed its preference for regression to the norm.

China was, however, a limited meritocracy. The examinations tested candidates' ability to master officially prescribed interpretations of the Confucian classics and to reproduce them in appropriately stylised forms. This in turn required that candidates had a formal, lengthy and orthodox education, and the state provided little of this. There were many instances of poor boys being sponsored by a wealthy relative or kinship organisation, but as a general rule education was restricted to children of the well-to-do who could afford to pay. Those who successfully passed the gruelling series of examinations joined the ranks of officialdom and occupied themselves with the usual governmental tasks of an agrarian society. They collected taxes, raised forced labour and conscripts as required, saw that irrigation systems were repaired and extended, and settled disputes. In general they acted in conjunction with, and in the interests of, the local landlords.

This was due partly to the fact that they were drawn from the same strata of society, and local landlords who had failed to obtain official positions for themselves tended to constitute the 'natural' leaders of rural China on whom the magistrates relied. It was also a result of corruption; for official stipends were small. Some officials were content to retire 'with only wind in their sleeves'. Many, however, resembled the man who was so rapacious that 'even an egg was smaller when it passed through his hands'. Therefore they sold 'favours' to the local gentry, who could afford them and saw to it that exactions fell most harshly on the peasantry.

The landlord class was, then, in a favoured position, just below the ranks of officialdom in the hierarchy. Chinese landlords rarely owned vast estates, and landholdings were extremely modest compared with those in Tsarist Russia. But landlords were a leisured class nevertheless. One of the less attractive features of Confucian culture was the widespread belief that a gentleman should not engage in manual work, and landlords left the actual farming to others. They themselves pursued interests appropriate to persons of education: they wrote poetry, painted, practised calligraphy and, of course, studied antiquity.

It was the peasants who did the work. The bulk of the population, they ranged from persons who hired labour to assist them to landless labourers who lived by selling their labour power. In terms of Confucian ideology they enjoyed an honourable position. So, too, did artisans. This still left a number of groups in society who were officially regarded with contempt, among whom were merchants. Merchants lacked education and, unlike peasants, did not actually 'produce' anything, but managed nevertheless to create wealth for themselves. They were often regarded as parasites, an attitude which was ultimately to marry nicely with Marxist theories of capitalist exploitation. Commerce did flourish but it was subject to official regulation and, if an activity were particularly profitable, would then be made an official monopoly. Consequently, it was not until the middle of the nineteenth century that a bourgeoisie of any real significance began to appear and that came about only as a result of foreign penetration.

Soldiers, too, found little favour. Dynasties were founded by force of arms, and martial emperors and great generals were accorded respect. But this did not extend to the common soldiery. The contempt of the scholar-officials for them was epitomised in the saying, 'One does not use good iron to make a nail, nor a good man for a soldier.' There were also the *déclassé* elements. These included common criminals, those like fortune-tellers and prostitutes who earned their living by dubious means, and itinerant fishermen, boatmen and coolies. There were also the secret societies. These existed throughout Chinese history and were to be found in both secular and religious varieties. They were a refuge for the unwanted and the disaffected, providing the lowly members of society with what has been termed a 'surrogate kinship organisation'. With heterodox beliefs and esoteric rituals, the societies were outside the law. Their activities ranged from operating as Chinese Robin Hoods to mounting full-scale rebellions, and they participated in the overthrow of several dynasties. Generally, however, their influence was limited.

Finally, there was the family. This, too, was meticulously structured and children were brought up to recognise their own place and that of their relatives within a framework which stressed male dominance and, above all, the utmost respect for the aged. Within the home given names were rarely used; instead family members addressed each other in terms of rank: 'elder brother', 'younger sister' and so on. The stress was on duties rather than rights and, in the event of disputes, the young were expected to subordinate themselves to their elders and to 'swallow bitterness' and endure their lot without complaint. Self-assertiveness was actively discouraged and the interests of the group took priority over those of the individual.

The ideas that man possessed innate goodness, and that the proper education would enable him to achieve his full potential, were among the most ancient in Chinese thought. In practise, however, 'goodness' was equated with those attributes which the imperial authorities deemed desirable for the maintenance of the existing social order, and the use of education to inculcate 'correct' ideas were fully accepted as part of government policy. Under the Ming and Qing dynasties particularly, great efforts were made to promote official orthodoxy. Those who received a lengthy formal education in order to compete in the imperial examinations were, of course, taught to value conformity. But the imperial authorities were not content to leave matters there. The Qing dynasty, especially, tried to indoctrinate the masses also by establishing a lecture system. In every district lecturers were appointed on the basis of their scholarship, age and good character, and were required to expound imperial maxims twice a month. Edicts of a morally uplifting nature were provided by the emperors themselves for the edification of their subjects and attendance at the lectures was compulsory. An interesting feature of the system was that lecturers were required to use examples of virtuous behaviour for purposes of emulation. Equally, those deemed guilty of anti-social behaviour were criticised, their names were posted in public places and remained there until they showed contrition for their acts. Thus the communist glorification of moral exemplars and vilification of 'negative examples' has an imperial past.

Confucianism, therefore, fulfilled many of the functions of organised religion in other societies and, especially in its official version, contributed to the maintenance of social order just as state churches have done elsewhere. Ordinary Chinese did not consider they had any right to participate in government and, being fully conscious of the fact that government meant demands, tended to minimise their contacts with it. Nevertheless there was a widespread acceptance of the 'rightness' of the state's institutional arrangements, and Confucianism was the basis for the value system to which most subscribed. For much of the time the bulk of the population was passive, and foreign visitors commented on the 'easy governability' of the Chinese people.

The harsh authoritarianism of the imperial system was somewhat mitigated by the officials themselves. The lengthy education they had undergone laid emphasis on moral virtue and, just as the good subject and the 'filial son' were inseparable, officials were supposed to act as the 'fathers and mothers' of the people, strict but fundamentally benevolent. They were also expected to remonstrate with higher authority, including the emperor himself, if they considered that injustices and oppression were occurring. Many did, even at the risk of exile or death for themselves and their families. Thus in 1959, when Peng Dehuai remonstrated with Mao for the hardship inflicted by the Great Leap Forward and suffered disgrace for his pains, he was acting in a noble tradition.

Wu Han, a playwright, promptly drew attention to this by writing a play entitled 'Hai Rui Dismissed from Office'. This dealt with the life of a Ming dynasty official who had similarly spoken up on behalf of an oppressed peasantry and had been dismissed by the emperor for so doing. 'Emperor Mao' was among those who recognised the analogy, and in 1965 Wu Han became the first target in the Cultural Revolution and paid the price.

In fact, if a dynasty refused to listen to those who remonstrated on the people's behalf, there was little alternative but rebellion. If the rebellion were successful, a rebel leader would establish a new dynasty and it would be explained that his predecessor had lost the 'Mandate of Heaven'. Reforms would be instituted, including a more equitable distribution of the land, and the new dynasty would embark on a new era of greatness before succumbing, eventually, to decay and overthrow. This dynastic cycle repeated itself until the nineteenth century, when the Qing dynasty entered its period of decline. Internally a growth in population occurred, and in the absence of significant technological advance this resulted in considerable land hunger. Landlords and officials benefited from the pressure on fixed resources, rural misery increased dramatically and there was a marked rise in social unrest. There was, however, a new element in the equation – foreign intervention.

Within fifty years of the Macartney mission Britain inflicted on China a humiliating defeat in the Opium War of 1839–42. The Treaty of Nanking of 1842 forced China to cede to Britain the island of Hong Kong and to open up to British trade. From then on China was at the mercy of any foreign power, and throughout the nineteenth century the Western nations (and eventually Japan) used force to secure trading rights, established themselves in 'concessions' on Chinese soil and made what became known as the 'treaty ports' their base for commercial and ultimately industrial operations. Foreign penetration was also religious and cultural, in that it included massive (and unwanted) missionary activity and the establishment of Western educational institutions. Chinese attempts to resist were defeated by military means, followed by the imposition of financial indemnities.

The Western onslaught transformed Chinese attitudes of superiority into xenophobia and, ultimately, into a more positive sense of nationalism. This became particularly strong in the aftermath of the First World War, when a cultural and nationalistic renaissance known as the 'May 4 Movement' began, taking its name from anti-Japanese demonstrations which occurred on 4 May 1919. The coming of the West also initiated a debate on how China should adapt, which in some respects is still continuing. In the nineteenth century Chinese statesmen and intellectuals argued fiercely as to how far Westernisation should go. Protagonists ranged from those who believed that minimal change was necessary to those who saw salvation in the establishment of a constitutional monarchy. One important viewpoint was that it would be possible to combine Chinese 'essence' with Western 'utility', taking from the West its technological achievements while leaving Confucian values and structures relatively untouched.

In fact no suitable combination of the two was achieved during the lifetime of the Qing dynasty. Unable to cope with either foreign interference or domestic discontent, the Qing elite was assailed by peasant rebellions throughout the nineteenth century. In the treaty ports the nascent bourgeoisie became amenable to Western political ideas which gave rise to a small but influential republican movement led by Sun Yat-sen which saw the overthrow of the Qing dynasty as a prerequisite for China's national salvation. In 1911 the imperial system was overthrown and in 1912 a republic was proclaimed.

The Republic lasted until 1949 on mainland China (and continues to claim to be the rightful government from its island stronghold of Taiwan). However, in many respects it is best regarded as a watershed between two eras. Its early years were characterised by warlord rule in which power was fragmented and was exercised by men offering diverse solutions to China's problems. Eventually Chiang Kai-shek succeeded in imposing a new unity. However, because of the Sino-Japanese war of 1937–45 and the rise of Chinese communism, Chiang's regime could do little to forge lasting institutions and distinctive values. It represented an uneasy amalgam of Western ideals, attempts to revive Confucian principles, and a strong element of dictatorial practice. Reforms rarely got further than the statute book, and the mass of the population remained deprived of any effective voice. It was left to the Chinese communists to try to lead China into the modern world and to attempt to provide new institutions and values.

Chinese political culture in the post-revolutionary period

Although socialist ideas were entering China from the late nineteenth century, knowledge of Marxism began to make a significant impact only after the First World War. At a time when the victors were demonstrating that their concern for nationalism and democracy was largely confined to Europe, the Bolsheviks' success in seizing power, their superb organisational capability in subsequently defending their state, and their promises that they were quite different from the 'imperialists' exerted a powerful influence. In its early days Sun Yatsen's Nationalist Party sought Soviet assistance, and in 1921 the Chinese Communist Party was established.

Initially communist successes were minimal as the party attempted to follow slavishly ideas and practices formed in a European context. But Mao Zedong succeeded in 'sinifying' Marxism by tying it to the criticism of specific features of the traditional Chinese culture. What Mao did, in essence, was to exploit the dissatisfaction with Confucian values and institutions which had become widespread during the decline of the Qing dynasty. In part he did so by making use of the 'counter-culture' of peasant rebels and secret societies which had always existed alongside the dominant orthodoxy of the Confucian elite. Of rich peasant stock himself, Mao came to emphasise the revolutionary potential of the peasant masses when he investigated their opposition to the traditional political and economic power structure in his home province. His 1927 'Report on an Investigation of the Peasant Movement in Hunan' concluded that in the last analysis the peasants were the best judges of those placed in power over them. He held that peasant violence was greatest in those areas where the local gentry and landlords had been most oppressive and that the masses could be trusted to distinguish between their various exploiters. He wrote:

> The peasants are clear-sighted. Who is bad and who is not, who is the worst and who is not quite so vicious, who deserves severe punishment and who deserves to be let off lightly – the peasant keeps clear accounts and very seldom has the punishment exceeded the crime.

Mao's appreciation of peasant consciousness convinced him of the value of political participation as an instrument for attitudinal change. He was impressed by the speed with which traditional attitudes of passivity could be cast aside and how peasants were able, more or less spontaneously, to establish their own political organisations. He was also quick to note the value of violence in facilitating changes, and argued that it was essential to go beyond polite debate:

> To put it bluntly, it is necessary to create terror for a while in every rural area, or otherwise it would be impossible to suppress the activities of the counter-revolutionaries ... Proper limits have to be exceeded in order to right a wrong or else the wrong cannot be righted.

Thus, in contrast to old ideas of hierarchy, Mao put forward a populist faith in the ability of ordinary people. He saw the masses as China's greatest asset in building the revolution, an enormous reservoir of creative power. Whereas Confucian China had insisted that the educated should rule, Mao made a virtue out of the very backwardness of much of China's population. Thus he was to write in 1958:

> China's 600 million people have two remarkable peculiarities: they are first of all poor, and secondly, blank. That may sound like a bad thing, but it is really a good thing. Poor people want change, want to do things, want revolution.

Mao's respect for the peasantry in particular and for the masses in general was further strengthened by the circumstances by which the communists came to power in China. In contrast to the Bolsheviks, the Chinese Communist Party had to fight a protracted war and had to do so in the villages of the rural hinterland. There, desperately short of manpower and material, the party could only survive by developing techniques of 'people's war'. To gain support guerrillas must offer a better deal than their enemies are able to do. Hence in the rural areas, and particularly in the great base area centred on Yan'an in the years 1937–45, Mao concentrated on creating a political and military machine which had a genuinely popular base. This was embodied in a style of leadership and participation designed to ensure that leaders and masses remained united, the famous 'mass line'. In his most celebrated statement on the subject, Mao in 1943 defined the 'mass line' when he instructed that:

> In all the practical work of the party, all correct leadership is necessarily from the masses, to the masses.
>
> This means: take the ideas of the masses (scattered and unsystematic ideas) and concentrate them (through study turn them into concentrated and systematic ideas); then go to the masses and propagate and explain these ideas until the masses embrace them as their own, hold fast to them and translate them into action, and test the correctness of these ideas in such action. Then once again concentrate ideas from the masses and once again go to the masses so that the ideas are persevered in and carried through. And so on, over and over again.

This approach, with its rejection of bureaucratic practices, gave the party a distinctive political style which did much to bring it to power in 1949. Thereafter it helped it to consolidate that power by mobilising the populace in a host of mass campaigns. These were directed at human targets such as 'counter-revolutionaries' and landlords, but also natural ones: pests and diseases and the Chinese earth itself. Through involvement many Chinese underwent attitudinal change and learned to 'take the attitude of being the masters', whether by attacking former 'exploiters' or by learning, through participation in water conservancy campaigns, that the forces of nature could be tamed.

The 'mass line' was about consultation, education, persuasion and eliciting an enthusiastic response. It was not, however, necessarily concerned over-much with democracy. Mao and his colleagues were Leninists and the party was the revolutionary 'vanguard', not simply an agency for implementing the wishes of the people. The weakness of the 'mass line' was, ironically, that it reflected in part a traditional view that the masses would accept the leadership's interpretation of their true interests if only these were properly explained. Chinese communist theory did acknowledge that differences of interest could exist; but in practice the leadership, especially Mao, was unable to accept this.

From the late 1950s to Mao's death in September 1976 acute difficulties arose, especially in the Great Leap Forward and the Cultural Revolution, when Mao's attempts to impose a particularly utopian interpretation of socialism conflicted with the view of their best material interests held by the masses and, increasingly, large sections of the party leadership also. In place of persuasion the 'mass line' degenerated into hectoring, bullying and resort to purges. In the face of widespread opposition to his radical policies in virtually every area, Mao blamed everyone and everything but his beloved 'masses' and the policies themselves, and attacked not only individuals but the institutions of the People's Republic also. The immediate result was widespread violence, near-anarchy in many places, and the reappearance of many of the more unpleasant aspects of traditional patterns of thought and behaviour. Mao himself sought to bolster his position by permitting, and probably encouraging, a personality cult which bestowed upon him the awesome attributes of a traditional emperor. Other political leaders banded into highly polarised factions which brought to Beijing an era of palace intrigues reminiscent of imperial dynasties in their days of decline. In an uncertain world ordinary citizens sought a measure of security by resorting to particularist loyalties based on 'connections'.

Faced with a damaged economy and widespread demoralisation, the leaders who have ruled China since Mao's death in September 1976 have, by voluntary or imposed choice, dismantled most of his policies and have, tacitly at least, rejected many of the principles underlying his desire to produce a thorough and irreversible transformation of traditional attitudes. The mobilisation style of politics has been discarded and attention has been given to creating effective political institutions centring round the party itself. In the country-side, the 'production responsibility system' leaves agriculture collectivised in theory but in practice has restored individual household farming. In both town and country private commerce flourishes again. The collectivist, egalitarian and class-based jargon of the Cultural Revolution has not disappeared entirely and still commands some support in minority sections of the leadership and populace. But the emphasis of official pronouncements since the late 1970s has been on economic development and the need to harness the skills of the talented to achieve it. Enterprising peasants and 'advanced' workers have their place, but greater stress has been laid on the need to produce graduate manpower and give it responsibility throughout society. In a curious sense China is again turning to the 'scholar official'. Even Confucianism has been harnessed to the causes of economic development, with Chinese historians producing articles on how Confucian scholars of the late Song dynasty had much to say of direct relevance to China's modernisation.

Further reading

The classic study of political culture is Pye and Verba (1965), which contains a chapter on Soviet Russia by Frederick Barghoorn as well as further more analytic discussions. There are shorter introductions to the concept in Kavanagh (1972) and Rosenbaum (1975). The political cultures of a number of communist states are surveyed in Brown and Gray (1979); a further more methodological discussion, focusing particularly upon the USSR and Czechoslovakia, is available in Brown (1984).

The fullest available study of the political culture of the USSR is White (1979). Glazov (1985) is a stimulating *émigré* account. See also the classic study by Inkeles and Bauer (1959) based upon interviews with post-Second World War *émigrés*; the results of interviews with more recent *émigrés* are presented in Gitelman (1977) and White (1978b). On patterns of Soviet historical development, Tucker (1977), Bialer

(1980), Cohen (1985) and Hosking (1985) are particularly helpful. White and Pravda (1987) deals with developments in the official ideology. On the national question in the USSR, see Katz (1975), Carrère d'Encausse (1979), Lapidus (1984), Connor (1984), which deals with Marxist regimes generally, Akiner (1985), which deals with Soviet Muslims, and Karklins (1986). On religious and nationalist movements, see Dunlop (1983) and (1985), and Ellis (1986). Memoirs which may particularly be recommended include Ginzburg (1967) and (1981), Yevtushenko (1963), Etkind (1978) and Khrushchev (1971–74).

Two classic accounts of the inter-war period in Eastern Europe are Seton-Watson (1986) and Rothschild (1974). There is no one synoptic work on the political cultures of the post-war period, but a number of country studies are useful. Among them are Ulč (1974) on Czechoslovakia, Toma and Volgyes (1977) on Hungary, Pavlowitch (1971) on Yugoslavia, Zukin (1975) and Doder (1978), also about Yugoslavia. Mićunović (1980), which is primarily about foreign policy but which also contains valuable insights on Yugoslav attitudes, Oren (1973) on Bulgaria, and the relevant sections of Jowitt (1971) on Romania. Shafir (1985) and Heinrich (1986) provide more recent surveys on Romania and Hungary respectively, with a first chapter in each dealing with history and political traditions. Hirsowicz (1986) offers an interpretation of coercion and control in communist societies which is of general application. Memoir literature and novels which should be noted include Kohout (1972), Illyés (1967), a brilliant account of the pre-war Hungarian peasantry, Brandys (1981), which offers an analysis of Polishness, and Mlynár (1980), which is interesting on the Czechoslovak leadership's perceptions of the Soviet Union in 1968.

An immensely detailed and valuable study of Chinese political culture is Solomon (1971). A more narrowly conceived but useful study is Liu (1976). On patterns of Chinese historical development and contemporary trends, Schram (1973, ch. 1) and (1981) are particularly helpful. On recent doctrinal developments, see Schram (1984) and Brugger (1985). Major studies of Mao include Schram's biography (1970), his study of Mao's political thought (1969) and his collection of more recent Mao writings (1974). See also Starr (1979) on Mao's political thought. Useful studies of recent developments include Watson (1984), which deals with social stratification, Gold (1985), which considers personal relationships since the Cultural Revolution, and Maxwell and McFarlane (1984), Schell (1986) and Prybyla (1986), all of which deal with the wider reorientation of policy under the current Dengist leadership.

3

Structures of Government

The formal structures of government – constitutions, legislatures and executives – have not normally been accorded much attention in the study of communist political systems. There are good reasons for this. In the first place, the electoral system is closely controlled in these countries, and, although there is sometimes a choice of candidate or even of party in local or national elections, the whole process is closely controlled by the communist party and no candidates openly opposed to Marxist–Leninist principles are allowed to stand. The legislatures to which the deputies are elected meet infrequently, their votes are normally unanimous, their legislative output is fairly meagre, and no direct challenge is ever issued to the government which are nominally responsible to them. The communist or ruling party normally provides a majority of deputies in these assemblies, its members constitute a party group or caucus which is expected to take a leading part in their proceedings, and party members, all of them subject to party discipline, dominate the key positions at all levels. Although there is some variety among them in terms of institutional form (see Table 3.1) and, as we shall see, in organisational effectiveness, it has been conventional, for reasons such as these, to regard communist legislatures as mere 'rubber stamps' and formal government structures more generally as of little consequence for the domestic political process.

Valid though these criticisms are, it has become apparent in recent years that they equally be taken too far. Communist legislatures, certainly, do not challenge the governments they

TABLE 3.1

Legislatures in the communist states

Country	Name of legislature	No. of chambers	No. of deputies	No. of parties	Electoral choice
Albania	People's Assembly	1	250	1	No
Bulgaria	National Assembly	1	400	2	No
China	National People's Congress	1	2978	9	Yes*
Cuba	National Assembly	1	499	1	Yes*
Czechoslovakia	Federal Assembly	2	350	5	No
GDR	People's Chamber	1	500	5	No
Hungary	National Assembly	1	352	1	Yes
Kampuchea	National Assembly	1	117	1	Yes
Korea	Supreme People's Assembly	1	615	3	No
Laos	People's Congress	1	45	1	No
Mongolia	Great People's Khural	1	370	1	No
Poland	Sejm	1	460	3	Yes
Romania	Grand National Assembly	1	369	1	Yes
USSR	Supreme Soviet	2	1500	1	No
Vietnam	National Assembly	1	496	3	Yes
Yugoslavia	Federal Assembly	2	308	1	Yes*

* Elections to legislatures in these countries are indirect and a degree of choice is permitted at the preliminary stage only.

Sources: International Centre for Parliamentary Documentation of the Inter-Parliamentary Union, *Parliaments of the World*, 2nd ed. (Aldershot, Hants, 1986); *Ezhegodnik Bol'shoi Sovetskoi Entsiklopedii 1986g.* (Moscow, 1987); and current press reports.

nominally elect, still less the communist party authorities; and they accept the official doctrine by which the party rules, or decides 'political' questions, leaving state institutions the task of governing or of carrying out the decisions that the party has approved. Communist legislatures, however, are not thereby condemned to an entirely negligible role in the political system. They help to legitimate the system, by providing it with at least an appearance of electoral endorsement by the people to whom all power theoretically belongs; they are widely representative of all sections of the community and play a role of some significance in involving (for instance) women, young people and ethnic minorities in the workings of the political system; they provide a 'school of government' for a substantial proportion of the population, particularly at the local level where the rate of turnover of deputies is most rapid; and they provide a useful means by which the party authorities can give at least the impression that the issues that concern the population are being seriously discussed at a policy-making level. Above all, through their developing committee structures they provide a means of investigating matters of public concern as well as of checking upon the performance of government and discussing the annual economic plan and state budget. It is difficult to establish empirically the extent to which representative institutions in the communist states now dispose of a substantial measure of independent authority; in Poland, Hungary and Yugoslavia, at least, they would appear to do so, and in the other states the influence of representative institutions is by no means negligible. In this chapter we shall look at the situation in a number of the communist states in more detail in order to provide the basis for such an assessment.

The USSR: constitution, legislature and government

The largest of the communist states, the USSR, is officially a federation consisting of a voluntary union of fifteen nominally sovereign union republics (the RSFSR or Russian Republic, the Ukraine, Belorussia, Latvia, Lithuania, Estonia, Moldavia, Georgia, Armenia, Azerbaidzhan, Kirgizia, Kazakhstan, Uzbekistan, Turkmenia and Tadzhikistan). The RSFSR is by far the largest of these republics, accounting for about 76 per cent of the total area and for about 52 per cent of the total population. All the other republics are far smaller and most of them have a population of no more than two or three million. The union republics are described in the present Constitution, adopted in 1977, as 'sovereign Soviet socialist states', and they have a considerable range of formal powers, including the right to secede and the right to establish diplomatic relations with foreign powers. (Two of them, the Ukraine and Belorussia, have in fact been members of the United Nations since its foundation.) The laws of the USSR as a whole, however, take precedence over those of the union republics, the decisions of the national government are binding throughout the USSR, and the state as well as the party is officially committed to the doctrine of democratic centralism by which the decisions of higher bodies of state authority are binding upon lower ones. The union republics, accordingly, are rather less than sovereign states; but they do provide a formal expression of the multi-national character of the state (in each of them a particular nationality is supposed to be predominant), and, as we shall see, they exercise a substantial number of devolved powers of government.

The principle of democratic centralism applies not simply to relations between the federal government and the union republics, but also to relations between the union republics and the lower levels of government that are subordinate to them. The most important of these sub-divisions are the regions (*oblasti*) into which the eight largest republics are divided, and the districts (*raiony*) into which the regions, larger cities and the other union republics are divided. A simplified representation of these divisions is set out in Figure 3.1. A number of nationalities which are not sufficiently numerous to have their own union republics exercise a more limited range of powers within an autonomous soviet socialist republic (ASSR), an autonomous region or an autonomous area. There were 121 regions in the USSR in 1987, which together with the twenty ASSRs, eight autonomous regions, ten autonomous areas and six territories (*kraya*) form the

FIGURE 3.1 The state structure of the USSR (simplified)

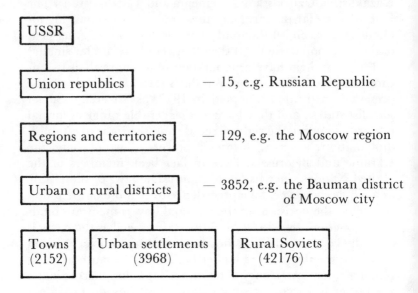

'provincial' level of government in the USSR. Below them come the urban and rural districts (641 and 3211 respectively in 1987), and then the towns, urban settlements and villages which constitute the lowest level of state authority, or local government proper. At all levels of this system soviets or councils are elected, usually for two and a half years at a time. In 1987 more than 2.3 million citizens were serving on elected bodies of this kind at various levels, and more than 30 million citizens were associated with their work, usually by unpaid work on a voluntary commission of some sort. The soviets in turn elect executive committees or (at the union or autonomous republican level) councils of ministers to carry on the day-to-day work of government.

At the national level the representative body is known as the Supreme Soviet of the USSR, and it is constituted as shown in Figure 3.2. It consists of two chambers formally equal in powers, one of them, the Council of the Union, elected by the population at large (approximately 1 deputy for every 300 000 of the population), and the other, the

FIGURE 3.2 The USSR Supreme Soviet and government structure (simplified)

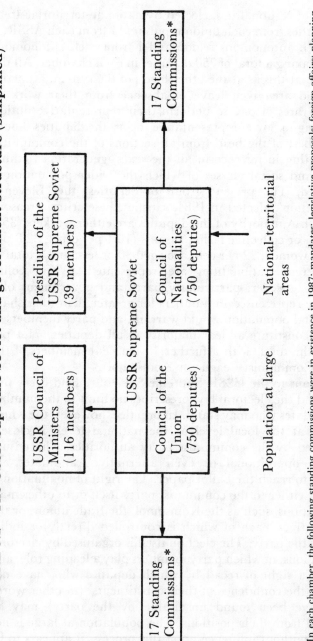

*In each chamber, the following standing commissions were in existence in 1987: mandates; legislative proposals; foreign affairs; planning and budget; industry; power engineering; transport and communications; construction and the building materials industry; agro-industrial complex; science and technology; consumer goods and services; housing and municipal services; health and social security; education and culture; women's work and social conditions and the protection of motherhood and childhood; youth affairs; and conservation and the rational use of natural resources.

──→ : elected by and formally subordinate to lower body.

Council of Nationalities, elected by national–territorial areas (32 deputies from each union republic, 11 from each ASSR, 5 from each autonomous region and 1 from each autonomous area), making a total of 750 deputies in each chamber. All the deputies, at this as at the other levels of the system, are part-time, and are given leave of absence from their work at average rates of pay to perform their representative duties. According to Soviet representative theory the deputies should be the 'best of the best' from all sections of the community, representing in microcosm all the sexes, generations, ethnic groups and social classes of which the wider population is composed. The present group of deputies, the 'Eleventh Convocation', elected in 1984, satisfies these criteria reasonably well. A majority of the deputies are either workers (35.2 per cent) or collective farm peasants (16.1 per cent); 32.8 per cent are women; 22 per cent are aged 30 or less; and a total of 61 different nationalities are represented. White collar workers, however, particularly party and government officials, are represented in numbers far greater than their share of the total population would warrant, and party members in general constitute a clear majority of all deputies (71.4 per cent of the total, with a further 15 per cent members of the Young Communist League or Komsomol).

Elections to the USSR Supreme Soviet are held every five years, and the electoral law prescribes no limit to the number of candidates who may stand. In practice, however, the whole process, at the local level as the national level, is closely controlled by the communist party authorities, who ensure that no oppositional or even alternative candidates are allowed to reach the ballot paper. The right of nomination is reserved either to the communist party itself or to other mass organisations, such as the Komsomol, the trade unions or the co-operatives, each of which is controlled directly or indirectly by the party. The election itself is organised by electoral commissions, in which party members play a leading role, and there is a right of recall by which deputies who 'have not justified the confidence of their constituents' (in other words who have been found unsuitable by the party) may be removed from their positions. The population at large is not entirely without influence upon this process: it appears to be possible, for instance, to exercise some influence upon the choice of the single individual who is to be nominated, and cases are known when a particularly unpopular choice has had to be withdrawn in the face of the obvious dissatisfaction of those who were supposed to nominate him. It is also possible to exert some leverage by threatening not to vote until a number of local grievances are attended to (voting is not in fact compulsory, but the authorities in each area are under considerable pressure to secure a near-universal turnout), and by writing comments upon the ballot paper, all of which are collated subsequently and passed to the relevant authorities for their consideration. By and large, however, Soviet elections are not of great significance as a means of bringing the political preferences of the Soviet public to the attention of the leadership, and they certainly provide no opportunity for the choice from among genuinely competing candidates and parties which is the essence of elections in the liberal democracies.

The election itself is held on a Sunday, usually in March at the national level, and it is preceded by a prolonged publicity campaign in which the press, radio and television, as well as electoral 'agitators', bring party and government policies to the attention of the voters and establish precise electoral registers. All citizens over the age of 18 have the vote, apart from the 'legally certified insane', and every effort is made to secure the maximum possible turnout on the election day itself. The polling stations are open from 6 a.m. until 10 p.m., and in addition ballot boxes are brought to the sick in their beds, to shepherds in distant pastures, to passengers in long-distance trains and to Soviet ships in foreign waters. Even cosmonauts in outer space are enabled to telegraph their vote to earth, though hardly to keep it secret as the electoral law requires. An affirmative vote for the list of candidates, the 'bloc of Communists and non-party people', requires a voter to do no more than drop the ballot paper, unmarked, into the box; a negative vote, however, normally requires a voter to make use of the screened-off booth in the polling station, and most voters appear to think that it would be unwise to draw attention to themselves in this way. The level of turnout is accordingly very high; in 1984, for instance, 99.99 per cent of the registered electorate took part in the elections, and of these 99.94 and 99.95 per cent respectively voted for the single list of candidates for the Council of the Union and the Council of Nationalities. At the local level candidates are occasionally defeated by failing to secure a majority of votes cast; at the national level, however, all the candidates are invariably elected.

The deputies, once elected, keep in touch with their constituents in a variety of ways. One of the most basic is by means of reports upon the fulfilment of the mandates (*nakazy*) that they adopt when they hold their nomination meeting with their constituents. These mandates, which will normally have been agreed beforehand with the party authorities but which would serve no purpose if they were entirely meaningless to the electors, normally concern matters such as the improvement of the local transport system or the availability of shops or kindergartens in the locality, and deputies are legally required to report back upon their fulfilment. Deputies also hold regular surgeries in their constituencies to which citizens can bring problems, they are required to hold general meetings with their constituents at least once or twice a year, and they normally both receive and engage in an extensive correspondence. They may be asked to intercede with the relevant authorities in the case of an unlawful dismissal from a factory, for instance, or to try to secure a family a larger flat. In some areas local soviets have conducted opinion polls to discover what the public thinks about the matters they are considering, and in at least one case some enterprising deputies have established a regular television programme, 'Deputies' reception', at which local issues can be discussed. Being part-time and without much in the way of secretarial or research assistance, however, deputies are usually at a disadvantage in their dealings with the government bureaucracy, and despite periodic efforts to bolster their authority, such as the 'Law on the Status of the Deputy' which was adopted in 1972, the individual deputy in the USSR – as indeed elsewhere – is not normally a political actor of great consequence.

Deputies, as already mentioned, take part in formal sessional activity on a relatively infrequent basis. For instance, the national legislature, the USSR Supreme Soviet, is required by the Constitution to meet twice a year, with the possibility of further sessions if they are specifically convened by the Presidium or requested by a union republic or by one-third of the deputies. No particular length is specified for any of these sessions, however, and in fact the average length of meetings in recent years has been about two or three days on each occasion or a total of about five days a year, making the USSR Supreme Soviet one of the world's least frequently convened assemblies. One of the two annual sessions is normally devoted to a different policy area each year, while the other is normally reserved for a consideration of the annual plan and budget. Over the past few years, for instance, the Supreme Soviet has adopted basic principles of legislation on environmental pollution (June 1980), housing (June 1981) and education (April 1984), as well as an important series of measures following the adoption of the new constitution in October 1977 covering matters such as the electoral system (July 1978), citizenship (December 1978), the Supreme Court and legal profession (November 1979) and the state frontier (November 1982). The number of deputies who can take part in the discussion of any of these matters, however, is limited for purely practical reasons to about 30 or 40, and for the most part these formal sessions are occasions for the explanation of government policy to deputies and to the country at large rather than for the detailed formulation of policy or the examination of government performance.

The second session of the year, which is normally devoted to the budget and the economic plan, is usually the longer of the two and gives the deputies slightly more opportunity to intervene in the discussion. About forty deputies were able to take part in the discussion of the plan and budget in the November 1979 session, for instance, and most of them were able to raise issues of particular importance to their constituents as well as matters of more general significance. A deputy from north Kazakhstan called for greater investment in the coalmining industry in his republic and for the building of more schools in country areas; a deputy from Belorussia called for more technical colleges, housing and clinics to be built in his republic, and for more staff to be allocated to the railways in that area; and a deputy from Georgia raised the issue of the supply of raw materials to factories in his republic and criticised the ministries responsible for their shortcomings in this connection. Other deputies raised matters such as the irrigation of agricultural lands, the pollution of the Black Sea, labour turnover in Siberia, the quality of urban architecture and the work of the construction industry in general. Deputies do not carry their objections so far as to vote against the government, or even abstain, when policies are formally submitted to the vote at the end of these debates; but their remarks are usually specific and directly worded, and if the whole process is to serve even propagandist purposes the party cannot allow observations of this kind to be entirely ignored.

The standing commissions of the Supreme Soviet

The most considerable influence exerted by deputies upon government policy, however, is probably through the standing committees or commissions, of which there are at present seventeen attached to each chamber. When the Supreme Soviet was first established in 1938 there were only four commissions attached to each chamber with no more than 8 per cent of deputies serving on them; but particularly since 1966, when the system of commissions was reorganised, both the number of commissions and the number of deputies sitting on them have increased considerably. The present total is 34 commissions in both chambers with 1210 deputies (80.7 per cent of the total) as members. The commissions cover all the main areas of policy, such as international affairs, planning and the budget, agriculture, industry, health, education and science (see Figure 3.2). They meet somewhat more often than the Supreme Soviet itself, about three or four times a year in most cases, and in addition their members form subcommittees for preparatory investigations which meet more frequently again. All in all the expansion in the number and authority of the standing commissions is perhaps the most significant development to have occurred in Soviet legislative politics over the last couple of decades, and it is the respect in which the 'rubber stamp' stereotype is most obviously inadequate.

The standing commissions, broadly speaking, perform

three functions. In the first place, they have the right to initiate legislation and to propose amendments to draft legislation submitted to them by the Presidium for their consideration. The first of these powers is used relatively infrequently (over the past ten years, for instance, the commissions have submitted only two items of legislation to the Supreme Soviet in this way). The commissions, however, are much more active in scrutinising draft legislation, and they normally propose extensive amendments in the reports which they submit on the drafts to the Supreme Soviet itself. The commissions are assisted in this work by academic and other institutions, to which relevant pieces of legislation are usually submitted for consideration, and also by the public debate and correspondence which takes place when (as is frequently the case) a piece of draft legislation is published in draft form in the press and comments are specifically invited. More than 110 million citizens were reported to have taken part in the discussion of the 1983 labour collectives law, for instance, and about 120 million took part, through meetings and correspondence, in discussion of the 1984 educational reforms. The commissions take these comments into account in preparing their recommendations upon the legislation in question, which are then presented to the Supreme Soviet in a 'co-report' after the legislation concerned has been presented by a government spokesman. Most items of legislation are modified to some degree, and some are altered considerably. About a 100 corrections, additions or other changes were made in the draft educational reform of 1984, for instance, and many additional proposals were referred to the Ministry of Education and other bodies for further consideration.

The commissions, secondly, exercise a supervisory or monitoring power over the work of government and state bodies, a power known in Russian as *kontrol'*. The forms this takes are very varied. It may involve, for instance, investigating the performance of ministers in matters such as the operation of the transport system, the development of new building materials, the increased output and improved quality of consumer goods, the improvement of services in rural areas and the construction of greater numbers of children's pre-school institutions; or it may involve an inquiry into the observance of legislation on matters such as pollution or the employment of women and juveniles. The relevant commissions, separately or jointly, usually appoint a preparatory group to conduct an initial investigation into such matters, which will typically arrange for its various members to look into the situation in their own localities and then report back to the committee. ('A commission meeting usually takes several hours, but the preparation for it usually takes several months', as the chairman of one of the commissions has put it.) The preparatory group than presents its findings to the full commission at which ministers and officials from the departments concerned are normally in attendance, and a series of recommendations is agreed with a view to putting an end to the shortcomings that have been discovered. The length and thoroughness of the initial investigations, the use of outside experts, the support of the Presidium bureaucracy and (not least) the presence on many commissions of leading party officials usually ensures that these recommendations are not entirely without consequence.

The commissions, thirdly, have an important role to play in the examination of the plan and budget every year. The annual economic plan, together with the state budget, must be presented to the standing commissions at least a month before they are presented to the Supreme Soviet itself, and the evidence suggests that they are examined with some care. In 1978, for example, sixteen preparatory commissions were elected from among the standing commission members to take part in this work, with about 200 deputies as members. They were assisted by a similar number of specialists from the State Planning Committee (*Gosplan*), the Central Statistical Board and other bodies, and they held 65 meetings over a three-week period at which more than 190 reports and other communications from ministries, state committees and union republican governments were considered. The chairmen of the plan and budget commissions then reported the commissions' conclusions to the Supreme Soviet itself after the government's proposals had been presented, recommending a number of changes involving an additional 138 million rubles (about 100 million dollars) of both income and expenditure. The commissions' recommendations were accepted and the government's plan and budgetary proposals, as amended, were then passed into law. The extra spending approved by the commissions in recent years has been devoted increasingly towards socio-cultural purposes such as schools, the health service and social benefits rather than towards the economy, defence and administration, suggesting that in making these changes the commissions are probably reflecting the political preferences of their constituents.

The Council of Ministers and Presidium

At its first session after each election the Supreme Soviet elects a new Council of Ministers of the USSR and also a Presidium. The Council of Ministers is in effect the government of the USSR and its chairman, currently Nikolai I. Ryzhkov, holds an office equivalent to that of Prime Minister. The Council of Ministers is a large body, with a total membership of more than a hundred, including the chairman of the councils of ministers of the union republics as well as ministers and chairmen of state committees and other bodies, and it normally meets in full session no more often than once every three months or so. Its day-to-day activities appear to be devolved upon a rather smaller body, the Presidium of the Council of Ministers, which was first mentioned in the Constitution in 1977. This consists of the chairman of the Council of Ministers and its thirteen vice-chairmen, and is intended, according to the Constitution, to function as a 'standing body of the Council of Ministers of the USSR to deal with questions relating to the guidance of the economy, and with other matters of state administration'. The Council of Ministers itself is described in the Constitution as the 'highest executive and administrative body of the USSR', and it is responsible and accountable to the Supreme Soviet and, between its sessions, to the Presidium of the Supreme Soviet. Its specified responsibilities include the direction of economic, social and cultural development, the drafting of current and long-term economic plans and of state budgets, the regulation of money and credit, social security, the maintenance of public order and the conduct of international relations. It has the power to issue decrees (*postanovleniya*) and ordinances (*rasporyazheniya*) within its areas of competence but not to adopt statute laws (*zakony*); this is the exclusive prerogative of the USSR Supreme Soviet.

The detailed administration of individual enterprises and of construction firms, state farms and institutions of all kinds is the responsibility of the ministries themselves. There are at present about seventy ministries in the USSR, and they may be divided into three categories. The most important, particularly where the management of the economy is concerned, are all-union ministries. These include, for instance, the ministries of the oil and gas industries, of defence and foreign trade, of the railways and the merchant marine, the various machine-building ministries, the ministries of the automobile industry, the chemical industry, the electrical engineering industry and so forth, all of which are managed centrally from Moscow. The other ministries are either union-republican in status, which means that they are managed both by a central ministry in Moscow and by corresponding ministries in the union republics (examples are the ministries of health, culture, education, food, light industry and finance), or else republican, which means that they are wholly devolved to the republican level of government (there are relatively few of these, and they are not represented in the USSR Council of Ministers; examples are the ministries of consumer services, inland water transport and social security). The ministers themselves are normally professional administrators rather than figures of independent political standing, and they have tended to serve for long periods of office (the Minister of Finance, Vassily Garbuzov, for instance, from 1960 until his death in 1985). The 1980s have, however, seen a greater emphasis upon the appointment of younger and more professionally qualified figures and the nature of ministerial appointments is likely to change accordingly.

The Supreme Soviet also elects a Presidium, variously described as a collective presidency or as a standing committee of the legislature. It has a total of 39 members, a chairman (who is in effect the President of the USSR, currently Andrei A. Gromyko), a first vice-chairman, 15 vice-chairmen (one from each of the union republics), 21 members and a secretary. The Presidium, according to the Constitution, is a 'standing body of the Supreme Soviet of the USSR, accountable to it for all its work and exercising the functions of the highest body of state authority of the USSR between sessions of the Supreme Soviet, within the limits prescribed by the Constitution'. It performs two main functions. In the first place, it discharges the ceremonial tasks that have to be performed in any political system, such as the conferment of honorific titles, the granting and deprivation of citizenship, the declaration of amnesties and the acceptance of the credentials of foreign ambassadors. It also supervises the work of state institutions generally, convening sessions of the Supreme Soviet itself, co-ordinating the work of the standing commissions, and forming and abolishing ministries and state committees of the USSR on the recommendation of the Council of Ministers. The Presidium holds a formal meeting about every two months, and it can issue edicts (*ukazy*) and decrees (*postanovleniya*) on its own authority. The Presidium also decides matters of war and peace, and it appoints the members of the Soviet High Command and of the Defence Council of the USSR, chaired by the party General Secretary, which is understood to oversee defence and security affairs in a manner roughly equivalent to that of the National Security Council in the USA.

It has been conventional to regard state institutions generally, and the Supreme Soviet in particular, as potential rivals to the party for supreme authority, and therefore as condemned to a subordinate and essentially decorative role to the extent to which the party monopolises ultimate decision-making powers within the society. A more considered judgement suggests that state institutions such as the Supreme Soviet and its standing commissions may in fact be complementary to the party's authority rather than in competition with it. The party can use its substantial representation in the soviets, for instance, to carry out the close scrutiny of government bodies that it has no constitutional authority to do itself, and the soviets can also serve as a means of giving at least the appearance of a public debate, and of concessions to popular preferences, in areas that do not directly threaten the party's authority, such as education, environmental pollution, the health service or public transport. The party authorities have in fact generally taken the initiative in extending the powers of the soviets in recent years, and they have repeatedly affirmed that the soviets should exercise those powers in such a manner that (as Brezhnev put it in 1979) 'every, I repeat, every Soviet citizen should feel involved in state affairs, that his opinion, his voice will be heard and taken into account in the making of both major and minor decisions'. Short of a direct challenge to party dominance, which would certainly be resisted and for which there appears in any case to be little public demand, there would seem to be no reason why the party leadership should not find it appropriate to make at least as much use of the democratic potential of the soviets in the future as they have done in the recent past.

Structures of government in Eastern Europe

The formal structure of governments in Eastern Europe, as might be expected, shows certain variations from state to state, although, of course, they are all in some form subordinated to the leading role of the party. These variations reflect the survival of pre-communist traditions, different styles of rule and to some extent alternative political concepts developed in the communist period. As far as the last is concerned, party leaderships have found that a measure of relaxation in the institutional arrangements concerning, say, legislatures and elections can provide a politically inexpensive method of giving recognition to the competition of interests – above all, because reforms in this area are easily reversed.

The constitutional framework

In the communist world, constitutions play a rather different role from their function in most Western democratic societies. Instead of encompassing the political system and laying down a consensual framework in a relatively 'neutral' fashion, thus being the formal expression of legitimacy, communist constitutions are overtly programmatic. They are intended to map the direction towards which society will evolve, i.e. the construction of socialism, and thus to create a normative rather than a neutral framework. Nowhere is this approach better illustrated than in Yugoslavia, which has adopted five constitutions (in effect) since 1946, each one corresponding to a phase of political development. The most important justification for constitutional change of this kind in Eastern Europe has been the move from people's democracy to socialism, a higher stage of development roughly corresponding to industrialisation. Czechoslovakia adopted a 'socialist' constitution (in this sense) in 1960, and the state was formally renamed the Czechoslovak Socialist Republic. However, to confuse matters, Romania and Albania also declared themselves 'socialist', in this instance as part of their campaign of differentiation from the Soviet Union, although they could scarcely be said to have become industrialised.

The original model of all East European constitutions is the Soviet Constitution of 1936 (since superseded), but a variety of modifications have been introduced to them. Although East European constitutions may appear to play only a very limited role in the political process it is not an altogether negligible one, though it differs markedly from that in other types of political system. A clear illustration, already referred to, is the repeated changing of the constitution in Yugoslavia. The 1946 Constitution followed the Soviet model closely and corresponds to Yugoslavia's 'Soviet' period; in 1953, after the break with Stalin and the move towards self-management, a new constitution was issued to take account of the shift; and ten years later, a third constitution set the scene for far-reaching devolution and decentralisation. This document was further amended very significantly in 1966, 1967 and 1968, to such an extent as to be tantamount to a new constitution, for it transformed the Yugoslav system into a *de facto* confederation by vesting sovereignty in the republics rather than the centre. The 1974 Constitution followed the recentralisation of Yugoslav politics in 1972 and returned some, though not all, of the powers devolved to the republics back to the centre. In many ways the role of the constitution in Yugoslavia is analogous to that of a party programme, in that it is not regarded as a permanent framework but as an instrument with strong political imperatives.

An equally programmatic document, though pointing in a

very different direction, is the Albanian Constitution of 1976. Whereas the 1946 Constitution followed the standard model, the 1976 document sought to stress the differences between the Albanian version of communism and that of the other East European states, and, further, to incorporate the ideological and political aims of the Hoxha leadership. It was intensely nationalistic and emphasised the defence of the country as 'the highest duty and greatest honour' of the citizen; it made Marxism–Leninism the official and sole ruling ideology, implying the duty to struggle against all other value systems; it proclaimed a commitment to radical, revolutionary politics and to continuing modernisation; and it enjoined a disciplined and tight central control by the party over society, in its role as 'the sole leading political force of the state and society'. Private property was declared liquidated and religion abolished.

The debate in 1975–76 over the amendments to the Polish Constitution illustrates another aspect of the relationship between constitutions and the political system – in this instance, that a programmatic constitution can run into opposition from members of the society. In December 1975, the Polish leadership announced amendments to the Constitution which would have (i) formally entrenched the leading role of the party; (ii) made civic rights dependent on the duty of constructing socialism; and (iii) stressed the permanency of the country's links with the Soviet Union. Against all expectations, this elicited strong protests from sections of the intelligentsia and the country's powerful Roman Catholic church. Objections were raised on all three grounds. It was argued that these provisions were incompatible with the country's sovereignty, with the rule of law and the freedom of the individual (all formally guaranteed in the Constitution), and in the event the Polish authorities made some concessions in the final wording of the amendments. The underlying explanation for the campaign was the myth value of constitutions in the Polish political tradition. The modern political era in Poland is dated from the '3rd of May Constitution' of 1791, which sought to transform the archaic feudal Polish system into a modern polity and which was frustrated by the second and third partitions. The fact that Russia had been one of the partitioning powers and was felt to be introducing alien elements into the Constitution in 1975 undoubtedly influenced the responses of the campaigners.

The role of representative institutions

Although no East European state ever developed parliamentary institutions with sovereign powers over the executive before the communist period, none the less these polities did enjoy parliamentary traditions and the political elites perceived their political systems as having such tradition. Some of this survived the communist revolution, although in different forms and with different levels of intensity. In periods when the power of the party has been weak, clear-cut attempts have been made to revive parliaments as genuinely representative institutions. Likewise, when party control was somewhat relaxed after 1961 during the second de-Stalinisation, some official efforts were made to upgrade legislatures from the purely ritualistic charades of the high Stalinist period and to modify them in such a way as to provide for at least a small measure of choice. This process applied both to elections and to the functioning of legislatures.

Elections

At no point during periods of weakened party control (Czechoslovakia 1968, Hungary, 1956, Poland in 1980–81) did elections take place, so that only officially sponsored modifications need be considered. The official theory is that in communist polities competitive elections are unnecessary because the societies are founded on consensus, a set of ideas which is derived from the myth of unanimity embodied in Marxism–Leninism. However, choice between individual candidates, all of them subscribing to official policy, does not seriously undermine consensus and has been felt to be a useful way of raising the level of citizen participation in several East European countries at different times.

In the case of Poland this had its origins in the 1956 reforms, and it allowed a modicum of competition in the 1957 and 1961 elections as well as in the 1958 local elections. Non-communist parties, particularly the Roman Catholic Znak, were able to make nominations, and in several cases their candidates outstripped the communists. In one instance a communist candidate was not elected because he had failed to receive the necessary minimum of 50 per cent of the vote. Voter disapproval was expressed by the deletion of names of official candidates; in 1957, 10.6 per cent of voters cast a negative vote in this way. The Hungarian electoral system which emerged in the late 1960s had similarly the desire of the party leadership to permit controlled interest articulation behind it; in particular, it was accepted that the economic reform, the New Economic Mechanism of 1968, which encouraged economic decentralisation and differentiation, should be accompanied by some political changes. Hence the 1966 electoral law provided for the possibility of multiple candidacies in single-member constituencies, in which all those who stood subscribed to the programme of the party-backed People's Patriotic Front's (PPF) programme, offering a choice of personalities if not of policies.

In the 1967 elections this process was not especially successful, as PPF officials continued to control the nomination process and discouraged unofficial nominations. Accordingly changes were introduced for the 1971 elections, and on that occasion there were double candidacies in 48 constituencies and 1 triple candidacy out of 352 constituencies. A few of the unofficial candidates, i.e. those not backed by the PPF, were in fact successful. A further modification to the electoral system was the basis of the elections in 1985. In this case, all elections, local as well as national, had to be fought by at least two candidates. To ensure that senior national figures remained in parliament and avoided the indignity of scrambling for votes a special reserve list of 35 seats was created. Otherwise, there were contests in all the remaining 352 seats. In the event, the rather unexpected outcome was that local coteries of power found themselves able to strengthen their positions against the centre and only in a few instances did entirely independent candidates find themselves elected to parliament (for a more detailed account see Racz, 1987).

Special circumstances brought elections in Yugoslavia in the 1960s close to genuine political contests in which central control was relatively weak. The 'liberal' 1963 Constitution, the defeat of the conservative secret police chief Ranković in 1966, and the needs of the 1964 economic reform all contributed to creating a fairly open attitude towards elections in 1967. Thus in the elections for the Federal Chamber of the Federal Assembly in that year, the communal assemblies (which were the scene of direct elections) put forward 82 candidates for 60 seats; and in Serbia, there were 41 candidates for 25 seats. Ironically, those who benefited from the liberal electoral regime tended to be representatives of the conservative hardline, standing on a populist–nationalist platform against the younger liberal–technocratic official candidates. The 1969 elections involved all legislative bodies with a total of 620 deputies; it marked the maximum extent of the liberalisation and indicated how far the party had withdrawn from exercising its power over society. In a majority of seats voters were offered a choice, although the nomination procedure had been tightened up in order to prevent the election of 'unsuitable' candidates as had happened in 1967. In the event, this attempt at control proved relatively unsuccessful and a significant number of 'undesirable' deputies were elected, either as the result of local bargains struck by different interest groups or of populist conservatives winning over officially-favoured candidates. This election sowed doubts in the minds of party leaders about the suitability of popular electoral processes, and they subsequently ensured that 'spontaneity' would not find expression in this way. When it came to the 1974 elections the system had been changed to a local level direct election involving some 65 000 units, in which those successful were mandated delegates subject to recall; this was followed by a complex series of indirect delegate elections to produce all legislative bodies at communal, republican and federal levels, without the possibility of electoral choice at any of these levels.

In none of the other East European states did elections come to offer even the moderate choice found in Hungary or Poland, let alone Yugoslavia. The 1975 and later elections in Romania, it is true, were held under limited choice conditions, but this had little significance. Elsewhere (Bulgaria, the GDR, Czechoslovakia since the 1970s and Albania) voters have a single list of candidates to accept or, exceptionally, reject. In the first three of these states the lists were drawn up between the communist party and the other façade parties (see Table 3.1). After the 1978 elections, the Albanian authories proudly announced a 100 per cent turnout, with not one negative vote; the picture was marred only by 1 voter who managed to abstain and 3 spoiled ballot papers.

Legislative behaviour – in periods of weak party control

The short-lived, hectic attempt to revive party life during the Hungarian revolution of 1956 failed to produce any significant data on legislative behaviour – the experiment was over when it had barely begun. But both during the 1968 Prague spring and the Polish events of 1980 and after, a significant revitalisation of parliamentary activity could be discerned, parallel with the contraction of party control. The 1963 Yugoslav Constitution ushered in an analogous state of affairs, where the leading role of the party was so attenuated that legislative behaviour, at both the federal and republican levels, could be regarded as semi-autonomous.

All three experiences tend to bear out the proposition that when allowed to perform their ostensible roles, communist legislators begin to adapt to and attempt to perform their assigned tasks. At the same time, because these legislators perceived that their true relationship with their supposed electorates was weak, given that they had been elected by a process in which choice had been artificially limited, they lacked the self-confidence and sense of legitimacy which would have encouraged them to withstand renewed pressures upon their autonomy. The experience of the Czechoslovak National Assembly illustrates this two-phase process clearly: it moved only rather cautiously into the newly competitive political arena in 1968, then performed a fairly useful function in subjecting the government to criticism, but returned to habitual obedience to the party after the invasion.

There was certainly a feeling at the outset in Czechoslovakia that the National Assembly, formally the supreme organ of state power, should strive to make a reality of these extensive powers. The communist party itself accepted this in part by indicating that its leading role should be expressed solely through communist members of the legislature. The National Assembly then endorsed the principle that the government should be subject to recall and turned itself into an open chamber of debate and criticism, not least thanks to the urging of Josef Smrkovský, the Assembly's radical president (i.e. speaker). Thus between April and August 1968, the government was often subjected to vigorous criticism, and many times proposals from deputies were incorporated into the final version of a law. The Assembly even went so far as to set up a Committee on Defence and Security, a highly sensitive area, and the Minister of the Interior was questioned on topics like telephone tapping and censorship of the post. Unanimity was abandoned when the law abolishing censorship was passed. All in all, by the summer of 1968 the National Assembly was well on the way to securing its sovereignty over the government. When the invasion occurred the Assembly went into a six-day permanent session and repeatedly called on the Soviet Union and its allies to withdraw their forces from Czechoslovak soil. Yet within three weeks the Assembly had accepted restrictive legislation banning institutions outside the National Front, i.e. beyond the control of the party, and also reintroducing censorship. The last gasp of parliamentary activity showing signs of independence was the negative vote by four deputies against the Soviet–Czechoslovak treaty to legalise the occupation on 18 October 1968.

The Polish experience of 1980–81 had many similarities to this. Rather cautiously, well after the Gdańsk agreement of 31 August 1980, the Sejm (Parliament) began to assert itself. As the mood of the country changed during the latter months of 1980, deputies began to press more vigorously for the implementation of their ostensible role. In November there were calls for the resignation of the Ministers of Agriculture and Food Processing, both areas of extensive mismanagement. A debate in February 1981 was televised live and showed the sometimes biting criticism of the government by deputies. 'The period of plastered-over unanimity has gone for good . . .' prophesied one deputy, wrongly as it turned out. The critical attitude and apparent commitment of deputies to a genuinely supervisory role over government persisted until General Jaruzelski's takeover on 13 December 1981. After that the Sejm was rapidly brought to order, although several deputies continued to voice their disagreement with government policies. In a session of some symbolic importance in January 1982 the Sejm endorsed the state of emergency – the device used to justify the takeover – with only one vote against and six abstentions. After that, the Sejm was used by Poland's rulers for two purposes. Over the four years that followed, a great mass of legislation was pushed through to empower the local and national authorities to take whatever measures they saw fit against anyone whom they deemed antagonistic. Furthermore, as the Polish party failed to recover from the defeat it had suffered in 1980–81, some of its deliberate and debating functions were assigned to the Sejm, so that its role was somewhat less ceremonial in the late 1980s than it had been before 1980.

In Yugoslavia the rise of the power of the Federal Assembly lasted roughly from 1967 to 1970. In the 1963 Constitution a highly complex five-chamber legislature was created as part of the anti-centralist strategy of the temporarily ascendant liberals. The structure of the Federal Assembly consisted of the Federal Chamber and four specialised chambers, each representing a specialised interest. The Federal Chamber, with 120 deputies elected directly and representing territorial constituencies, was the basic political chamber. The Chamber of Nationalities, with twenty delegates from each of the six republics and ten each from the two autonomous provinces, was part of the Federal Chamber. The other four chambers were the Economic, the Educational–Cultural, the Health and Welfare and the Organisation–Political, each with 120 members delegated by appropriate interest groups such as the trade unions. The operative practice of the Federal Assembly was to function bicamerally; the Federal Chamber acted together with one of the corporate chambers as appropriate. In 1967, the Assembly proposed a number of constitutional amendments with the aim of furthering decentralisation. One of these upgraded the Chamber of Nationalities and remitted to it all economic matters where national equality was involved. In effect, this transformed it into an independent chamber, something which was confirmed by the abolition of the Federal Chamber in 1968 and the transfer of its powers to the Chamber of Nationalities, which then became known as the Social–Political Chamber. At the republican level this five-chamber pattern was reproduced and the Croatian assembly, the *Sabor*, introduced direct elections for four of its five chambers.

Ironically, just as its independence was increased, the power of the Federal Assembly declined with the passing of the locus of real power to the republics. The result was stagnation, as the republics were able to block federal initiatives through the Chamber of Nationalities. Eventually, the log jam was resolved by the creation of an extra-constitutional Inter-Republican Consultative Committee, which reduced the role of the Federal Assembly to the margins. The post-1972 recentralisation of Yugoslav politics included the complete restructuring of the Federal Assembly, the return of bicameralism, and the renewed subordination of the Assembly to the party. The experiment with competitive politics had not been a success.

Legislative behaviour – in periods of effective party control

The principal characteristic of periods of effective party control, which are the norm in Eastern Europe, is that legislatures have only as much scope for action as they are accorded by the party. If this scope is increased they can perform deliberative roles, act to some extent as sounding boards for popular opinion, and perform the manipulative function of giving society the illusion of participation. The pattern has varied from the orchestrated unanimity of Albania to the comparative freedom allowed to the Hungarian parliament between 1968 and 1973. In between these two extremes there may be found a variety of cases, mostly of dependence, indicating that the different applications of the party's leading role in Eastern Europe since the 1960s has tended towards a restrictive, relatively formal role for legislatures not unlike the situation in the Soviet Union. Thus in the East German Volkskammer only one instance of non-unanimity has ever been recorded: in 1972, fourteen members of the (façade) Christian Democratic Union voted against a bill introducing abortion. The Romanian and Bulgarian legislatures have behaved in an equally ceremonial fashion.

In the 1970s, however, in line with the slightly looser control over institutions exercised by the Polish party under Edward Gierek, the Sejm did take part in various supervisory activities and sought to carry out certain control functions, although mostly in non-contentious areas and often to little effect. In the late 1960s, the Hungarian party similarly embarked on an experiment in relaxation of control over institutions parallel with the economic reform which was taking place at that time, and this led it to look for ways of revitalising parliament. This resulted in an increase in the legislative activity of the National Assembly, and each year from 1967 onwards it considered at least one major piece of legislation, like the 1972 Youth Law and the Code of Criminal Procedure. Significantly, however, the politically sensitive law on passports and foreign travel was issued as a decree-law by the Presidential Council (a collective presidency equivalent to the Presidium of the USSR Supreme Soviet). On the whole, the bulk of legislative work, in the Hungarian legislature as in the other legislatures in Eastern Europe, was undertaken in committees rather than plenary sessions, and occasionally drafts were amended as a result of scrutiny. The revival of the pre-war institution of interpellations – questioning ministers on the floor of the house on their activities – was intended as a further move in the same direction, but these rarely lost the character of ritual. On one occasion in 1969 an answer to a question by the Minister of Labour was rejected by the vote of the house and was then referred to a standing committee; such exchanges petered out during the 1970s. However, the parliament elected under the new regulations of 1985 appeared to be more prepared to scrutinise government activity than its predecessor and several deputies have abstained from voting on a range of more or less contentious topics.

The governing authorities

Here again the pattern follows closely on the model inherited from the Soviet Union. East European governments are basically the executive arm of the party, but there have been periods when governments have succeeded in gaining a measure of autonomy for themselves. This corresponds to the pattern discussed under legislatures. Typically, communist governments tend to behave in a 'bureaucratic' rather than a 'political' fashion, and conflicts of interest generally take place behind a smokescreen from which the public is excluded. One noteworthy feature of communist governments is that technical or branch ministries have tended to proliferate over time. These may be set up on an *ad hoc* basis to resolve a temporary problem, but then remain in being until a new reallocation of competences is made. Sometimes branch ministries are highly specialised: Bulgaria and Poland, for instance, have a Ministry for the Chemical Industry, while Czechoslovakia has a federal Ministry of Electrical Engineering and Electrotechnics, indicating the importance attached to this branch of industry. A more recent trend in the reverse direction has been away from proliferation: in December 1980 three of the industrial branch ministries in Hungary were merged into a super-Ministry of Industry, and this was copied in Poland in June 1981. One curiosity, again evidence of more deep-seated political attitudes, is that the Bulgarian ambassador to the Soviet Union sits as Minister without Portfolio in the Bulgarian government. In several East European countries the heads of certain important government agencies – the Office of Religious Affairs, the State Planning Commission, the Statistical Office – might also hold the rank of minister or deputy minister.

Those appointed to governmental portfolios, as in the Soviet Union, have tended to be specialist administrators and executives rather than politicians, and under normal circumstances they can expect to hold office for many years. Although after elections are held the Council of Ministers (government) submits its resignation to the legislature and a new government is formed, substantial turnover of individuals is normally rare. Some ministers, therefore, especially if they hold government office concurrently with a high party post, can expect their personal standing and influence to grow over the years. This applies most notably to the police and the secret police – the Ministry of the Interior. The East German equivalent, the Ministry of State Security, has been held by Erich Mielke since 1957, and he held a junior post in the same ministry before that, since 1950. Despite his advanced age (b. 1907), he appears irremovable. It was this growth of personal standing and influence – personal in the sense that it cannot be transmitted to a successor – that the principle of rotation, applied in Yugoslavia and Romania, was supposed to prevent. In Romania it has led to a bewildering spectacle of musical chairs without any apparent rationale as Ceauşescu has moved his administrators rapidly from one post to another. In Yugoslavia rotation was more meaningful, especially in the State Presidency, where the head of state held office strictly for one year only after Tito's death, but certain individuals, notably Nikola Ljubičić, Federal Defence Minister from 1967 to 1982, were less subject to this than others.

Occasionally, an individual may suffer a decrease in personal influence – he may be held personally responsible for some event or misfortune over which he may have had no control. For example, a poor agricultural or industrial performance will generally require the sacking of at least one minister with some kind of responsibility in the area. This practice of finding a scapegoat instead of looking for the deeper causes of failure is widely found in Eastern Europe (as indeed elsewhere), as it is regarded as politically simpler to dismiss individuals than to embark on major structural change. Incidentally, not all ministers need necessarily be members of the communist party. In 1980 as part of the Polish renewal and in recognition of the importance of Roman Catholicism in Poland the neo-Znak Roman Catholic deputy, Jerzy Ozdowski, was appointed deputy prime minister with special responsibility for social affairs. The chairman of the nominally independent Democratic Party, Edward Kowalczyk, was appointed to a similar position in 1981. Similarly the Hungarian Foreign Minister from 1961 to 1973, János Péter, was a bishop of the Hungarian Reformed Church on his translation and only joined the party later.

As concerns the functioning of communist governments, a much repeated theme, which arose both in Czechoslovakia in

1968 and in Poland after 1980, has been the need to establish some distance between them and the ruling party. In practice the party prefers to supervise the work of governments closely, thus effectively duplicating their work, and often the efficiency of government is reduced through informal intervention and pressure. In conditions where the party has redefined its leading role to allow governments some room for manoeuvre, efforts to secure greater autonomy have been made and governments have been allowed to acquire some measure of genuine authority.

An example of the first of these trends – the striving towards greater independence from the party – may be found in Hungary during the period of high liberalisation (1968–73), when under the energetic premiership of Jenö Fock government ministers claimed and were accorded palpable independence from the party. Individual ministers no longer took instructions from relatively junior party officials, sometimes insisted on implementing policies despite the known displeasure of middle-level party cadres, and generally sought to promote an autonomous governmental or sectional interest – something which Fock, in his resignation speech, described as 'portfolio chauvinism'. The prosperity of Hungarian agriculture, for example, derived in no small part from the strong agricultural lobby in the government, which had sufficient backing in the central party apparatus to overcome opposition from regional party officials. It was to bring the government to heel and end its relative autonomy, as well as to terminate other manifestations of sectional independence, that the recentralisation of 1974–75 took place. This resulted in the resumption of tighter party control over government activities.

Perhaps the most far-reaching claim to autonomy yet made by a communist government can be found in the Yugoslav republic of Slovenia. Although it was a republican government and not that of an entire state that was involved, the circumstances were none the less remarkable: on 7 December 1966, the Slovene government was defeated in the Health and Welfare Chamber, one of the five chambers of the Slovene assembly, when a draft law on health insurance payments was rejected by 44 votes to 11. The Slovene premier, Janko Smole, thereupon resigned, arguing that if the government did not have the confidence of the legislature it could not continue in office. In the event a compromise was reached, and the Slovene precedent has not so far been followed anywhere else in the communist world.

China: constitutions, participants and bureaucrats

The People's Republic of China (PRC) has been governed by four constitutions. The years immediately following the establishment of the regime were a time of radical political, social and economic restructuring and it was not until 20 September 1954 that the first Constitution was adopted. This effectively ceased to operate in 1966–67, when the Cultural Revolution resulted in the disruption of established institutional arrangements and produced new structures and processes which had little, if any, constitutional validity. The second Constitution was adopted on 17 January 1975. This was replaced by the third of 5 March 1978. At the time of writing China is governed under the fourth Constitution, adopted on 4 December 1982.

In its first constitution the PRC defined itself as a 'people's democratic dictatorship'. This formula had been enunciated by Mao throughout the 1940s in order to broaden the appeal of the communist party among socio-economic groups who were neither workers nor peasants, but who were nevertheless regarded as having 'progressive' features and who were disenchanted with the Nationalist rule of Chiang Kai-shek. In communist parlance these were a somewhat amorphous amalgam of strata of the 'petty bourgeoisie' and the 'national bourgeoisie'. Consequently, they were regarded as being among the ranks of 'the people' as opposed to 'enemies of the people', and were to be permitted to share power. In the 1950s, however, it was assumed that the 'transition to socialism' had begun in 1949 and that the 'people's democratic dictatorship' was actually synonymous with the 'dictatorship of the proletariat'. Consequently, the 1975 Constitution defined the PRC as a 'socialist state of the dictatorship of the proletariat led by the working class and based on the alliance of workers and peasants'. When the 1978 Constitution was promulgated China was only just feeling its way out of the Maoist era and this phase was repeated. But since then it has been acknowledged that excessive and misdirected attention to the 'class struggle' in the Cultural Revolution decade caused the 'dictatorship of the proletariat' to be interpreted with undue severity at a time when, in fact, exploiting classes no longer really existed as such. In a bid to heal wounds, to raise the morale of groups like intellectuals, scientists and managers whose real or imagined 'bourgeois' status had caused them to be persecuted, but who are now regarded as having a key role to play in China's modernisation, the wheel has come full circle. In the 1982 Constitution it is stated that the people's democratic dictatorship, 'which is in essence the dictatorship of the proletariat', had been consolidated and developed. It is also acknowledged that 'exploiting classes as such' have been eliminated.

The right of 'the people' to be represented and to participate in affairs of state is by no means seen as being inconsistent with party leadership, but the emphasis placed on the party has varied over time. In 1975 and 1978 (when Maoist influence remained strong) the Constitution referred to the party as the 'core of leadership', the 'vanguard' through which the working class experienced leadership over the state. By 1982, however, determined efforts were being made to delineate more precisely the functions of party and state, and to reduce the former's interference in the day-to-day work of the latter. This found constitutional expression in general statements about party 'leadership' and the 'guidance' of Marxism–Leninism and Mao Zedong Thought.

Unlike the USSR, the PRC has always been a unitary multinational state. Constitutionally, all nationalities are equal and 'big-nation chauvinism' and 'local-nation chauvinism' are equally opposed. All nationalities are free to use their own languages and there are constitutional arrangements for regional autonomy in areas inhabited by the non-Han minorities. But there is no right to secede: 'All the national autonomous areas are inalienable parts of the PRC.'

Administratively, the PRC is divided into provinces, autonomous regions and municipalities directly under the central government in Beijing. There have been various administrative reorganisations and boundary changes over the years but as of 1986 there were 29 administrative units at this level (30 if one includes Taiwan). Of these 21 are provinces: Liaoning, Jilin, Heilongjiang, Hebei, Shanxi, Shandong, Jiangsu, Anhui, Zhejiang, Jiangxi, Fujian, Henan, Hubei, Hunan, Guangdong, Sichuan, Guizhou, Yunnan, Shaanxi, Gansu and Qinghai. Five are autonomous regions: Tibet, Inner Mongolia, Guangxi (home of the Zhuang, China's largest minority), Ningxia (inhabited by the Hui, who are Chinese Muslims), and Xinjiang (where the principal minority is Uighur). The centrally-administered cities are Beijing, Shanghai and Tianjin. The 1982 Constitution contains an article permitting the state to set up 'special administrative regions' which, implicitly, will be different from the rest of China. This is designed to facilitate the return of Hong Kong and, ultimately, Taiwan.

Provinces and autonomous regions are divided in autonomous prefectures, counties, autonomous counties and cities. Counties and autonomous counties are divided into townships, nationality townships and towns. Beijing, Shanghai and other large cities are divided into districts and counties. These divisions are analogous to those in the other communist states.

At all levels upwards state power is vested in people's congresses. The highest organ of state is the National People's Congress (NPC) which is composed of deputies elected by the provinces, autonomous regions and municipalities directly under the Central Government, and by the armed forces. The NPC is elected for a term of five years and holds one session in each year.

The 1982 Constitution vests in the NPC a wide range of powers and functions. It has the power to amend the Constitution, to make laws, and to supervise the enforcement of constitutional and legal enactments. It elects the President and the Vice-President and is given some say in determining who the senior officials of the state shall be, although the constitutional formulation used to describe its precise role is somewhat convoluted. Thus it is laid down that the NPC shall 'decide on the choice of the Premier of the State Council upon the nomination of the President'. (In 1978 it was 'upon the recommendation of the Central Committee'.) Similarly it shall 'decide on the choice' of vice-premiers, state councillors and ministers upon nomination by the Premier. Some offices, however, are at the NPC's disposal without such constraints. Thus it is empowered 'to elect' the Chairman of the Central Military Commission, the President of the Supreme People's Court and the Procurator-General. It has the power to remove from office all the persons listed above, from President downwards. The NPC is also entitled to examine and approve the national economic plan, the state budget and report on its implementation, to 'decide on questions of war and peace', and to 'exercise such other functions and powers as the highest organ of state power should exercise'.

The NPC elects a Standing Committee to act when it is not in session. This body conducts the election of deputies to the NPC and convenes it. It interprets the Constitution on laws and enacts decrees, and supervises the work of the State Council, the Central Military Commission, the Supreme People's Court and the Supreme People's Procuratorate. The Constitution gives the Standing Committee the power to annul rules, regulations and decisions of the State Council and lower bodies which contravene the Constitution and it can, when the NPC is not in session, appoint and dismiss ministers and other senior office-holders.

The State Council is the actual government, being 'the highest organ of state power', and is constitutionally responsible to the NPC and its Standing Committee. It is composed of the Premier, a number of vice-premiers, state councillors and ministers (who head either ministries or 'commissions'). These are roughly equivalent in function to the Presidium and Council of Ministers in the USSR.

From 1954 to 1964 the NPC did meet once a year, except in 1961. However, it could not be regarded as a major decision-making body. In 1957, for example, Luo Longji, Minister of the Timber Industry and Vice-Chairman of the China Democratic League (one of the major 'democratic' parties permitted to exist after 1949), took advantage of the 'Hundred Flowers' campaign (discussed in Chapter 6) to observe:

At the Standing Committee meetings of the NPC ... the democratic parties and groups could not voice any effective opinion on matters under discussion because they were not informed in advance of the matters to be discussed, and they had no time to study them at the moment of discussion.

Although subsequent developments, discussed later in this chapter, gave the NPC a somewhat more important role in Chinese politics from the late 1970s onwards, during the last twelve years of Mao's life the NPC met only once (1975) and on that occasion conformed entirely to the 'rubber stamp' stereotype of communist legislatures.

Mass campaigns

This lack of effective participation in decision-making might appear to contradict Mao's insistence upon bringing 'the masses' into political involvement, which was discussed in Chapter 2. The answer, however, is that Mao preferred to institutionalise participation through other channels. For the distinctive feature of the PRC during his lifetime was the 'mass campaign'. The importance of this device was evidenced by Premier Zhou Enlai in 1959 when he observed that:

The party has always paid attention to combining its leadership with broad mass movements guiding the masses to raise the level of revolutionary consciousness constantly, and to organise their own strength to emancipate themselves step by step, instead of imposing revolution on the masses or bestowing victory on the masses as a favour.

Therefore, in the years following the establishment of the PRC, the mass campaign was extensively utilised as a participatory device. Numerous campaigns were instituted whereby millions of ordinary Chinese citizens were able to acquire political knowledge and to play a part in implementing policy. Campaigns could be organised for political, social or economic objectives, but all of them tended to display common characteristics which are worthy of mention.

First, each campaign was preceded by a stage in which the leadership gave considerable attention to propaganda matters. Once it had decided that a certain course of action was desirable it would embark on a careful programme to make its views known to the mass of the population. The leadership's views would be spelled out in the greatest detail by the media at all levels. Cadres from central to village level were expected to spend much of their time addressing meetings which varied in size from huge mass rallies to face-to-face contacts with half a dozen people. Organisational support was provided by the publication of massive amounts of relevant literature, much of it in pamphlet form, ranging from relatively sophisticated selections of Marxist writings deemed to be particularly relevant to material dealing with such *minutiae* as the respective merits of such propaganda tools as blackboards, slogans, cartoons, and wallposters. Even that old standby of politicians everywhere, the 'question-and-answer' book, would be provided, so that cadres would be familiar with the points likely to be raised by members of their audience and would have memorised in advance the 'correct' answers to them. The actual quality of Chinese propaganda was of a relatively high order in that, while the message might be simple and crude, it would be readily comprehensible and would use examples with which 'the masses' were familiar.

The aim of the propaganda barrage which initiated each mass campaign went beyond ensuring that the masses knew what was wanted of them; they were also expected to reveal their own feelings on a particular issue. An essential aspect of Chinese propaganda techniques was that they demanded discussion within the organisational context of the 'small group'. Virtually everybody was a member of at least one unit, whether based on factory, school, office, or place of residence, through which they were in regular contact with a cadre. Cadres would see to it that everyone became aware of policy by arranging such activities as collective newspaper-reading or radio-listening; they also had the task of making people declare their opinions in front of their peers. In this way it was possible to identify those individuals who appeared 'progressive' and to carry out 'systematic education' towards those who had doubts, apprehensions, and 'erroneous ideas'.

Where a basic-level cadre was faced with widespread opposition to a policy as, say, in the case of the collectivisation campaigns, he could either recommend to his superiors that it be modified or else appeal for moral and practical support from the higher echelons who might, for example, send a high-powered propaganda team to visit an area where local cadres were unable to create the necessary degree of willing support. It should be noted here that it was common practice to try out new policies on a local basis in order to test their efficacy before launching them nationally. This was supposed to ensure that by the time a campaign was launched throughout the country many of its teething troubles had been solved.

The next stage was to 'mobilise the masses' to implement the given policy line. Vast numbers of people who may have had little or no previous involvement in any form of political activity were exhorted to carry out tasks under the guidance of cadres. In many cases special *ad hoc* organisations would be set up to facilitate participation. For example, in the Land Reform of 1950–52, 'peasant associations' and 'tribunals' were established to deal with such matters as conducting investigations in patterns of landownership in a particular village, the implementation of directives on the confiscation and redistribution of land, and the penalties to be meted out to those 'local despots' whose 'exploitation' and 'oppression' had placed them outside the ranks of 'the people'. Similarly, in the 'five-anti' campaign of 1952, hundreds of thousands of workers, shop assistants and students were mobilised to denounce, investigate and punish private businessmen and industrialists allegedly guilty of bribery, theft of state assets, cheating on government contracts, tax evasion and the theft of state economic secrets. Other campaigns were geared to government-inspired 'self-help' policies, particularly in the field of public health.

Mass campaigns did not give ordinary citizens the opportunity to participate in the formulation of major decisions: this always rested with the senior leadership. But they had important functions nevertheless. One of these was educative. For the first time in China's history 'the masses' were made conscious of what their government's policy was. The unremitting propaganda barrage, and the insistence that 'the masses' involve themselves with political affairs, produced a degree of awareness probably unequalled in the economically under-developed world. Nor was the fact that only one 'correct line' was allowed to flourish entirely without its merits, although repugnant from the Western point of view. After more than two millennia in which the Chinese state had been sustained by the integrative moral code of Confucianism, the disruption and turmoil of the nineteenth and twentieth centuries produced a situation in which Sun Yat-sen could describe his country as a 'sheet of loose sand'. After the forty years of violence, warlordism, invasion and civil war which followed the collapse of the Qing dynasty, it was essential to provide a new integrative myth to replace anarchic conditions and to harness the energies of the Chinese people to the tasks of economic reconstruction and industrialisation.

Furthermore, mass campaigns did give ordinary citizens the right to participate in some decisions which, elsewhere, would have been left to the law courts and the central government. For example, peasants had some flexibility in deciding which of the ex-landlords in their villages were to be punished harshly and which to be treated leniently; in some cases they could press for a modification of national policy in the light of local conditions. Some were able to break away from the traditional attitude that 'a poor man has no right to speak'. The campaigns also served a valuable recruitment function in that they were a means by which millions of Chinese could rise to positions where they could take relatively important decisions. With the close of each campaign there would be a recruitment drive to bring into positions of responsibility those activists who had 'bubbled up' during its course.

And, on occasion, the mass campaigns were used to exert control over party and state bureaucrats. In 1951–52, for example, the 'five-anti' was accompanied by a 'three-anti' campaign which used similar methods to attack cadres guilty of 'corruption, waste and bureaucracy'. In the early 1960s a 'socialist education' campaign was waged, partly in an attempt to control rural cadres. Most important of all was the Cultural Revolution. For in 1966 Mao did, in effect, assert that officials must be accountable to the people. In place of the considerable, but in fact largely fictitious, powers enjoyed by the NPC to that date, Mao advocated 'extensive democracy', in which 'the masses' were invited to criticise, dismiss and replace their government (and party) leaders on a scale, and with a degree of violence, that was unprecedented in China or in any of the other communist states.

The Cultural Revolution

The Cultural Revolution was, in large measure, an attack on bureaucracy and bureaucratisation. By 1966 Mao had concluded that many officials were no longer revolutionary or responsive to the needs of 'the masses', and that the latter should rectify this problem by direct action. Initially, the campaign was directed at certain individuals, but in 1967 it widened into an attack on institutions themselves. Although the party was severely affected, so, too, was the government apparatus. The State Council, and the ministries under its control, became a prime target for attack. By 1966 the State Council controlled 49 ministries and commissions, and consisted of 366 persons who were ministers or vice-ministers. Half of them had been ministers of vice-ministers in 1949. They were also heavily involved with work in the party bureaucracy. The State Council was, in fact, representative of a trend, evident throughout the political system, for the party to become in effect a managerial instrument, staffed with personnel who thought in terms of day-to-day administrative practicalities rather than serving as a power-house of creative, radical ideas.

In 1949 the party had been able to postpone too close an involvement with the machinery of government for the simple reason that it consisted largely of uneducated peasants and, moreover, wished to stress the 'united front' with those socio-economic groups who, as it happened, were the main source of highly qualified manpower. Thus of the ministers and vice-ministers of the Government Administrative Council (the State Council's predecessor) in 1949, only 58 per cent were communists and the rest were 'non-party persons'. Thereafter, however, the party was able to develop its own specialists, and as it gradually extended its control over all aspects of government and society, the state bureaucracy grew. The number of ministries actually doubled between 1949 and 1966 and so, too, did the 'interlocking directorate' system, an arrangement whereby it became common for party cadres to assume positions of responsibility in state organisations.

These would usually, though not always, be related to their party function. Thus, for example, a senior member of the Central Committee's Propaganda Department might become an official in the Ministry of Culture. Donald Klein, in his study of the State Council and the Cultural Revolution, has calculated that by 1966 at least 81 per cent of ministers and vice-ministers were party members. As some three-quarters of the ministries and commissions were concerned with economic matters, many State Council officials inevitably devoted their time to the efficient running of the economy. And, with the passage of time, increasingly elderly cadres settled comfortably into their functional specialisations. They began to manifest the characteristics found in all bureaucratic organisations: a concern for hierarchy, a belief in orderly procedures and a dislike of radical change.

Thus, the radicalism of the Great Leap Forward was followed in the early 1960s by policies designed to foster steady growth at the expense of social transformation. This was done by rewarding the highly-skilled, whether they were managers, technicians, skilled workers or enterprising peasants. This in turn created a large group of 'have-nots' in society, like unskilled labourers who received very low wages and no welfare benefits, and who had minimal security of employment. Similarly, the Ministry of Public Health was condemned by Mao in 1965 for concentrating on providing well-qualified doctors for the urban areas, while ignoring the health needs of the peasant majority. The Chinese bureaucracy, in short, was beginning to resemble the over-padded bureaucracies to be found elsewhere in the Third World, and like bureaucratic organisations everywhere was beginning to view the 'public good' in terms of its own departmental interests.

Hence, one aim of the Cultural Revolution was to cut the

bureaucracy down to size both metaphorically, by subjecting it to mass criticism and a greater degree of mass control, and literally, by reducing the numbers of government agencies and their employees, especially at the central level. Precisely because Mao saw the problem in ideological terms, ministries like Education and Culture suffered particularly severely for their failures to inculcate the correct revolutionary attitude. But few remained unscathed. Klein has demonstrated that by February 1968, roughly half of China's ministers and vice-ministers had not appeared in public since the end of 1966. Most of them, we now know from official Chinese sources, had not simply been dismissed but had been subjected to harsh treatment for offences real and, very often, imagined. A number of ministries entirely ceased to operate until 1975. Even then, when the fourth NPC met in January of that year and provided the first comparative list of State Council ministries for nearly a decade, it was discovered that, as a result of amalgamation and administrative streamlining, there were only 29 ministries functioning at that time.

Developments in the post-Mao era

This peculiar attempt to control bureaucracy, not by a legislature, but by making it directly accountable to 'the masses', resulted in considerable human misery, grave political instability and economic disruption. It was an astonishing radical experiment but, at the practical level, it created many more problems than it solved and it did not, in fact, survive Mao's death. Since 1976 the PRC has attempted to develop an organisational format and political style which, although it has distinctive features, would be readily recognised by communists from the USSR. Since the late 1970s it has been reiterated on a number of occasions that the age of mass campaigns is definitely over and that, while they may have served a valuable purpose especially in the early 1950s, they long outlived their usefulness and have no part to play in China's present modernisation strategy.

Deng Xiaoping's approach rests, on the one hand, on encouraging the growth of an efficient state bureaucracy with a managerial ethos, staffed by well-educated and relatively young professionals. It is now argued that party and state should be more distinct and that the practice of having a relatively small number of people monopolising the key jobs in each should cease. After various reorganisations, the situation in July 1986 was that the State Council presided over 45 ministries, commissions and similar bodies. These are:

Foreign Affairs
National Defence
State Planning Commission
State Economic Commission
State Commission for Restructuring the Economic System
State Science and Technology Commission
Commission for Science, Technology and Industry for
National Defence
State Education Commission
State Nationalities Affairs Commission
Public Security
State Security
Civil Affairs
Justice
Finance
Auditing Administration
People's Bank of China
Commerce
Foreign Economic Relations and Trade
Agriculture, Animal Husbandry and Fisheries
Forestry
Water Reserves and Electric Power
Urban and Rural Construction and Environmental
Protection
Geology and Mineral Resources
Metallurgical Industry
Machine-Building Industry
Nuclear Industry
Aviation Industry
Electronics Industry
Ordnance Industry
Astronautics Industry
Coal Industry

Petroleum Industry
Chemical Industry
Textile Industry
Light Industry
Railways
Communications
Posts and Telecommunications
Labour and Personnel
Culture
Xinhua News Agency
Radio and Television
Public Health
Physical Culture and Sports Commission
State Family Planning Commission

On the other hand, serious attempts have been made to make the NPC a far more effective body, and since the convening of the fifth NPC in February 1978 there is growing evidence that its role should be taken more seriously. Meetings have taken place annually since 1978, the fourth session of the sixth NPC having convened in March 1986. The work of the NPC may be illustrated by reference to the third session of the sixth NPC which convened from 27 March to 10 April 1985. This adopted a number of draft proposals covering a wide range of issues including the report on the work of the government, the 1985 plan for national economic and social development, the 1984 state settlement of accounts and the 1985 state budget, the ratification of the Sino-British joint declaration on Hong Kong, the establishment of a committee to draft a 'basic law' (effectively, a mini-constitution) for the projected Hong Kong Special Administrative Region, the granting of authority to the State Council to make provisional regulations for economic reforms and the opening of China to the world, and the PRC's inheritance law.

The session concerned did show signs of genuine 'parliamentary' activity. The premier's report came in for mild criticism and two finance and banking ministers were taken to task for lax control over credit in the previous year. The draft inheritance law provoked a lively debate on the serious issues involved. And deputies from various parts of the country were vociferous in pressing for the material interests of their own areas. All of this is modest enough in terms of major decision-making, even in comparison with the other communist states, but it is a beginning none the less.

Further reading

The constitutions of the communist states are collected together with brief introductions in Simons (1980a). The role of legislatures on a comparative basis is considered in Nelson and White (1982), which devotes particular attention to Yugoslavia, Poland, Romania, Czechoslovakia, the USSR and China. On electoral arrangements in the communist states, see Pravda (1986). Two useful recent surveys of the state in communist societies are Holmes (1981a) and Harding (1984). The works of Marxist theory that bear most closely on the state are Karl Marx's *Critique of the Gotha Programme* (1875) and V. I. Lenin's *The State and Revolution* (1917), both of which are available in a variety of modern editions. These and other works of Marxist theory are of course open to a number of interpretations and do not necessarily correspond with, still less justify, all the actions that communist governments have taken in their name.

General treatments of state institutions in the USSR include Vanneman (1977), Friedgut (1979), Hill (1980), White (1982a) and Jacobs (1983). The 1977 Soviet Constitution is widely available in pamphlet form and is reprinted together with extensive introduction in Sharlet (1978), Feldbrugge (1979) and Unger (1981a), which also contains the texts of earlier Soviet constitutions. The electoral process is considered in some detail in Zaslavsky and Brym (1978); the role of the Supreme Soviet in budgetary matters is examined in White (1982b). Gureyev and Segudin (1977) and Krutogolov (1980) provide representative Soviet statements on such matters.

An assessment of governmental structures in Eastern Europe, as well as in other communist countries, is available in

Szajkowski (1981). General surveys of Eastern Europe in this connection include Rakowska-Harmstone (1984) and Volgyes (1986), as well as the contributions on Poland, Czechoslovakia and Romania in Nelson and White (1982). On particular countries , Czechoslovakia up to 1968 is dealt with very fully in Skilling (1976) and also in Golan (1973). On Yugoslavia, Rusinow (1977) is outstanding. Singleton (1976) has a useful chapter on constitutional changes, and Ramet (1984) examines the operation of the federal system, up to 1983. The reform period in Hungary is fully covered in Robinson (1973); an admirable and more recent survey is Heinrich (1986). On the 1985 elections in Hungary, see Heinrich (1986, ch. 2) and Racz (1987). Shafir (1985) provides a well-informed and up-to-date survey of Romania. Polish political developments up to the Solidarity crisis are well covered in Leslie (1980). On the more recent period, see the works cited at the end of Chapter 6, and also the research reports produced by Radio Free Europe in Munich, West Germany.

The Chinese Constitution of 1982 is available in pamphlet form and may also be found in *Beijing Review*, no. 52 (1982). The most thorough study of the NPC is Gasper (1982). More generally, Barnett (1967) is an immensely detailed and classic study and Schurmann (1968) is also invaluable. On the impact of the Cultural Revolution on the central state bureaucracy, see Klein (1970). An excellent study of the Maoist era is available in Harding (1981). The political decision-making process in more recent years is discussed in Oksenberg (1982) and Barnett (1985). Recent developments in terms of the development of 'socialist democracy' are considered in Goodman (1985) and in Nathan (1986).

4

The Communist Parties

One of the defining characteristics of a communist state, it was suggested in Chapter 1, is the existence of a communist or Marxist–Leninist party exercising dominant political authority within the society in question. Not all the parties we shall consider in this chapter in fact call themselves communist. The Polish party, for instance, is called the Polish United Workers' Party, and the Albanian party is called the Party of Labour of Albania (see Table 4.1). Nor are these parties necessarily the only parties that are permitted to exist in their respective societies; almost half of them, in fact, permit more than one party to exist, with seats in the legislature and a formally independent status (see Table 3.1). In none of these states, however, is any genuinely competitive political party permitted to exist, and the non-communist parties in these countries are generally of a more or less 'puppet' character, contesting elections together with the communist party on the basis of a common list of candidates and with a common manifesto. The dominant role of the communist party within the political system, and within the party of its central leadership, is indeed the essential characteristic of a communist state not just to political scientists but also so far as the communist party authorities themselves are concerned; it was to resist any challenge to that role that the Soviet Union and its allies intervened in Czechoslovakia in 1968 and appeared likely to do so again in Poland in 1980–81.

The 'leading role of the party', as this dominant role of the party in the society is known, derives from a number of circumstances, including the existence in a number of these

TABLE 4.1

The ruling communist parties in the late 1980s

Country	Name of Party	Membership (c. 1986)	% of population	Party leader (in 1986)
Albania	Party of Labour of Albania	147 000	5.1	Ramiz Alia
Bulgaria	Bulgarian Communist Party	932 055	9.3	Todor Zhivkov
China	Communist Party of China	44 000 000	3.6	Hu Yaobang
Cuba	Communist Party of Cuba	523 639	4.4	Fidel Castro
Czechoslovakia	Communist Party of Czechoslovakia	1 650 000	10.5	Gustáv Husák
GDR	Socialist Unity Party of Germany	2 300 000	13.2	Erich Honecker
Hungary	Hungarian Socialist Worker's Party	870 992	8.0	János Kádár
Kampuchea	People's Revolutionary Party of Kampuchea	7 500	0.1	Heng Samrin
Korea	Workers' Party of Korea	3 000 000	15.6	Kim Il Sung
Laos	Lao People's Revolutionary Party	42 000	0.9	Khaysone Phomvihane
Mongolia	Mongolian People's Revolutionary Party	88 150	4.2	Dzhambiin Batmunkh
Poland	Polish United Workers' Party	2 126 000	6.0	Wojciech Jaruzelski
Romania	Romanian Communist Party	3 500 000	15.0	Nicolae Ceauşescu
USSR	Communist Party of the Soviet Union	19 037 946	6.8	Mikhail Gorbachev
Vietnam	Communist Party of Vietnam	1 750 000	3.0	Truong Chinh
Yugoslavia	League of Communists of Yugoslavia	2 200 000	3.0	Vidoje Žarković

Sources: Richard F. Staar, 'Checklist of Communist Parties in 1985', *Problems of Communism*, March–April 1986; *Ezhegodnik Bol'shoi Sovetskoi Entsiklopedii 1986g.* (Moscow, 1987); and current press reports.

countries of a tradition of autocratic rule and the establishment of a centralised system of economic management. It derives also from a number of ideological sources, in particular from the doctrine of the 'vanguard party', formulated most fully by Lenin in works such as *What is to be Done?* (1902). In *What is to be Done?*, Lenin argued that socialism would not necessarily come about through the automatic extension of trade union and other forms of economic activity by the working class. Strikes, Lenin argued, represented the class struggle in embryo, but 'only in embryo', because the workers did not as yet have an awareness of the irreconcilable nature of the conflict between their interests and those of the capitalist class. This, Lenin went on, could 'only be brought to them from the outside', by the 'educated representatives of the propertied classes – the intelligentsia'. 'There can be no revolutionary movement without a revolutionary theory,' Lenin insisted, and the role of the vanguard could be fulfilled only by a party which was guided by this advanced theory. The struggle for socialism, in Lenin's view, must therefore place at least as much emphasis upon raising workers' political consciousness as upon bread-and-butter economic issues, and within this struggle a role of particular importance devolved upon the intellectuals who possessed a knowledge of and commitment to the revolutionary theory by which the wider movement must be guided.

No less important was the question of party structure and organisation, and it was upon this issue that Lenin and the Bolsheviks (majority group) split from the remaining Russian Social Democrats, thereafter called the Mensheviks (minority group), at the Second Congress of the Russian Social Democratic Labour Party in 1903. Lenin argued in *What is to be Done?* that the first and most urgent practical task was to 'create an organisation of revolutionaries able to guarantee the energy, stability and continuity of the political struggle'. Such an organisation, Lenin insisted, must embrace 'primarily and chiefly people whose profession consists of revolutionary activity'; and it must 'inevitably be not very wide and as secret as possible', since it was essential to avoid police penetration. Lenin added that the professional revolutionaries must 'serve' the mass movement, not dominate it or 'think for everyone'; he held that professional revolutionaries would be thrown up by the mass movement itself in 'ever-increasing numbers'; and he insisted that his proposals were intended to be valid for Russian autocratic conditions only, in which an open organisation would simply create a 'paradise for the police'. Lenin's principles have, none the less, been taken as the organisational basis of the ruling communist parties of today, and it is to his concept of a 'vanguard party' – a relatively small group, centrally organised, of professional revolutionaries – that they are still officially committed.

The structure and role of the Communist Party of the Soviet Union

The Communist Party of the Soviet Union (CPSU), in words at least, conforms closely to Lenin's precepts. The party is described, in its revised Rules adopted in 1986, as the 'tried and tested militant vanguard of the Soviet people, which unites, on a voluntary basis, the more advanced, politically more conscious section of the working class, collective farm peasantry and intelligentsia of the USSR'. It is not, in other words, a mass organisation, admitting all those who might wish to join it, but an elite group which, at least in theory, consists of those who have the highest levels of political knowledge and commitment in the society and who have been admitted into the party on that basis by the existing membership. The party is described in the Rules as the 'highest form of socio-political organisation' and as the 'leading and guiding force of Soviet society'. It is based, officially speaking, upon what are called 'Leninist norms of party life', in other words democratic centralism, collective leadership, inner-party democracy, the creative activity of party members, criticism and self-criticism, and broad publicity. The Rules, however, also make clear that the party is committed to 'ideological and organisation unity, monolithic cohesion of its ranks, and a high degree of conscious discipline', and any form of group or factional activity is specifically prohibited. Party activity, finally, is supposed to be based on Marxist–Leninist theory and upon the party Programme, which defines the party's tasks as the 'planned and all-round perfection of socialism' and the 'further progress of Soviet society towards communism'. The party also regards itself as an 'integral part of the international communist movement'.

The Rules lay down the organisational structure of the party, a simplified version of which is set out in Figure 4.1. At the bottom of the structure are the primary party organisations (PPOs), formerly called 'cells', which are formed at workplaces and at a few residential locations throughout the USSR, wherever three or more party members are present. There were over 440 000 of these bodies in 1986. The PPO is the organisational basis of the party; it admits new members, carries out agitation and propaganda work and seeks generally to improve the economic performances of the institution within which it is located. Meetings of members are held at least once a month, and a party secretary and (in all but the smallest PPOs) a party bureau are elected, who hold office for a year. Each PPO elects representatives to the level of the party immediately above it, the district level, which in turn elects to the regional level and then to the republican level of the party. At each of these levels conferences or congresses are held every two-and-a-half or five years at which party committees, bureaux and secretaries are elected, the latter consisting of full-time officials responsible for various areas of party work. At the apex of this system is the all-union Party Congress which meets every five years, and which elects a Central Committee which in turn elects the party's ruling bodies, the Politburo and the Secretariat.

Membership of the CPSU, according to its Rules, is open to any citizen of the USSR who accepts the party's Programme and Rules, takes an active part in communist construction, works in one of the party organisations, carries out all party decisions and pays his or her membership dues (up to 3 per cent of monthly earnings). Admissions may be made from the age of 18, though those aged up to 25 inclusive may join only through the party's youth wing, the Komsomol. Applicants must submit recommendations from three existing members who have been members of the party for not less than five years and who have known the prospective member, professionally and socially, for not less than a year. Membership is

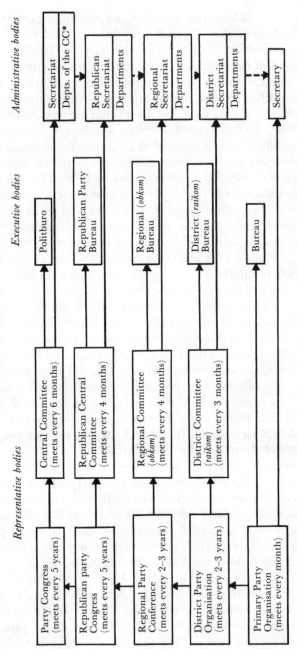

FIGURE 4.1 The organisational structure of the CPSU (simplified)

*In 1986, the following 24 departments were known to be in existence: administration of affairs; administrative organs; agriculture and food industry; agricultural machine building; cadres abroad; chemical industry; construction; culture; defence industry; economic; general; heavy industry and power; international; international information; letters; liaison with communist and workers' parties of socialist countries; light industry and consumer goods; machine building; organisational party work; propaganda; science and educational institutions; trade and domestic services; transport and communications; Main Political Directorate of the Soviet Army and Navy.

Note: ——→ election; - - - - - → supervision and control

initially for a year-long probationary or 'candidate' state, after which a decision on full membership is taken by the members of the primary party organisation to which application has been made. Once admitted, a member gains the right to elect and to be elected to party bodies, to discuss party policies at party meetings and conferences and to uphold his opinions until a decision is taken, to 'criticise any party body and any Communist, irrespective of the position he holds', to address any question, statement or proposal to any party body up to Central Committee level and to demand an answer, and to attend any party meeting at which his conduct is discussed (Party Rules, Art. 3).

Party members are required at the same time to set an example at their place of work, to carry out party policies and explain them to the masses, to take an active part in political life, to master Marxist–Leninist theory, to observe the norms of communist morality, to combat nationalism and chauvinism, to strengthen the party's organisational and ideological unity, to 'wage an unflagging struggle for peace and friendship among nations', and, as if all this were not enough, to 'develop criticism and self-criticism' and 'combat ostentation, conceit, complacency and eyewash' (Party Rules, Art. 2). Party members are also liable to be sent to far-off places on party missions, and they must seek the permission of the local party organisation if they wish to change their place of work or take up residence in another part of the country. Party members, however, are more likely than non-members to be given permission to travel abroad, their sources of political information may be somewhat better than those of non-members, and, above all, their career prospects are likely to be considerably improved since party membership, though no guarantee of a leading position, is often in practice a necessary qualification for such positions and non-members will be at a serious disadvantage in seeking to obtain them. Despite periodic warnings from the leadership that nominal or self-seeking members will not be permitted to remain within the ranks it seems clear that it is the career advantages of party membership that presently attract many applicants, and warnings from the leadership and occasional expulsions are unlikely to alter this situation significantly so long as the party effectively monopolises the leading positions in the society.

The party's total membership has grown steadily in size since the 1950s, both absolutely and as a proportion of the total population, although the central authorities have been attempting to hold down the rate of growth over the last couple of decades in order to preserve the party's elite or vanguard character. The total membership in 1986 was just over 19 million, or about 10 per cent of the adult population. Some 45.0 per cent of members were workers by social origin, a proportion which has been increasingly steadily over the past couple of decades as a result of a deliberate decision by the party leadership to maximise recruitment from this section of the population. Collective farm workers accounted for about 11.8 per cent of party members at the same date, a proportion which has been falling slowly over the years, and white-collar workers accounted for the remaining 43.2 per cent. Women are rather under-represented in the party, at 28.8 per cent of all members as against just over half of the total population, but their proportion of total membership has been steadily increasing, and compared with political parties in other countries the present level of female membership may be considered fairly high. Of the nationalities, Russians account for rather more than their share of total party membership, at 59.1 per cent of all members in 1986 as compared with 52.4 per cent of the total population, but Georgians (and Jews) are relatively more heavily over-represented than Russians. The level of party membership is lowest in the Central Asian republics and in Moldavia.

The leading party organs

The 'supreme organ' of the CPSU, according to the Rules, is the Party Congress, which is held every five years. (It is also possible to convene extraordinary Congresses if the circumstances require it.) The Congress hears and approves the reports of the Central Committee and of the other leading party bodies; it reviews and amends the party's Rules and Programme; it elects the Central Committee and the Central Auditing Commission (a largely honorary body which is responsible for overseeing the party's accounts); and it 'determines the line of the party in matters of domestic and foreign policy, and examines and decides the most important questions of party and state life and of communist construction'. The Party Congress is too large and meets for too short a time, however, to serve as a policy-making body of the kind that is implied in the Rules, and in practice it serves mainly as a means of ratifying policies decided in advance as well as a periodic rally and morale-booster, particularly for those, supposedly the 'best of the best', who are sent to the Congress as delegates by their local party organisation. The Central Committee's report to the Congress, normally presented by the General Secretary, is the most important item of business considered by the Congress; it also receives a report delivered by a government spokesman on the performance of the economy and on the new Five-Year Plan. These are approved unanimously after a rather perfunctory debate, although individual speakers, as in the Supreme Soviet, sometimes take this opportunity to press the interests of their own particular institution or area.

Of rather more significance in a policy-making sense is the Central Committee, which is elected by the Party Congress to discharge its responsibilities in the intervals between Congresses. The Central Committee elected by the 27th Party Congress in March 1986 had 477 members, of whom 307 had full membership and 170 had candidate or non-voting status. The Central Committee is required to meet not less often than once every six months; its responsibilities include the direction of the activity of the party and of its local bodies, the selection and appointment of leading functionaries, and the management of party institutions, the party press, and of the party budget. Its members constitute the closest approximation to the Soviet political elite, including – often, it appears, as of right – the leading party officials from the republican and regional levels as well as leading government ministers, trade union officials, diplomats, generals and heads of academic and scientific institutions, and a small number of 'genuine' workers and peasants. The proceedings of the normally Central Committee are not published, but it seems clear that its periodic meetings serve as sounding-boards for the consideration of policy alternatives as well as occasions for the party leadership to announce new policies or to administer authoritative warnings about shortcomings in various areas of policy. The Central Committee played a role of some importance in 1957, when its members were hurriedly convened in Moscow in order to overrule a hostile majority by which Khrushchev was at that time confronted in the Politburo; but it cannot normally be said to hold the party's leadership to account in any way, and this is not surprising when it is remembered that the leadership itself is largely responsible for its selection.

The party's two supreme decision-making bodies are the Politburo (or Political Bureau) and the Secretariat, both of which are formally elected by the Central Committee. The Politburo is supposed, according to the Rules, to 'direct the work of the party' between meetings of the Central Committee. It is, in fact, the functional equivalent of a cabinet in a British-style political system, meeting once a week and taking the key decisions in all areas of policy. The Politburo elected after the 27th Party Congress in 1986 consisted of nineteen members, twelve full and seven candidate or non-voting members; all of them are men, and their average age is about 64, with four members old enough to have been born before the October Revolution of 1917. The Politburo may be thought of as representing a number of key institutions in Soviet life. In 1986, these included the ministries of defence, foreign affairs and the KGB, the Council of Ministers in the person of its chairman, a number of larger urban and republican party organisations, and a number of Central Committee Secretaries representing the party's central apparatus. The degree of overlap between party and government leaderships at this level is so extensive that it may often make sense to regard them as a single hierarchy. The Politburo reportedly works on a consensual basis; votes are rarely taken and contentious questions are usually referred to sub-committees, which are expected to resolve the matters in dispute and then report back to the full Politburo with their conclusions.

The party's supreme administrative body is the Secretariat of the Central Committee of the CPSU, also elected by the Central Committee, each of whose members takes responsibility for a particular area or areas of policy. The Secretariat meets weekly as a body, and it also supervises the work of the party's full-time bureaucracy, the twenty-four departments of the Central Committee, which monitor all areas of Soviet life. (These departments are listed in Figure 4.1.) The Party Rules say no more than that the Secretariat 'directs current work, chiefly the selection of cadres [leading officials] and the verification of the fulfilment of decisions'. This central bureaucracy, with its counterparts at lower levels, is in fact an institution of the utmost importance, the instrument by which the party's decisions are put into practice, a source of advice and information to the Politburo, and the administrative hub of the whole Soviet system. The head of the Secretariat is the General Secretary, currently Mikhail S. Gorbachev, who is separately elected by the Central Committee; he takes the chair at meetings of the Politburo and the Secretariat, and in addition has a small personal staff of his own. The post of General Secretary is conventionally regarded as the most important one in Soviet politics, a view which is supported by the fact that its present occupant is also a member of the Supreme Soviet Presidium and *ex officio* chairman of the Defence Council of the USSR.

All the party's leading bodies are in principle elective and accountable to those who elect them, but in practice they largely dominate the congresses and conferences to which they are supposedly responsible as well as each lower level in the party hierarchy. There are several reasons for this. Perhaps the most important is the principle of democratic centralism, enshrined in Article 19 of the Party Rules, which requires that all party bodies be elective and accountable but also that there be 'strict party discipline and subordination of the minority to the majority' and that 'the decisions of higher bodies are obligatory for lower bodies'. The decisions of leading party bodies cannot therefore be openly challenged, at least without the risk of expulsion and other sanctions, and any attempt to form organised groupings or to establish direct links between party bodies at the same level in the hierarchy is explicitly prohibited. The Party Rules also specify various ways in which each level of the party structure controls the level immediately below it. Of particular importance is the influence that is exerted over the election of leading officials at each level of the party by the level immediately above it.

Although there is a secret ballot and though members have the 'unlimited right to challenge candidates and to criticise them', it is normal for a single list of candidates to be 'recommended' by the party level immediately above and for it to be elected without opposition. Each level of the party hierarchy is also supposed to 'direct' and 'inspect the work' of the party bodies immediately subordinate to it, and to hear regular reports upon their performance.

The leading officials at each level, accordingly, can usually count upon the support of the party officials immediately superior to them and by whom they have been recommended, and they need therefore pay rather less attention to the wishes and opinions of those who nominally elect them. The Party Rules do in fact provide for the 'free and business-like discussion of questions of party policy in individual party organisations or in the party as a whole', for the right of any member to criticise the conduct of any other member regardless of what position he might hold, and for special party-wide discussions of controversial matters if the circumstances require them. These are held to be basic principles of inner-party democracy, and severe penalties, even expulsion, are attached to any attempt to suppress criticism or to victimise those who have expressed it. The party press, however, is full of cases of this kind, with critics being forced to undertake less pleasant work or even to leave their jobs as a result of having spoken out frankly at party meetings, and it often requires the intervention of a much higher level of party authority before the injustice can be put right. It is presumably clear to most members that only 'constructive', that is to say mild and unspecific, criticism will be encouraged, and that any more thorough-going criticism may well have adverse consequences for the careers of those who express it, perhaps even placing their personal liberty in jeopardy. In the circumstances it is not surprising that the CPSU tends in practice to function in a centralised and hierarchical manner rather than in the internally democratic manner for which the Party Rules ostensibly provide.

The 'leading role' of the CPSU

The party's 'leading role' extends to virtually all areas of

Soviet life, with the single and fairly nominal exception of the church (which is constitutionally separate from the state and responsible for its own affairs). It includes, in the first place, the party's ideological work. This takes two main organisational forms. The first of these is agitation and propaganda (*agitprop*), which is intended for the mass of the population and consists of political talks or lectures given by 'agitators' or 'political informers' on a weekly basis at workplaces throughout the USSR, attendance at which is in theory voluntary but in practice difficult to avoid. The subjects covered include economic, political, cultural and international matters; for instance, the economic significance of the decisions taken by the most recent Party Congress, or the imperialist nature of US foreign policy in Latin America. The second main organised form of ideological work is the system of political education, which consists of classes in Marxist theory and party policy intended primarily but not exclusively for party members, and is conducted at three main levels, primary, intermediate and advanced. There are currently about 21 million people enrolled in these classes, more than a third of whom are not party members, studying subjects such as the biography of Lenin, the history of the CPSU and, at the higher levels, more vocationally-oriented topics such as economic management and agricultural policy. Apart from this there is a considerable political content in the educational curriculum in schools, particularly in subjects such as history and civics, and the party is also supposed to exercise general ideological guidance over art, literature and music and over the mass media.

A good deal of sociological research has been conducted into the effectiveness of this vast effort. Political classes and lectures, it appears, are often attended unwillingly and as a result of party or trade-union pressure, and they have a very limited effect in changing political values and behaviour, or even in raising levels of political information, since they tend to be attended disproportionately by those who have a better than average level of political knowledge in the first place. International affairs and topical issues are consistently more popular than economic or theoretical questions, and there are frequently complaints about the lack of novelty, excessively abstract character and lack of convincing argumentation in the political lectures and classes that are provided. There is also some evidence that the party's ideological efforts may not be reaching all sections of the community, particularly those who live in rural areas, young people and pensioners. The improvement of ideological work has been given a good deal of attention in recent years by the party leadership, partly, no doubt, in response to such surveys. There had been too much emphasis upon the customary 'gross' approach, Gorbachev told the 27th Party Congress in 1986. The relevant statistics were indeed impressive: hundreds and thousands of lecturers and propagandists, massive newspaper circulations, and audiences in their millions. And yet real, living people were all too easily forgotten in this 'playing around with figures and with "coverage"'. Party propagandists have been instructed in future years to pay much more attention to work with individuals, and to rebutting the 'psychological warfare' unleashed by the capitalist countries; the mass media have also been urged to respond more promptly and convincingly to current national and international developments. Reforms of this kind have, however, been called for before and it remains to be seen how much difference these latest injunctions will make.

A second and not less important way in which the leading role of the party is exercised is through the party's guidance (*rukovodstvo*) of the soviets and of elected bodies of all kinds. As we have seen in Chapter 3, the party effectively controls the electoral system, by regulating the choice of candidates and in other ways. In addition, the party exercises a leading role within elected bodies of all kinds, wherever there are three or more party members, by means of the formation of party groups or caucuses within them. According to the Party Rules, the CPSU, acting within the framework of the Soviet Constitution, 'exercises political leadership of state and public organisations' and 'directs and coordinates their work'. This leadership role is carried out through the party groups, which are required to promote party policy within the organisation in question and to 'verify the fulfilment of party and government directives', and which are guided in their work by the Central Committee or by a lower level of the party organisation. Party groups meet beforehand to coordinate their tactics, mobilise support for party policies within the body within which they work, and report back upon its activities to the party committee to which they are responsible. Party groups are supposed to develop the activity and initiative of the bodies within which they work, not to command them or attempt to usurp their authority, but at the same time they are supposed to play a leading or guiding role within all such bodies and to ensure that their activities conform to the requirements of party policy. Party groups function, in effect, as means by which the party's authority can be extended to elected state and public bodies of all kinds.

A third and most important form of party control is the party's effective monopoly of appointments to key positions at all levels of society. In the Soviet Union this is usually known as the party's 'cadres policy', or as the 'selection and allocation of cadres'. It is more usually known in the West as the *nomenklatura*, the list of positions at various levels which require the approval of the party before they can be filled (a parallel list or card index of the people who hold these positions, 'nomenklatura workers', is apparently also maintained). The party as such has no authority to make appointments to any positions that are not within its own ranks, but it can exercise a decisive influence over all other appointments through the party committee within the institution in question, which will normally consult with party officials at the appropriate level before making its recommendations in any matters of this kind. The list of positions at the national level which are believed to be controlled in this way by the party include, for instance, all ministerial appointments, the editors of newspapers, generals and the more important ambassadorships, the heads of the trade union, cultural and scientific bureaucracies, the directors of the largest factories (those of 'all-union significance'), rectors of the major universities and so forth. Parallel lists of positions are maintained by the party apparatus at lower levels of the system, from the republican down to the district level, and all appointments to these positions are similarly regulated. In all it is estimated that about 3 million executive positions throughout the USSR are controlled in this way.

It does not necessarily follow that only party members will

be appointed to positions that are on the party nomenklatura, or that a purely arbitrary choice will be made and then imposed upon the organisation in question regardless of the wishes of its members. Party approval may in some cases amount to no more than the routine endorsement of the candidate preferred by the institution in question; and account will certainly be taken of the professional as well as party-political credentials of all potential candidates. It has also been known, moreover, usually at the local level, for the party's recommendation of (for instance) a collective farm chairman to be rejected and for a more acceptable alternative candidate to have to be found instead. The Academy of Sciences, the prestigious institution within which most Soviet scientific research is conducted and which admits its members by secret ballot, has also been known to reject particularly unpopular candidates despite the fact that they have party backing. In the last resort, however, the party can exercise decisive influence in all matters of this kind if it decides to do so, and those who hold leading positions at all levels cannot fail to be aware that their continued tenure of their position depends to a very large extent upon the support of party officials at the relevant level in the hierarchy rather than upon the continued favour of those to whom they are nominally responsible. This is not a situation calculated to encourage unorthodoxy, initiative or responsiveness to local needs.

Fourthly and finally, the party apparatus plays a role of key importance in monitoring the performance of government and state bodies at all levels. At the national level this monitoring or supervision – the Russian word is *kontrol'* – is performed by the departments of the Central Committee, under the guidance of the Secretariat. At the republican and lower levels it is performed by the elected officials and full-time party bureaucrats through a comparable but rather smaller network of departments. The Central Committee Department of Agriculture and the Food Industry in Moscow, for instance, monitors the performance of the State Agro-Industrial Committee (which incorporates the former Ministry of Agriculture) in this way, making sure that it is fulfilling its plan targets, minimising energy losses, introducing new technology and undertaking whatever other tasks the party considers to be of particular importance within the area of policy for which it is responsible. The Central Committee Department of the Chemical Industry supervises the work of the USSR Ministry of the Chemical Industry in the same way, and the Heavy Industry and Power, Construction and other Departments take a comparable interest in the work of the ministries and state bodies that undertake responsibilities within these areas.

The Central Committee departments, and the corresponding departments at lower levels in the party hierarchy, carry out this monitoring function in a variety of ways. Of particular importance in this connection is the party committee within the ministry or institution in question, which under the Party Rules has the responsibility of checking upon the fulfilment of party and government decisions by the institution within which it is located and of 'inform[ing] the appropriate party bodies in good time of shortcomings in the work of such institutions and of their individual employees, regardless of what posts the latter may occupy'. Party committees, it appears, may be rather reluctant to undertake duties of this kind, and they may sometimes identify with the position of the ministry rather than with that of the central party apparatus upon the issue in question. Indeed even Central Committee departments may sometimes associate themselves with the interests of the ministries they supervise, if necessary at the expense of other party priorities, since it is upon the performance of the ministries for which they are responsible that they themselves will be judged.

The central party apparatus, however, does have very considerable powers through mechanisms of this kind, ranging from the ability to call an individual minister, as a party member, to account before the party committee in his ministry, to the ability to summon leading party and government personnel from Moscow and the provinces to occasional meetings or conferences in the Central Committee offices at which their performance may be critically scrutinised and at which they may also receive authoritative instructions upon future party policies within the area for which they are responsible. These powers are usually sufficient to ensure that the central party apparatus dominates the policy-making process. Party officials are supposed to refrain from intervening in the day-to-day work of government departments and other bodies, reserving their influence for the selection of leading personnel and general strategic guidance. Often, however, the distinction between a policy and its detailed implementation is a difficult one to draw, and party bodies frequently become involved in routine matters such as the resolution of a transport bottleneck or the procurement of some scarce raw materials, since their authority is often greater than that of the government and economic bodies they supervise and since party bodies are in turn responsible for their satisfactory performance.

The leading role of the party is accordingly a fairly complicated matter, varying a good deal from one policy area to another, from one period of time to another and from one part of the country to another. Party organisations are supposed to guide the work of representative institutions, but not to supplant them; they are expected to make sure that suitable candidates are chosen to fill leading positions, but not to ignore the wishes of those who are nominally responsible for doing so; and they are supposed to refrain from involving themselves in the routine administrative tasks which are the responsibility of governmental and economic institutions, though it will often prove impossible to achieve the party's long-term objectives in the area of policy in question without a good deal of detailed intervention of this kind. The party's exercise of its leading role will, of course, also be influenced by other factors, such as the special interests of various sections of the party bureaucracy itself, the pressures exerted by major institutions such as the trade unions and the military, and by the Soviet public through the various channels that are available to them for this purpose. We shall consider the various forms assumed by party leadership in other communist states in the remainder of this chapter, and then turn to the interaction of these various interests and pressures in Chapter 5.

The communist parties of Eastern Europe

Structures and practices

In this sphere the East European parties have followed the Soviet model closely, with the important exception of Yugoslavia, as far as formal organisation is concerned. Thus in matters of structure and procedures East European parties invest party congresses with an authority similar to that of CPSU, and politburos, central committees and lower-level party organisations ostensibly play virtually the same roles. However, because in general politics in East Europe have been less stable than in the Soviet Union, the content and functioning of these institutions have varied from the original model. The spectrum of leadership stability, for instance, runs from Albania and the GDR (two leaders each since 1944) to Poland (seven leaders over 42 years), and the actual methods of change have included death, purge, resignation and being voted out of office. As a general proposition, leadership change in Eastern Europe tends to be associated with instability whether from within the party or more broadly from society.

A further feature of the East German, Polish, Czechoslovak, Hungarian and Bulgarian parties is that their leaderships appear to be subject at least to a Soviet veto; possibly the Soviet Union even enjoys a *de facto* right to initiate appointments. An example of this was the removal of Walter Ulbricht, the well entrenched and long-serving leader of the East German party (1945–71), who was dismissed at the behest of the Soviet Union because he opposed the policy of *détente*. Turnover in central committees shows no clear overall pattern; in some parties rejuvenation is regular, e.g. in Hungary where individuals are encouraged to retire at 60, whilst in others the turnover is much lower, for example in Bulgaria. Nevertheless in general a new party leader will usually seek to fill the central committee with individuals who can be counted on to give him support, and the same usually applies to lower-level party functionaries (for example, district party secretaries).

Although East European parties pay lip service to the concept of being an elite party, the interpretation of 'elite' has been so wide as to be virtually meaningless. If one takes the CPSU as the norm as far as percentage of party members in the total population is concerned (see Table 4.1), then it will be seen that five out of eight East European parties are above the Soviet figure of 6.8 per cent; Romania is more than double and the GDR is almost double. It is significant that the Romanian leader Nicolae Ceauşescu has expressly sought to redefine the nature of the vanguard party as applied to Romania and to broaden the implication of this term. Another noteworthy feature of East European parties is that their memberships generally tend to grow at a rate higher than the growth of total population, despite fairly regular scrutinies of the fitness of individuals to retain their member-ship (known as the 'exchange of party cards'). To take one example: the Hungarian party, which is at the conservative end of the spectrum in this respect, lost 56 332 members through death, resignation, exclusion and expulsion and gained 91 956 members net (an increase of 13.9 per cent) between 1970 and 1975. Over the next five years the party made a further net gain of 57 480 members (an increase of 7.6 per cent) and lost 48 245 members. Both these net increases were well above the population growth rate. In the 1970s the most striking aspect of recruitment policy was the strategy of proletarianisation – a rise in the proportion of active workers in the membership. By the end of the decade all these parties had registered an increase in working-class membership, although the levels of industrialisation and the differences in statistical enumeration and their reliability made closer com-parisons difficult (see Table 4.2).

Finally, East European party memberships have on the whole shown greater instability in numbers than that of the CPSU, sometimes by design, sometimes not. An extreme case was the disintegration of the Hungarian party in 1956, the membership of which dropped from about 900 000 in October 1956 to about 30 000 two months later in conse-quence of the revolution. But other fluctuations have been recorded. The Czechoslovak Communist Party, for instance, has varied between 22 per cent (in 1948) and 8.5 per cent (in

TABLE 4.2

The social composition of East European communist parties
(percentages)

		Workers	Peasants	White-collar employees	Others*
Albania	1966	32.9	28.6	37.1	1.4
	1981	38.0	29.4	32.6	0.0
Bulgaria	1971	40.1	26.1	33.8	0.0
	1986	44.4	16.3	39.3	0.0
Czechoslo-	1973	44.1	4.7	31.6	19.6
vakia	1984	45.0†			
	1965	45.6	6.4	28.4	19.6
GDR	1976	56.1	5.2	20.0	18.7
	1986	58.1	4.8	22.4	14.7
Hungary	1967	34.9	7.8	38.1	19.2
	1985	42.6	7.8	42.4	7.2
Poland	1970	30.3	11.5	42.3	5.9
	1985	38.5	9.1	51.0	1.4
Romania	1969	43.0	28.0	23.0	6.0
	1984	56.0	16.0	21.0	7.0
Yugoslavia	1984	30.1	4.9	39.1	25.9

*Others is a mixed category which variously includes pensioners, students, members of the armed forces, but not all East European parties use the category in the same way.
†Estimate:
Source: Compiled on the basis of figures in Bogdan Szajkowski (ed.), *Marxist Governments: A World Survey*, 3 vols (London, 1981), and reports to party congresses.

1980) of the total population. In the immediate aftermath of the communist takeover all East European parties, including the Czech party, were swollen with Social Democratic members who were soon to be purged. The Czechoslovak party experienced a further purge after 1969 which resulted in the expulsion of over 400 000 members, or between a fifth and a quarter of the total. By 1980 over 40 per cent of the membership had joined after the Prague Spring and the purge that followed.

The Polish party has also experienced periods of considerable turnover, such as 1958 (the removal of Stalinists and Revisionists), in 1971–72 (when over 140 000 members were lost as Gierek consolidated his hold), and 1980 (when approx-imately 300 000 members left in the aftermath of the crisis). The post-martial law regime has seen a steady erosion in party membership, though official data on the losses were not regarded as reliable. The League of Communists of Yugosla-via (LCY) was similarly slimmed down after the reassertion of party control in 1971–72, with the membership dropping from a high of 1 146 000 in 1968 to 1 010 000 in 1972 to begin a steady climb thereafter.

The internal affairs of communist parties have been a frequent subject for debate, and the evidence of the post-war period is that a viable compromise between creative initiative from below and the needs of Leninist democratic centralism has still to be reached. The party leaderships are aware of the potential dangers they face if they permit the membership a genuine voice in decision making, which can result in div-isions and undermine party unity. At the same time excessive control results in formalism and apathy, and also careerism and a general absence of idealism in what is, after all, supposed to be a party of ideals. However, the overall trend in the 1970s and 1980s was away from idealism and towards routine despite the risks of formalism – the Polish reform movement of 1980 and after, quintessentially deriving from grass-roots pressure, was the only example of a trend in the opposite direction. It was, however, interesting that the democratisation of the party has been regarded as an import-ant area of discussion throughout and that a number of experiments in party reform have been attempted.

The 1968 Czechoslovak events threw up one of the most important variants of party reform. A poll of some 38 000 people, published in May 1968, showed that among party members with higher education 45 per cent regarded democ-ratisation of the party as a first priority (66 per cent with only primary education). The draft of the new party statute published just before the invasion envisaged a fairly similar party structure to that which had existed previously, retaining the hierarchical pyramid, but it was suffused by the new spirit of membership participation. Thus party bodies were to be genuinely responsive – the Congress to the membership, the Central Committee to the Congress, and the Presidium (in other words the Politburo) to the Central Committee – whilst there was to be an equal opportunity for all party members to express their standpoint towards the party's policy and to define their views in party organs. There was to be democratic election of officers by secret ballot, a ban on multiple office-holding in party and state institutions and rotation and independence of lower party organs, and, most importantly, the draft of the new statute came close to recognising the right of minorities to continue to press their views though not to organise – defined in Soviet orthodoxy as factionalism. The draft read: 'The minority is subordinated to majority opinion and carries out decisions taken', but the minority had 'the right to formulate its standpoint, to require that it be recorded in the minutes, to persist in its views and to require, on the basis of new information and experience, a fresh examination of its standpoint.' With hindsight this draft can be regarded as less radical than it appeared at the time because it largely slides over the problem of accountability of the leadership to the members and simply assumes that the party leadership will conduct itself in such a way as to obviate accountability.

This attitude did not commend itself to the radicalised membership of the Polish party in 1980–81 when it launched a grass-roots reform movement with the specific goal of creating a system in which the leadership would at all times be accountable for its actions to the members. Among other schemes devised, a system of regular reporting back by all party leaders at every level to their basic organisations was put forward, coupled with a strict limitation on the length of office-holding; in addition there was strong pressure from below for secret ballots at all party elections, something which was conceded by the leadership in the election of delegates to the Extraordinary Ninth Congress of the party which was held in July 1981. In consequence approximately 95 per cent of the delegates were new, a thorough and far-reaching purge of the higher reaches of the *apparat* testifying to the intensity of membership feelings. The most striking organisational innovation thrown up by the Polish crisis was the creation of horizontal organisations cutting directly across Leninist organisational norms. Instead of the customary hierarchical organisations in which each factory party cell was responsible to a district or town party organisation, resulting in powerlessness of the membership and reliance on instructions from above, the horizontal movement consisted of direct, unmediated links between party organisations in the same locality, embracing individual party cells in large and small enterprises as well as educational institutions. Thus the horizontal movement linked manual and non-manual workers, provided the membership with a greatly increased pool of information, and gave it the self-confidence to stand up to pressures from higher levels of the hierarchy (which was itself demoralised by the defeat of August 1980). There was also indications that the horizontal movement in some places sought to involve non-members of the party at large-scale open meetings in the discussion of problems common to all.

A third attempt at democratisation, this time under the control of the party leadership and at its behest, took place in Hungary in 1968–73. The Hungarian experiment was interesting because it showed an awareness of the dilemma posed at the opening of this section, of the need to balance central controls against grass-roots initiative. In the event, the experiment petered out when the tensions within the dilemma proved impossible to reconcile and central control was re-established. The attempted reform originated with a Central Committee resolution in December 1969 on the further improvement of the party's methods of work in the period up to the Tenth Congress which was to be held eleven months later. Local party secretaries were warned that their proposals to the centre should be concrete and specific and that they should concentrate on the actual implementation of policy rather than on general statements. Party elections were to be as broadly based as possible and the membership was to be consulted in the choice of candidates – consultation was even to extend to non-members, seeing that it was not 'a matter of indifference to them who is selected as party secretary . . . in a village, enterprise or office'. Permission was given for multiple candidacies in such elections.

Further attempts to give the membership greater say were made at the Congress itself in November 1970. Replies to comments made at the party forum had to be made at the same forum; members were to be protected against reprisals if they made critical remarks; appeals against expulsions were institutionalised; and generally the party authorities sought to create an atmosphere in which individual party members would not be afraid to voice their criticism and make a contribution to party work. The broad thrust of the Hungarian attempt at creating inner party democracy was to build up the morale of the rank and file and to create at least a minimal machinery for the expression and implementation of their views. This could be achieved only in a climate of sufficient central control over the middle level of the party apparatus, which was most directly threatened by an increased grass roots voice in party affairs; in the event such a climate disappeared with the growing recentralisation of 1973 and after. Since then the affairs of the Hungarian party have been characterised by apathy, although the leadership from time to time responds to particular expressions of opinion if this appears advisable.

The party and society

Since the end of the Stalinist period and the rejection of a monolithic conception of society in which the party was the sole initiator and aggregator, the East European parties have tried to find alternative forms of defining their leading role. As in the case of inner party democracy the problem is one of finding a balance between excessive central control, which results in stultification, and insufficient control, in which case the position of the party is threatened. But from the outset, the move from monolithism presented the East European parties – except Albania which still adheres to it – with a theoretical problem. If the role of the party is no longer to be a monolith, in which conflicts of interest are held to be illegitimate and even criminal, then conflicts of interest must be accepted as normal, though they may be termed 'non-antagonistic'. This raises a further problem of defining the role of the party in this new situation: what is to be the function of the party and how is it to be exercised? In essence, though not all the East European parties defined it in this way, the debate signified a move from monopoly over society to a more limited form of control, and the restriction of monopoly to the broad political sphere where it was to be regarded as a monopoly of initiative. One consequence of this was to withdraw party control from certain areas of life – the family above all – and to permit a range of individual choice over matters of consumption, i.e. economic choice (though not political choice).

The role of the party, therefore, was to determine the global interest of society as a whole (the societal interest), to arbitrate among competing sectional interests and to protect the individual interest wherever necessary. The party would continue to retain its claim to a monopoly of rationality in strategy (goal setting) and of efficiency in execution (policy implementation), though it would exercise this monopoly in conjunction with other interests, always reserving to itself the right of ultimate decision. This would enable the party to make better use of the technical intelligentsia and to reject the primacy of political reliability over expertise – in effect a switch from 'red' to 'expert'. This opened the door to real debates, as distinct from ritualistic denunciations, but it also imposed on the party a far more complex duty of decision-making, for the determination of the societal interest in any given situation proved to be far from straightforward.

The advantage of this shift, which can be dated from the second de-Stalinisation of 1961 (the 22nd Congress of the CPSU), was that it enabled the party to use the energies and resources of society in a more humane and efficient fashion than under the Stalinist model, but without abandoning control entirely. It created real hopes for a viable means of running post-revolutionary societies in which the initial task of concentrating energies for the beginning of industrialisation could be gradually redefined as involving the ever greater complexity and differentiation of economic maturity. The disadvantage of this conception was that it assumed that rational arbitration was at all times possible, and that the party had the ability to discharge this task on its own without becoming entangled in distortions through incompetence, corruption, the self-interest of officials or plain contrariness. Further, the conception was based upon another assumption, namely that the party could continue to exclude society from genuine political participation at a time when it was growing in sophistication and its claim to be included in a share of power could no longer be adequately met by largely token representation within the party itself.

This was the theoretical background against which the East European parties faced the years from the mid-1960s. The dilemmas involved weighed more heavily on the East European parties and societies than on their Soviet counterparts precisely because they had reached a higher level of political economic and social development and because their political traditions predisposed their peoples to a greater degree of involvement in the political process. The various strategies of political development adopted can be put into three categories: (1) political and economic reform pointing towards greater participation at different times (Czechoslovakia, Hungary, Yugoslavia, Poland); (2) economic reform only (the GDR and Bulgaria); (3) no reform (Romania and Albania). All these strategies (except Albania's) involved some redefinition of the relationship between party and society and the way in which the party would exercise its leading role.

In broad terms this redefinition followed the Soviet approach of controlling the institutions of the state relatively strictly and suppressing interests at variance with party control, for example the demand by the intelligentsia to express autonomous criticism of party policies. The party also retained an unchallenged and unchallengeable monopoly over the instruments of coercion (the armed forces, paramilitary forces, police, secret police and to some extent the judiciary), which formed the outer perimeter of the party's power. There were only a few isolated instances of questioning in this area. During the Croatian crisis of 1970–71, where the leading role of the party was directly impugned, spokesmen for the Croatian 'national euphoria' did suggest bringing at least a part of the armed forces under republican control and angered the army leaders by holding up the armed forces budget in the Federal Assembly. In Czechoslovakia in 1968 one of the developments that most seriously alarmed the Soviet leadership and was influential in precipitating the invasion was the decision by the Minister of the Interior to begin dismantling the secret police. The role of the police also came in for open debate in Poland in 1980 and after, notably following the Bydgoszcz incident in March 1981 when a number of members of Solidarity were reported to have been assaulted. The still rather murky attempt at a military coup in Bulgaria (1965) might likewise be worth a mention in this context. Otherwise party control over the means of coercion was deemed outside the area of politics in Eastern Europe and was not a legitimate target for differentiation, let alone social control.

The most effective instrument of party control over all other state and social institutions in Eastern Europe is the *nomenklatura*. The structure and methods of this institution in Eastern Europe are the same as they are in the Soviet Union (see above). However, there is good evidence that the nomenklatura expands or contracts according to the degree of control sought by the party at any one time. Thus when the party intends to supervise a wide range of activities, many of them in no way political, the size of the nomenklatura will increase enormously and will encompass even fairly low-level appointments. According to information from Poland in the early 1970s about 100 000 posts were filled at the behest of the party via the nomenklatura; by 1980 the number had risen to about 180 000. This not only meant that posts of the chief of the fire service for instance, were part of the nomenklatura, but also that the number of individuals needed to supervise the nomenklatura increased correspondingly, which explains the expansion of the Polish party bureaucracy. The equivalent figure for Czechoslovakia was estimated at around 100 000 posts at the end of the 1970s, whereas that for Hungary was significantly lower: possibly only 10 000 according to one source, although naturally the relative sizes of these societies affected these figures as well. The wider implications of party control and institutional autonomy need not be detailed – if a major (and even minor) decision-maker owes responsibility to the party, office-holders are left with very little room for independent action. An examination of this state of affairs has led one French scholar, Thomas Lowit (1979), to wonder if it is meaningful at all to write of 'the state' in Eastern Europe and, indeed, to rename the system the 'polymorphic party', i.e. one in which the party assumes a number of different forms.

The mass organisations, however, are another matter. Here at different times and while still retaining the ultimate right of intervention, the party has encouraged or at least accepted a measure of interest articulation. Of all the mass organisations or institutions of society, the press is the one which is most easily open to great differentiation with the least risk. Nothing is easier than to remove journalists who overstep the mark and infringe the newly re-defined leading role. Depending on the degree of room for manoeuvre permitted, the press has generally been given a kind of ombudsman role through providing publicity for isolated instances of abuse or else has served as a forum for debate on different policy alternatives. Apart from periods of weak party control (as previously defined), Hungary and Poland have provided the clearest examples of the operation of this redefined variant of the leading role. In both these countries the propagandistic role of the press was played down in favour of an informational one, though not to the complete exclusion of the former. On occasion this could allow genuine conflicts to surface, for example, on whether in a particular situation considerations demanded that a factory be built or environmental protection should take precedence.

Trade unions have been a more sensitive question, not least because the welfare of the working class lies close to the centre of the doctrines on which the party's legitimacy is based. In orthodox practice, the function of the trade unions was that of a transmission belt – they were supposed to explain party policy to the workers and to make propaganda in favour of higher production, as it was inconceivable that any conflict of interest could arise between the workers and the workers' party. This monolithic approach was jettisoned at least in part, after 1961, and trade unions were given some scope for the protection of the interests of their members. The conflicts involved could be quite stark: an enterprise manager's objective was to raise the level of output at all costs, while the workers had certain rights (working conditions, health, safety and so forth) to protect. Generally, trade unions tended to back the director in such cases, but in Hungary after 1968 the trade unions were given a veto over management decisions if these violated the collective contract between management and workforce. On the whole the threat of the veto was more effective than its actual deployment and by and large the right was used rather timidly, but there were well documented cases where the unions did intervene in this way. The leading role of the party was far from self-evident in such situations.

It was the insufficiency of interest protection and the failure of the party to exercise its leading role to the satisfaction of the workers that led to the pressure which eventually resulted in the formation of Solidarity, the autonomous trade union organisation, in Poland. The period after 31 August 1980, the date on which Solidarity was founded, represented a completely anomalous state of affairs in relation to the leading role of the party as traditionally interpreted. The Polish party continued to claim a monopoly of political control, but at the same time accepted the existence of a wholly autonomous trade union organisation with its own independent sources of power and legitimacy. A further anomaly of the Polish situation in the winter of 1980–81 was the absence of any mediation mechanism between the party and Solidarity, which had the effect of bringing conflict between them into the centre of the political arena. The imposition of martial law in 1981 – a radical departure in communist affairs – was an attempt to resolve the crisis by military means.

Special cases: Romania, Albania, Yugoslavia

The case of Romania deserves separate assessment in this context. According to the decision of the 1974 Romanian Party Congress and the programme it adopted, the role of the party would continue to increase throughout the process of socialist construction and would only wither away 'through its integration into the life of society by means of an ever more organic participation of party members in the whole of social life'. This corresponded to a trend visible in Romania since the 1960s, which had the aim of merging state and party functions in order to avoid parallelism and overlapping. The domination by the party over all state and social activities was in fact very extensive. The ideal type which the Romanian party leadership sought to create was that of the 'political manager' equally at home with ideology and with administration. Multiple-office holding in party and state was standard practice at all levels – unlike, say, the practice of the Hungarian party – and the heads of communal or town party organisations were also normally the heads of the corresponding local government units, a situation which has no parallels elsewhere in the communist world. Individuals were generally rotated freely between party and state posts. In the 1970s the Romanian party also began to create joint party–state institutions, like the Defence Council, the Council for Socialist Culture and Education, and many others. These bodies were simultaneously subordinated to both party and state organisations above them in the hierarchy – another unique innovation in the communist world. By the late 1980s the strategy of merging party and state functions was well advanced.

Albania diverged from the orthodox model through its determined adherence to Stalinism, both in terms of party control over state and social institutions and over individuals. While the size of the Albanian party relative to population was small its control of institutions was very far-reaching. Without having adopted a Romanian-style merging, there was extensive intertwining of offices. In 1978, seven out of twenty-two members of the government were members or candidate members of the party Politburo. A further eleven were members of the party Central Committee and the other four were party members. The Albanian party made no concession whatever to the concept of differentiation (as discussed above) and retained a monolithic approach to society. Policy continued to be implemented by means of mobilisation campaigns, militarisation and compulsory mass rituals, and terror was more widely employed than elsewhere in Eastern Europe. All adults are presently required to belong to one of the mass organisations, and, for example, purchases in shops are barred to non-members. It was this objective of controlling all manifestations of social life that led the party to abolish organised religion as a source of competing values.

Finally, special consideration should be given to Yugoslavia, where the nature of the leading role has been long
debated and several variants have been tried out in practice.
The Yugoslav variant began in 1948 after the break with the
Soviet Union. The rupture immediately forced the Yugoslav
leadership to make an ideological choice, one which has
continued to play a role ever since. Instead of abandoning a
Marxist system, the Yugoslav leadership chose to remain
Marxist but at the same time to challenge the Soviet monopoly of Marxism by evolving its own version. This gave
Marxism a home-grown quality in Yugoslavia and explains
why it has played a key role in legitimation. Equally it
clarifies the apparent ease with which ideological imperatives
have been changed with numerous political consequences (see
the discussion in the previous chapter on the various Yugoslav
constitutions). The Yugoslav model of the leading role of the
party emerged in the 1960s as one where the control function
had almost disappeared at the centre, though not in the
republics, being replaced by a guiding role or one aimed at
persuasion. Leninism had also vanished very largely from
Yugoslavia's ideological vocabulary.

There was some retreat from this after 1971, but full
Leninism has not been re-established. Instead an uneasy half-
and-half system has emerged, in which the party does not
enjoy a monopoly of power, although it does in ideology, and
where the relationship between party and society is mediated
by a variety of countervailing forces (for example, regional
disparity, the strength of other institutions especially at local
level, the nature of self-management, the possibility of emigration and ethnic nationalism). The upshot of this in the
late 1980s was that the Yugoslav party enjoyed a monopoly
in the field of politics – foreign and domestic policy, defence
and the means of coercion – but not in economics, manufacturing, services and the allocation of goods of collective
consumption. Interests had to be aggregated at the centre via
the party and state, through both federal and republican
institutions, and decisions had to be reached by consensus.
The death of Tito in 1980 removed a powerful element of
bonding in this and left the system significantly weaker.

There was growing evidence from several East European countries in the 1980s that the classical Leninist model of democratic centralism was evolving towards new forms. The party continued to insist on its leading role, but appeared to be less effective in exercising its aggregative and centralising function than before. In consequence, power was fragmented to a greater degree than previously, although this did not result in democratisation either in internal party procedures or in party–society relations. The loss of effectiveness showed itself in a number of ways. There was greater difficulty in elaborating strategies for the future and in enforcing them on other bureaucracies; the *nomenklatura* system was no longer a matter of purely central competence but increasingly the object of bargaining between centre and localities; and other institutions could accordingly launch occasional initiatives in the political sphere. The clearest illustrations of this trend were in Poland, Romania, Hungary and Yugoslavia, although the trend could be discerned in the other countries also.

In Poland, the post-martial law regime for all practical purposes pushed the communist party to the sidelines; indeed, there is an argument that the *coup* mounted by General Jaruzelski was directed not merely at Solidarity but also at the enfeebled and demoralised civilian branch of the party. Hence in the mid-1980s, the Polish ruling elite was primarily made up of an alliance between the defence bureaucracy (the Main Political Administration, the armaments industry and the security forces) and the economic bureaucracy. In Hungary, the local party organisation had greatly augmented their strength as against the centre and could resist central pressure to accept certain policies. In Yugoslavia, the core of the system was the coalition between the eight republican and provincial party organisations (plus the armed forces). Indeed, so far-reaching was the devolution of power to the republics that there was strength in the argument that, for internal purposes, Yugoslavia no longer constituted a single political system. The Romanian case, with the explicit abandonment of Leninism by Ceauşescu, has already been mentioned. With the economic crisis of the 1980s, the demoralisation of the party in that country was far advanced and it appeared to have lost much of its cohesiveness, let alone dynamism.

Other parties

The existence of non-communist parties is a curious anomaly left over from the immediate post-war coalition period. These parties, as a rule, are entirely controlled by the communist party and play no autonomous role in the political process; their function is therefore merely a manipulative and decorative one. In only one respect do they have any real significance under normal circumstances: occasionally an individual might not wish to join the communist party for personal reasons. In such a case membership of one of the façade parties is an accepted alternative as there seems to be a strict 'no poaching' convention. It is only in periods of weak party control that the façade parties begin to acquire lives of their own and to play something like an autonomous role. Both Czechoslovakia in 1968 and Poland in 1956–58 and 1980–81 provide examples of this. The sole exception among façade parties has been the small Roman Catholic group in the Polish Sejm, known as Znak. Znak deputies were allotted a number of seats in the Sejm but continued to sit independently after 1957 as a token gesture of recognition of the strength of Roman Catholicism in Poland; Pax (a pro-regime Catholic movement) has also held seats in the Sejm. Znak came under strong official pressure in the mid-1970s especially after its leader, Stanisław Stomma, abstained from voting in favour of the 1976 constitutional amendments. Znak's pro-regime's successor known as 'neo-Znak' enjoyed something of a revival in the early 1980s.

The Communist Party of China: ideology, organisation and leadership

Ideological transformation from Mao to Deng

The most striking feature of the history of the Communist

Party of China has been the influence upon it of one man. A founder-member in 1921, Mao became party leader in 1935 and dominated the party for the next 40 years. He led the party to victory in 1949, presided over its development until 1966, savaged it in the Cultural Revolution, and remained the source of its legitimation until his death and even beyond. At the 7th Party Congress in 1945 an incipient personality cult appeared. In the 1950s this was brought under control and the 8th Party Congress in 1956 produced a Party Constitution (the Chinese equivalent of the CPSU's Party Rules) which was quite orthodox in terms of its attitude to collective leadership. But during the Cultural Revolution the personality cult re-appeared to a grotesque degree. In 1969 Lin Biao told the 9th Party Congress that 'the Communist Party of China owes all its achievements to the wise leadership of Chairman Mao'. The Party Constitution of that year stated that the theoretical basis guiding its thinking was not simply Marxism–Leninism but 'Marxism–Leninism–Mao Zedong Thought', a formulation which carried through into the constitutions produced by the 10th and 11th Congresses in 1973 and 1977 respectively.

Thus Mao, having led a ruling communist party for longer than Lenin and Stalin combined, had become 'written in' to the Party Constitution. This imposed an intolerable burden on the leaders who survived and succeeded him. The way the Maoist legacy was handled is, of course, unique to the Communist Party of China. Yet it illustrates general problems of 'creatively developing' ideology which face all parties having such a commitment to an 'infallible' creed, and which cannot justify the factional disputes to which they are prone simply by reference to pragmatic considerations.

There is no doubt that at the time of Mao's death there was widespread distaste for the policies he had pursued since about 1958, and especially during the Cultural Revolution decade of 1966–76. However noble in conception they may have been, in practice they had led to economic hardship and personal misery for millions who had suffered through violent upheaval. The constant emphasis on 'struggle' had exhausted the population both physically and mentally. Mao had not only failed to take steps to ensure a peaceful succession but had made it impossible; first, by rejecting the 'successors' he had originally chosen (Liu Shaoqi and Lin Biao), and secondly, by switching his support from one leadership group to another in a manner which appeared arbitrary and which may have been due to senility as much as to rational intent. He left a party leadership which was bitterly divided. One group, centred round the 'Gang of Four' led by his wife, was if anything to the left of the Chairman. Another, consisting of veteran cadres who had suffered badly in the Cultural Revolution, looked to Deng Xiaoping. In the middle was a small group of leaders of whom Hua Guofeng was the most prominent.

The risk of a continuation of Maoism in its extreme form disappeared within a month of his death when Hua, with considerable support from the People's Liberation Army, led an allegedly 'pre-emptive' *coup* against the 'Gang of Four' and their followers. Hua sought to establish his authority by associating it with that of Mao, but also by producing a version of Maoism which was relatively moderate. In October 1976, he was not only appointed as Party Chairman but also took on a major ideological role when he took charge of the publication of Mao's works. He duly authorised the publication or republication of 'balanced' statements, as mentioned in Chapter 5, and in 1977 he edited a carefully-chosen fifth volume of Mao's *Selected Works* to add to the four that had been published during Mao's lifetime. This volume covered the years from 1949 to 1957 and thus avoided straying into the dangerous territory of the excesses of the Great Leap Forward. Use was also made of a cult which had developed around Zhou Enlai, in that the late premier's well-known moderation was officially linked to his supposedly close relationship with Mao. Within this framework Hua proclaimed that Mao's words and directives remained the basis for party orthodoxy. Thus in January 1977 Hua put forward the slogan, 'We must resolutely uphold whatever policy decisions Chairman Mao made and unswervingly carry out whatever Chairman Mao instructed.' This became known as the 'two whatevers' thesis.

Hua was not, however, strong enough to retain a monopoly of power for long. Deng Xiaoping, who had been purged at the start of the Cultural Revolution and again in 1976, commanded wide support. A persistent campaign to restore him to his posts was waged and, in March 1977, Hua was forced to agree to his return. Even before his 'public' reappearance in July Deng took issue with Hua's 'two whatevers' thesis. His supporters offered an alternative to it: 'Practice is the sole criterion for testing truth.' This formulation first appeared publicly on 10 May 1978, in a newspaper article which stated that 'only social practice can test whether a theory correctly reflects objective reality and is true'. It also went on to say that 'we must dare to touch and to get clear the rights and wrongs' regarding 'forbidden areas set up by the "Gang of Four" to shackle people's thinking'.

Deng was prepared to go much further than Hua in challenging Mao's infallibility. An interesting development came in July 1978, when the press published for the first time a speech which Mao had made in 1962. In it, Mao had said, 'Of all the mistakes made by the Central Committee I am responsible for those directly related to me, and I have a share of responsibility for those not directly related to me because I am its Chairman.' He also criticised those comrades who had attempted to keep hidden his 'shortcomings and mistakes'. Mao himself had admitted he could be wrong. There then ensued a major debate on just how wrong Mao might have been on various matters. In December 1978 Deng effectively established himself as China's political leader when the third plenum of the eleventh Central Committee initiated the programme of widespread reforms which has dominated all areas of policy ever since. In a statement of major importance the plenum announced: 'It would not be Marxist to demand that a revolutionary leader be free of all shortcomings and errors. It would also not conform to Comrade Mao Zedong's consistent evaluation of himself.' Party members were urged to follow Mao's own injunction and 'seek truth from facts', so avoiding a fundamentalist approach to ideology. This new slogan was in turn linked to demands that cadres who had been unjustly treated must be rehabilitated and, as they returned to positions of power, support for Deng's position, both ideological and political, increased.

The intra-party debate on Mao intensified and, as discussed in Chapter 6, many 'unofficial' contributions appeared also. In the autumn of 1979 the party leadership accepted that a definitive statement was essential and drafting began in March 1980. After extensive consultation both within and outside the party and much revision the 'Resolution on certain questions in the history of our party' was published on 30 June 1981. Predictably, the resolution was severely critical of Mao's role in Chinese politics from the Great Leap Forward and especially of his role in the Cultural Revolution. The illegitimacy of that movement was confirmed by the fact that the resolution referred to the term 'cultural revolution' in quotation marks throughout. It was deemed to have lasted from May 1966 to October 1976, and to have been 'responsible for the most severe setbacks and the heaviest losses suffered ... since the founding of the People's Republic'. It had been 'initiated and led' by Mao for reasons which the resolution completely rejected as conforming 'neither to Marxism–Leninism nor to Chinese reality'.

The Maoist thesis that the movement constituted 'a struggle against the revisionist line or the capitalist road' was flatly dismissed: 'There were no grounds at all for this definition.' Many things denounced as capitalist or revisionist during this decade were actually Marxist, socialist and correct. The 'cultural revolution' had confused 'the people' with 'the enemies of the people'. The 'capitalist roaders' thrown out were, in fact, 'the core force of the socialist cause'. Under socialism there was no justification for such a destructive upheaval. History had shown that the movement, 'initiated by a leader labouring under a misapprehension and capitalised on by counter-revolutionary cliques, led to domestic turmoil and brought catastrophe'.

There was, however, no attempt to vilify Mao completely. This was partly because it was genuinely felt that Mao's greatest errors had been concentrated in the last decade of an exceptionally long revolutionary life. There was also the warning provided by Khrushchev's de-Stalinisation. Hence the resolution attempted to strike a balance in three ways. First, it argued that although Mao had been hopelessly mistaken in the Cultural Revolution he had none the less acted on the highest revolutionary principles. He was a tragic hero. Second, party and society were also at fault, for they were under 'the evil ideological and political influence of centuries of feudal autocracy'. It was this which had permitted the over-concentration of power and the development of arbitrary individual rule. Third, the enormous achievements of Mao's earlier life were given due weight. Rather disingenuously it was argued that the ability of the party, state, PLA and socialist economy to weather the storm had been due in no small measure to Mao's earlier work in creating and strengthening them. The resolution dealt at length with Mao's role up to 1957, and particularly up to 1949. Mao was acknowledged as 'the most prominent' of the 'many outstanding leaders of the party', who had 'more than once' saved the revolution from disaster.

The party carefully salvaged its ideology by devoting considerable attention to 'Mao Zedong Thought', which the resolution defined as a 'valuable spiritual asset'. On the one hand, Mao was credited with having made numerous and lasting ideological contributions in the years up to 1957. On the other, the resolution made it absolutely clear that 'Mao Zedong Thought' was not to be confused with the sum total of Mao Zedong's thinking. His 'thought' consisted of those ideas which had been tested in practice and found to be valuable and correct. Hence the resolution could state that in the 'cultural revolution' the Chairman had actually gone against the 'Thought' which bore his name. It was made clear that Mao's achievements in ideology as in everything else could not be separated from those of the party as a collective entity. This thesis was duly enshrined in the Party Constitution produced by the 12th Congress in 1982 which defined 'Mao Zedong Thought' as the 'crystallized, collective wisdom of the Communist Party of China', a body of theoretical principles and a summary of experience which had been 'proved correct by practice'. The Constitution also followed the resolution by reverting to the formula 'Marxism–Leninism *and* Mao Zedong Thought', thus indicating that the latter was somewhat separated from (if not inferior to) the former.

Thus the resolution and the Party Constitution gave Deng Xiaoping room for manoeuvre by invoking those parts of the Maoist canon he found useful while rejecting those aspects of it he found inimical. In general Deng and his supporters have shifted the party's ideology away from what they consider to be unnecessary and harmful preoccupation with egalitarian concepts of distribution and towards more pragmatic problems of production. In July 1983 a volume of Deng's *Selected Works* was published, consisting of 47 speeches he had made between 1975 and 1982. These constituted the ideological justification for the formulas he had laid down for China's modernisation and became required reading for party members and the general public. A further collection of speeches, *Build Socialism with Chinese Characteristics*, was published in December 1984 and given comparable attention.

An interesting example of the new approach to ideology came in March 1983 when Hu Yaobang, the party's General Secretary, addressed a rally commemorating the centenary of the death of Karl Marx. This was an occasion of the utmost symbolic importance when a leader of the world's largest communist party could enlist the authority of the 'founding father' on behalf of any cause he wished. Hu chose the pursuit of knowledge, insisting that Marxism not be isolated from the cultural achievements of mankind, and that everyone must value science and knowledge. He condemned the tendency to separate intellectuals from the working class and called for the creation of an atmosphere in which they were valued. He also condemned the tendency to divorce party leadership from expert leadership and urged that all leading personnel must strive to become experts.

The emphasis on modernisation and the establishment of policies which are said to build 'socialism with Chinese characteristics', but which strike many observers as unsocialistic, has led China's present leaders to proclaim loudly and frequently that they remain Marxists but at the same time to insist on the need to deny the doctrine constantly. In December 1984, a leading official announced that Marx was a great revolutionary thinker but that he did not give much advice on the economics of revolutionary socialist construction. Early in 1985 *Red Flag* argued that Marx 'did not expect that there would still be commodity economy under socialist conditions. This is quite different from our practice today. It would be a big mistake to say ... that what the central authorities are practising is not Marxist simply because it is not what Marx had stated'. The article condemned a more dogmatic approach as 'trimming the foot to fit the shoe'. In similar vein it was stated in January 1986 that although the fundamental principles of Marxism still held true there were none the less a 'few conclusions' that were 'no longer valid'.

Mao himself referred to Marxism as 'a tree with many branches' and by self-definition China remains a Marxist and socialist state. However, Deng has succeeded in producing an ideology which can, albeit sometimes uneasily, preach the virtues of socialism while pursuing policies which, *inter alia*, have led to the effective privatisation of agriculture and the growth of an extensive private commercial sector. Not all party ideologists have accepted these changes wholeheartedly and some have warned of the dangers of slipping into capitalism. But, as of the late 1980s, those in favour of a liberal interpretation had prevailed over the strict construc-tionists.

Organisation and leadership

In organisational terms the Communist Party of China has borne a reasonable resemblance to the CPSU throughout most of its history as a ruling party, with the partial exception of the Cultural Revolution. Such deviations from the norm as did exist have largely disappeared since the death of Mao and especially since the convening of the 12th Congress in 1982. This is clearly shown by the Party Constitution of September 1982 which is presently in force. This describes the party as 'the vanguard of the Chinese working class, the faithful representative of the interests of the people of all nationalities in China, and the force at the core leading China's cause of socialism'. Like the CPSU it prides itself on its exclusivity and has never sought to incorporate more than a tiny percentage of the population within its ranks. Its constitution contains detailed rules governing the admission of members and the duties and behaviour required of them.

The actual criteria for membership have changed over the years, reflecting shifts in ideology and recruitment policies. In contrast to a number of its forerunners the 1982 Constitution acknowledges that class background is no longer a significant factor in China and provides an extremely broad definition of eligibility. Thus, membership may be sought by

> any Chinese worker, peasant, member of the armed forces, intellectual or any other revolutionary who has reached the age of eighteen and who accepts the party's programme and constitution and is willing to join and work actively in one of the party's organisations, carry out the party's decisions and pay membership dues regularly.

Duties are onerous in that members must, *inter alia*, undergo detailed ideological training and 'subordinate their personal interests to the interests of the party and the people'. They must be 'the first to bear hardships and the last to enjoy comforts' and shall 'accept any job or fulfil any task assigned them by the party'. They are to 'maintain close ties with the masses', consult them and listen to their views. They must oppose factionalism, practise criticism and self-criticism and 'play an exemplary vanguard role in production and other work, study and social activities'.

To become a probationary member an applicant must be supported by two existing members, accepted by a party branch after 'rigorous examination' and approved by the next highest level of party organisation. Probation normally lasts for one year during which time the candidate's progress is assessed and education is given. If all goes well, full membership will then be granted by the general membership meeting of the party branch and approved by the next highest level. Members who violate party discipline are subject to various sanctions including warnings of varying degrees of severity, removal from party posts, placing on probation and expulsion from the party. The party can also propose to 'the organisations concerned' that an offender should be removed from non-party posts. A member subjected to discipline has the right to be heard in his or her own defence and has a right to appeal to higher levels.

Although the high standards demanded by the Constitution are not necessarily met in practice, membership requires a high degree of commitment and considerable sacrifice of personal time. At times, party members have had the unpleasant task of implementing policies which were widely disliked. During the Cultural Revolution members were particularly vulnerable to the violent oscillations of the Maoist political process and were subject to savage criticism and much worse. Despite the condemnation of factionalism, the party was in practice heavily factionalised and the problem, though reduced, still exists. Many members have suffered simply by backing the losing side in a particular dispute. In the 1980s the penalties for losing were far less extreme than previously, but they were present none the less. Thus Deng's policy of party rectification, designed to reduce the influence of those unwilling or unable to support his reforms and to promote those who are, has resulted in massive personnel changes at all levels. Although expulsions from the party have been limited, groups of party members such as the elderly, the poorly-educated and 'leftists' have been retired, transferred, demoted or passed over in favour of younger and more skilled people. The attractiveness of party membership has also been diminished somewhat by its record of past failures and excesses which has tarnished its image, especially among the young. Recent policies towards agriculture, the emphasis on encouraging and rewarding the professionally competent and the insistence that the party should refrain from interfering in all aspects of day-to-day work have also made it increasingly possible for some sections of the population to pursue relatively well-paid and responsible jobs without joining.

Nevertheless, membership has always conferred great benefits and this remains broadly true. The party is still the locus of political power and few can achieve real political influence without membership and a record of political activism. Membership, moreover, has also always given enhanced access to desirable jobs. In the Maoist era the vast majority of responsible jobs in the state and mass organisations went to party members who, often, had few other qualifications. Deng's insistence on the need for an elite of competent modernisers in all walks of life has meant that political reliability alone is no longer regarded as a sufficient qualification for a senior appointment, but party credentials remain necessary for a wide range of sensitive positions and in a host of others will tip the balance in favour of those possessing them. Moreover,

wage scales in China are highly differentiated and those in
senior positions enjoying relatively high incomes, commensur-
ate pensions and superior accommodation. There is also a
range of 'informal' advantages as elsewhere in the communist
world. Although these have differed over time they have
always included access to information denied to the general
public; an increased ability to obtain 'good' education and to
use 'connections' to advance the careers of one's children;
opportunities to travel within China and, increasingly,
abroad; the right to use cars in a country where private car
ownership is extremely rare, and to travel 'soft' class on
trains; and the opportunity to enjoy a certain amount of
wining and dining at public expense. It may be noted that
there have been opportunities for corruption which appear to
have increased in scope as a result of the 'Open Door' policy
which has brought to China a wider range of foreign luxury
goods and foreign businessmen. Since 1982, the Chinese press
has published details of scandals similar to those of the Soviet
Union.

Although exclusive, party membership has risen steadily
since 1949. Then there were only 4 488 000 members. By 1955
membership had more than doubled to 9 393 000 and it rose
to 17 million in 1961. By 1973 it had reached 28 million and in
1977 stood at 'more than' 35 million. It increased to 38
million in 1980 and by 1986 was just under 44 million. These
figures of steady growth, however, disguise certain weaknesses
in past recruitment policies which now hinder the party's role
as an agent of modernisation. The basic problems are related:
the party paid insufficient attention to the recruitment of the
educated – especially in the Cultural Revolution – and the
young. In 1984 only 4 per cent of members had received
higher education and over 50 per cent were either illiterate or
had only been to primary school. Whereas in 1950 nearly 27
per cent of members were under 25, by 1983 this had fallen to
less than 3.3 per cent. At the higher levels, as will be discussed
below, the party has had great success in promoting the
educated and professionally competent. But at county level
and below the problem of elite renewal remains serious
despite leadership attacks on anti-intellectual sentiments and
lack of interest in recruiting the young.

Another weakness is the marked under-representation of women. By 1973 only 10 per cent of members were women and the few who had reached the highest echelons were, almost invariably, the wives of party leaders. Given China's 'feudal' and 'patriarchal' past this was not too surprising. But, despite advances at lower levels, the present leadership appears to attach limited importance to the promotion of women to the highest ranks. In September 1985 a national 'representative conference' (a rarely-used but perfectly constitutional body) met to elect new blood to the party's top bodies. The Politburo thereafter contained only one woman, an alternate member. Of 56 people newly elected to the Central Committee, only three were women.

The structures of the party have been broadly similar to those of the CPSU over the years. At the bottom there is a network of 'primary party organisations' based on work units or neighbourhoods, wherever there are three or more full party members. Above this is a hierarchy of organisation running upwards through county and provincial levels to the central bodies in Beijing. The National Party Congress is nominally the supreme decision-making body and meets every five years, the last occasion being 1982. However, as in other communist states, it is far too large for effective action and its functions are really to 'represent' the total membership in a symbolic sense.

In fact real decision-making authority begins with the Central Committee. As of September 1985 this had 209 full members and 133 alternates. In contrast to the situation a few years ago the Central Committee consists increasingly of relatively young leaders who have received a higher education. The Central Committee in turn elects a Politburo (20 full members and two alternates in 1985) and a Standing Committee of the Politburo. The Standing Committee consists of five men who are the most senior leaders of the party. Until 1982 the party differed from the CPSU in having a Chairman of the Central Committee. Mao had this post until his death in September 1976; Hua Guofeng from October 1976 to July 1981; and Hu Yaobang until September 1982 when it disappeared from the Party Constitution, as did the posts of vice-chairmen.

Theoretically the top post in the party thus became that of General Secretary. Significantly, however, Hu Yaobang who continues to hold this office clearly does not outrank the other members of the Standing Committee. The reason for these changes in 1982 was obviously to stress the collective nature of the leadership and to reduce the danger of a 'cult of personality' developing in the future. Another change introduced in 1982 was the creation of a 'Central Advisory Commission' to serve as 'political assistant and consultant' to the Central Committee. This was a device to permit and persuade elderly veterans to surrender real power while retaining a certain degree of status and influence. The emphasis in recruitment to leading positions in recent years has otherwise been on youth, technical competence and a higher level of turnover than has been customary in earlier periods or indeed in other ruling communist parties.

Further reading

The rules or statutes of all ruling communist parties are reprinted together with brief introductions and bibliographies in Simons and White (1984). No other studies are presently available which deal with all the ruling communist parties; Eastern Europe is, however, covered in Fischer-Galati (1979), and political leadership and succession in the USSR, Eastern Europe and China is considered in McCauley and Carter (1986). Lenin's writings on the communist party and its role include *What is to be Done?* (1902), which is available in many modern editions. The most useful general surveys of Leninist theory are Meyer (1957), Harding (1977) and (1981), and Lane (1981).

On the USSR more specifically, there are thorough studies of the CPSU in Hough and Fainsod (1979) and in Hill and Frank (1986). The Rules of the CPSU, as revised by the 27th Party Congress in 1986, are widely available in pamphlet form, together with the 1986 edition of the Party Programme. On the party's ideological work, see White (1979, chs 4–6 and 1985). On the party's role in economic management, which is considered further in Chapter 5, see Hough (1969) and more recently Rutland (1985). Two basic studies of party history are Schapiro (1970) and Rigby (1968), which should be supplemented by Rigby (1976). On the *nomenklatura*, see Harasymiw (1969) and (1984), and also Voslensky (1984). On the General Secretary and his role, see Brown (1980) and Gill (1986); on the Politburo more generally, see Löwenhardt (1982). On participation within the party, see Unger (1977–78) and (1981b), which are based upon interviews with *émigrés*.

On the communist parties in Eastern Europe, in addition to the works mentioned at the end of Chapter 3, the following may be consulted: King (1980) on the Romanian Communist Party, Kovrig (1979) on Hungary, Suda (1980) on Czechoslovakia, de Weydenthal (1986) on Poland, and Bell (1986) on Bulgaria, all of which are volumes in the 'Histories of Ruling Communist Parties' series produced by the Hoover Institution. In addition, McCauley (1979) on the GDR and Prifti (1978) on Albania are thorough and well documented. Lowit (1979) provides a useful theoretical perspective; Fischer-Galati (1979), already mentioned, provides a more general account.

On the Communist Party of China, Schurmann (1968) is a classic which is still essential reading. Chang (1978) is a valuable guide to policy-making. See also Teiwes (1979), which deals with the period up to the Cultural Revolution. More recent developments are considered in Saich (1984). The full text of the 'Resolution on certain questions in the history of our party', containing the party's assessment of the Mao era, is in *Beijing Review*, no. 27 (1981). The Party Constitution of 1982 may be found in *Beijing Review*, no. 27 (1981), and in Simons and White (1984). A useful source on policy changes in the post-Mao era is Deng Xiaoping (1984). The current leadership as elected by the 12th Congress of the Chinese Communist Party in 1982 is examined in Bartke and Schier (1985). An excellent study of the Chinese variant of the *nomenklatura* system is Manion (1985).

5

The Policy Process

Until relatively recently it was not generally believed that the communist states possessed anything that could properly be called a 'policy process'. The ruling communist parties, it was believed, simply issued decisions which were the handed over for implementation to the various subordinate bureaucracies – governmental, social and cultural, and economic. Party decisions were binding in all matters of this kind, and they were held to reflect the influence of ideology or of power politics within the leadership, but not, as in a Western country, of individuals or groups outside the leadership or of the institutions responsible for implementing the policies on which the leadership had decided. These institutions, after all, were staffed by communist party members, usually on the advice of the relevant party committee, and there was no shortage of sanctions, from the secret police to the threat of loss of employment, to make sure that they complied with the party's directives. Policies, moreover, were believed to be relatively simple, the overriding priority being the highest possible rate of economic growth and more particularly of heavy industry. This was clearly close to the view of communist politics held by those who adhered to the totalitarian approach, with its emphasis on party dominance. Modernisation theorists and many others, however, also accepted most of the assumptions of this 'directed society' image of the communist states, the central element in which was a small, monolithic and monopolistic party directing all aspects of society with little reference to the views and wishes of its members.

Most writers on communist politics would probably accept that there is still a substantial amount of truth in such a characterisation, and that there are important distinctions to be drawn between authoritarian forms of politics, such as those that exist in the communist states, and the forms of politics that are to be found in the Western liberal democracies. It has become apparent in recent years, however, that the 'directed society' image is, and perhaps always was, too simple. The leadership, it emerged, was often unsure of its priorities, or was even divided into rival factions. The government and other bureaucracies, moreover, were certainly staffed by party nominees, but it turned out that they often argued with the party in the interests of their own area or institution and did not simply implement whatever the party might propose. Party policies, in any case, were becoming increasingly complex and difficult to reconcile with each other, leaving a good deal of scope for the *de facto* selection of priorities by lower-level officials and various other forms of evasion of central control, and for specialist advice and influence. Major social institutions, such as the trade unions and the military, also turned out to have particular interests to defend, and even the public at large was not powerless – it could refuse to buy what was produced or to go where labour was required, and if its wishes were ignored it could engage in various forms of protest or direct action.

Even in the USSR in the Stalin period, it has become clear, economic and other policies were not unaffected by the special pleading of ministries and other bodies and by personal factions and followings. In the post-Stalin period the role of group and bureaucratic politics has become increasingly apparent, and few would now accept the adequacy of a view of the policy process in the communist states which failed to take account of the numerous and conflicting pressures upon the central leadership as well as of the considerable resources available to the central leadership in its efforts to ensure the implementation of its own priorities. A good deal of debate has taken place about the applicability of terms such as 'interest group' to the forms in which political pressures of this kind are exerted in the communist states, and about the extent to which terms such as 'bureaucratic' or 'institutional pluralism' can be applied to their political systems more generally. Clearly, potential interest groups have far less ability to organise and to take action than their counterparts in the liberal democracies, and few scholars would go so far as to suggest that terms such as 'pluralism' can usefully be applied to a political system in which the authority of the communist party is ultimately unchallengeable and in which individuals and groups lack most of the means by which governments elsewhere can (at least theoretically) be held in check, such as an independent judiciary, a free press and competitive elections. And yet a view of the policy process in the communist states which left out the role of bureaucratic and group interests and of popular pressures would, at least nowadays, be seriously incomplete and mis- leading. In this chapter we shall look at three different examples of the ways in which interests and policies interact in the communist states, beginning with the making of economic policy in the USSR and then turning to the politics of agriculture in Eastern Europe and the politics of education in China, in order to illustrate the various processes that are involved.

The USSR: the politics of the command economy

The management and performance of the economy is a central issue in any political system, particularly so in the case of a communist political system in which there are as a rule no private entrepreneurs and in which most of the economic activity of the society takes place in publicly-owned enter- prises under the direct supervision of the government. The economy, moreover, is perhaps for most writers the sphere of communist politics to which the 'directed society' image most obviously applies. Unlike Western societies, in which indivi- dual firms more or less autonomously decide what to produce, how to produce it, to whom to sell their produce and at what price, in the communist world it is commonly supposed that all matters of this kind are decided by the government by means of a comprehensive economic plan drawn up by the centre and then undeviatingly implemented. An economy of this kind is often described as a 'command', or at least as an 'administered' or 'managed economy'; it is an economy, in other words, in which the government directs most areas of economic life in accordance with its political priorities, rather than leaving them, as Western governments supposedly do, to be determined by the free play of self-regulating market forces. The management of economic activity is therefore not only a central area of policy-making in the communist states; it is also a particularly promising arena in which to consider the extent to which central directives are influenced, resisted, modified or even challenged by individuals, groups and institutions within and outside government and the implications that this has for the 'directed society' image of the policy process in these states more generally.

The Soviet planning process

It should first of all be noted that there is no necessary connection between communist rule and a centrally-planned economy. In the Soviet Union after the revolution a variety of forms of economic management were adopted, the most long-lasting of which, the NEP or New Economic Policy (1921–28), kept large-scale industry, foreign trade and finance in the hands of the state but allowed private entrepreneurs to run enterprises employing fewer than twenty workers and for the most part left agriculture and retail trade in private hands. This form of mixed economy, however, soon led to a number of social strains and tensions. The richer peasants, called *kulaks*, were believed to be getting richer, to be employing large numbers of their colleagues and to be threatening to withhold the supply of grain to the towns. A social group known as 'NEPmen' also sprang up, consisting of speculators, money-lenders and petty criminals as well as those who had lost their possessions and civil rights as a result of the revolution. Above all, the authority of the communist party itself was in question, as it was weakly represented in the countryside and vulnerable to political pressure both from its domestic political opponents and from the outside capitalist powers, which had invaded militarily after the revolution and were believed likely to attempt to do so again. An extended debate took place throughout the 1920s, in which the supporters of Trotsky, who wished to continue the revolution throughout Europe and to develop heavy industry, were ranged against those of Stalin, who were more sceptical of the possibility of a European revolution and initially more inclined to stress the needs of agriculture. A decision was eventually made, at the end of the 1920s, to resolve these various difficulties by adopting a centrally-directed economic plan. It is probably fair to say that there has been no more significant decision in Soviet post-revolutionary history.

The first Five-Year Plan was introduced on 1 October 1928, and pronounced achieved ahead of time at the end of 1932. It was followed by a second Five-Year Plan (1933–37) and then by a third Five-Year Plan, which lasted from 1937 until the Soviet Union entered the Second World War in the summer of 1941. For the first time anywhere in the world, at any rate in peacetime, the direct management of the economic affairs of the nation was taken into the hands of government, on a compulsory and centralised basis. Priority was given to industrialisation, with the lion's share of investment being allocated to heavy industry, producer goods, transport and military production; less attention was paid to quality, variety or waste or to the consumer goods sector generally. A quasi-military atmosphere prevailed: targets were 'stormed', areas of policy became 'fronts', and critics or doubters became 'spies' or 'wreckers'. In the countryside a parallel extension of state control was taking place, as more or less all private peasant households were moved 'voluntarily' – in fact with great violence and loss of life – into collective farms. Some 93 per cent of the rural population had been resettled in this way by 1939. The first five-year plans saw some heroic achievements, such as the construction of the Magnitigorsk iron and steel works, the Dnieper hydro-electric scheme and the Ural-Kuznetsk coal-mining complex. In overall terms the Soviet Union moved from a level of 7 per cent of American industrial production in 1928 to 45 per cent of the American level in 1938, at a time when most Western economies were experiencing slumps and mass unemployment. To many Soviet leaders the achievements of these years, followed by the Soviet victories in the Second World War, must have seemed to have vindicated the planning apparatus they had created, and it has survived, in more or less the same form, down to the present day.

The central institution in the Soviet planning system is *Gosplan*, the State Planning Committee, a body of union–republican status whose chairman is a member of the USSR Council of Ministers. It is Gosplan which is responsible for the preparation of draft proposals for each new five-year plan and annual plan, based upon the reports on plan fulfilment and requests for inputs for the following year that it has received from ministries and enterprises. Gosplan's proposals are submitted to and approved by the Council of Ministers and by the Central Committee of the CPSU, and are then submitted to the Supreme Soviet, together with the state budget of the USSR and a report on plan fulfilment for the current year. A number of relatively minor changes are made at this stage, as we have noted in Chapter 3; the final draft, incorporating these amendments, is then adopted as a formal law and is thenceforth binding upon all ministries, enterprises and any other bodies to which it makes reference. Gosplan is assisted in its work by *Gossnab*, the State Committee on Material–Technical Supplies, which is responsible for ensuring that the inputs and outputs of producing units, so far as possible, match up throughout the economy. The State Committee on Prices, which sets wholesale and retail prices, and the State Committee on Labour and Social Questions, which determines wage rates and job gradings throughout the economy, also have important roles to play. A simplified version of the planning process as a whole is set out in Figure 5.1.

The plan, as approved, is then passed for implementation to the ministries, which are responsible for ensuring that the targets in the plan are met by the factories, farms and other productive units that they supervise. The overriding aim of ministries, and of the enterprises themselves, is to fulfil the plan within the period allotted, and if possible to over-fulfil it by a small margin. Targets for each subsequent year are in turn based upon the levels previously achieved, with a few percentage points added on (the so-called 'ratchet principle'). The ministry entrusts its task of guidance to its chief administrations (*glavki*) which undertake the day-to-day management of productive units, appointing their key personnel in consultation with the party authorities and keeping a detailed

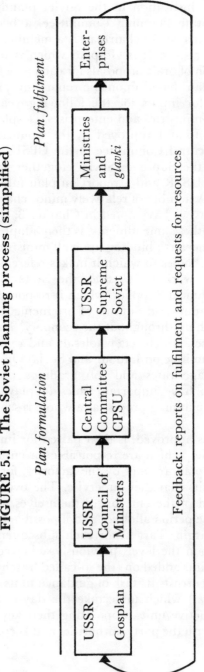

FIGURE 5.1 The Soviet planning process (simplified)

Plan formulation

USSR Gosplan → USSR Council of Ministers → Central Committee CPSU → USSR Supreme Soviet

Plan fulfilment

Ministries and *glavki* → Enterprises

Feedback: reports on fulfilment and requests for resources

watch over their activities. State farms (*sovkhozy*) are run by the central government in much the same way as other industrial enterprises; their managers are appointed by state officials and their employees have the same rights and duties as workers in other sectors of the economy. In addition to the state sector of agriculture there is also a co-operative sector, consisting essentially of the collective farms (*kolkhozy*). Collective farms are theoretically run by the collective farmers themselves with land that has been leased to them in perpetuity by the state, and they nominally elect their own chairmen. Collective farmers are also allowed to sell the produce of their private plots upon the open market, and collective farm markets, where this is done, account for a considerable proportion of the Soviet Union's agricultural production. The collective farms, however, are subject to the provisions of the national economic plan, and they must make certain compulsory deliveries to the state at prices that the state can fix. In general their independence is more nominal than real.

The plan that was sent to individual enterprises was formerly very detailed, specifying precisely what was to be produced, in what quantities, and with what inputs. This led to a number of problems. Enterprises might fulfil their plans, for instance, but with produce for which there was only a limited demand (such as pairs of right-footed or left-footed shoes). Enterprises might also attempt to fulfil their plans, which were usually specified in quantitative terms, in the easiest way possible: for instance, by producing excessively heavy steel or unduly heavy chandeliers. (A cartoon of this period, quoted by Alec Nove in his *Soviet Economic System*, showed an enormous nail hanging in a workshop. 'The month's plan fulfilled', said the director, pointing to the nail. And many other examples of this kind could be quoted.) As a result of these difficulties a series of reforms were introduced from the mid-1960s onwards. The first of these, the 'Kosygin reforms' of 1965, reduced the number of targets that enterprises had to meet and placed more emphasis upon output which was actually sold to consumers or other producers ('realised output') than upon gross output (*val*). Enterprises were also encouraged to earn a 'profit' or surplus upon their operations, part of which could be retained to finance additional investment and to provide a material incentive fund for employees. Further reforms in 1973 encouraged the formation of larger productive units, associations or *ob''edineniya*, in order to reduce the number of intermediate steps in the planning process, and in 1979 another round of reforms extended these principles further and attempted to make it easier for enterprises to innovate without jeopardising their plan fulfilment targets. The Soviet planning system, however, for all these modifications (most of which have in any case been implemented incompletely), remains essentially a command or administered one: the plan is a law, management is responsible to the government for its fulfilment rather than to shareholders or private owners, and capital and other inputs are allocated by the planners rather than obtained upon the market.

The politics of planning

The conventional view has usually been that a planning system of this kind is inherently inefficient because of the wasteful bureaucracy required to run it, and that it is retained essentially because it provides the central leadership with their monopoly of power. The real position is much more complicated and to a much greater extent reflects the various interests and preferences of the groups, individuals and institutions involved. The central party bureaucrats, for instance (the so-called *apparatchiki*), are normally supposed to have a vested interest in existing arrangements such that they will be unhesitatingly hostile to any kind of reform, particularly any reform that appears likely to reduce the extent of central control within the economy. A closer study suggests that the central party apparatus may not in fact be such dogmatic opponents of reform as this view assumes. Most market-type economic reforms that have been proposed in the USSR and Eastern Europe, for instance, stop short of the adoption of full-scale capitalism; they generally accept a considerable degree of central control over matters such as finance, foreign trade and large-scale industry, and the central political authorities would by no means necessarily be made redundant if they were adopted. Local party officials, similarly, would have every reason to favour a degree of economic reform if it involved some decentralisation and thus an increase in the powers that they could exercise at the levels of government for which they were responsible. All party officials, moreover, have an overriding interest in increasing production and improving economic performance, since it is upon this that their popular support to a large extent depends, and towards this end they may not be unwilling to contemplate some loosening of central control in the economy if this seems necessary (as it did when the Kosygin reforms were adopted). All in all, as the closest student of this question, Jerry Hough, has concluded, there is 'not the slightest evidence to support the hypothesis of a party appara- tus united on a conservative policy position – and a great deal of evidence to indicate that the hypothesis is wrong'.

If the central party authorities have different and some- times conflicting interests of their own to defend, the same is even more true of the instruments through which they rule, the ministries, republics and enterprises. Ministries, for in- stance, like the sections of the party apparatus with which they are associated, generally have preferences of their own in regard to the distribution of capital investment, in particular as between the producer goods sector ('Group A' in Soviet planning terminology) and the consumer goods sector ('Group B'). The defence and heavy industrial ministries, for instance, the so-called 'steel-eaters', appear normally and not surprisingly to favour the continued priority of Group A, while the light industrial and other ministries have generally promoted the claims of Group B, together with the party officials responsible for this area of policy and (in so far as they have influence at this level) the Soviet public. The heavy industrial lobby has generally had the better of this argument over the years, but in 1971 and again in 1981 and 1986 the five-year plans adopted in those years called for a more rapid rate of growth of consumer than of producer goods, perhaps indicating some increase in the relative influence of light industrial interests and of public opinion in recent years. The issue is one in which all ministries necessarily have a direct stake and it remains among the most hotly (though largely privately) contested in Soviet politics.

Ministries and enterprises also make every effort so secure as 'slack' a plan as possible from the central authorities so as to be sure, in conditions of shortage and uncertainty, that they will be able to fulfil it. They tend, for instance, to indent for more resources than they actually need, to conceal the resources that they have available, and to fulfil the plan by the smallest margin possible since it will be taken as the basis upon which the following year's plan is calculated ('planning from the achieved level'). Ministries tend also to take what Soviet sources describe as a 'narrowly departmental' view of their responsibilities. Typically they seek to build empires, responding to the needs of the enterprises for which they are themselves responsible but neglecting the needs of other sectors of the economy, and they generally attempt to provide as many inputs as possible within their own ministerial structure rather than become dependent for their inputs upon another ministry, which is likely to place the needs of its own enterprises first in the event of any shortages or difficulties in supplies. Ministries and enterprises tend also to fulfil the plan in the manner they find easiest, such as by producing adults' rather than children's clothing and finished goods rather than spare parts, despite the frequently-proclaimed need for greater production in both these categories and in many others. Given the practical impossibility of fulfilling all the plan targets harmoniously and at the same time, party officials in the localities have generally little alternative but to accommodate themselves to these choices of priorities provided total output targets are attained.

In 1957 Khrushchev sought to put an end to these problems by establishing 105 regional economic associations (*sovnarkhozy*) throughout the USSR, to which most of the functions of the industrial ministries were devolved. The reforms certainly reduced the 'narrow departmentalism' of the ministries concerned, but it led to an increase in the opposite fault of 'localism', or the tendency to place the needs of other enterprises in the same area above those of enterprises in the same industry but in other areas, and in 1965 the regional economic councils were wound up and a centralised ministerial system was restored. Tendencies towards 'localism', however, are still apparent at the republican and lower levels of government, the authorities responsible for each of which typically press the claims of their own areas rather than those of the USSR as a whole, and not necessarily insincerely or without justification. The centralised party structure should theoretically check any tendency towards localism of this kind; in fact, however, party officials at each level are concerned above all that the plan for their area should be fulfilled, and if this requires additional investment in railroads, mining equipment or energy extraction they may well be inclined to take the local rather than the national point of view upon such matters. Local party officials may also be influenced by the strength of nationalist sentiment in their area, or by the 'familyness' (*semeistvennost'*) or even corruption that can develop between party officials and the personnel that they are nominally responsible for supervising.

The allocation of resources is also influenced by a number of powerful lobbies both within and outside government, among them the military and the trade unions. The Soviet armed forces might not ordinarily be thought to represent any challenge to the party's dominance, or at least to its allocation of resources. The armed forces are run directly by the government, through the Ministry of Defence; they are staffed by party nominees who are in most cases also party members; there is a network of party-political officers at all levels under the control of the Main Political Administration of the Armed Forces, which is a Department of the Central Committee as well as part of the military command structure; and Gorbachev himself is chairman of the Defence Council of the USSR, which oversees all military and strategic matters. In practice, however, the military are not necessarily passive executants of the party's dispositions, at least in matters that concern them in their professional capacity. This emerges, for instance, from Khrushchev's autobiography. Things were very similar in the Soviet Union to the way such matters were conducted in the USA, he found out when he met President Eisenhower.

> Some people from our military department come and say, 'Comrade Khrushchev, look at this! The Americans are developing such and such a system. We could develop the

same system, but it would cost such and such.' I tell them there's no money, it's all been allotted already. So they say, 'If we don't get the money we need and if there's a war, then the enemy will have superiority over us.' So we talk about it some more; I mull over their request and finally come to the conclusion that the military should be supported with whatever funds they need.

Soviet military spending, as a result of these and other pressures, has increased substantially since the mid-1960s; it is presently estimated to account for about 11–13 per cent of Soviet GNP and for a similar proportion of the total Soviet labour force.

The manner in which the military intervene in the allocation of resources is not entirely clear. It appears, however, that the Main Political Administration is not necessarily as effective an instrument for the imposition of the party's dispositions upon the armed forces as might initially have been supposed. Party-political officers, it emerges from research such as Timothy Colton's, may often have a lower rank and status than the military men they are supposed to supervise, and they may often adopt the viewpoint of the armed forces or of the particular sector within which they work rather than that of the political authorities at the centre. Armed forces personnel are also well represented at the higher levels of party and state, and can presumably employ such opportunities as this provides to advance their institutional interests. The Minister of Defence, for instance, Marshal Sokolov, is a member of the Politburo, as were his two predecessors. Armed forces personnel also account for about 7 per cent of the full members of the Central Committee elected in 1986, and for about 4 per cent of the deputies to the USSR Supreme Soviet elected in 1984. The military, moreover, have a number of strong arguments to support them in their claims, such as the continued technological superiority of their NATO opponents and the need, particularly compelling in a country which has been invaded so often over the centuries, to be provided with the resources that are necessary to ensure the territorial integrity of the state. The evidence suggests that these arguments have not been without influence.

The trade unions constitute a lobby of a rather different kind. Formally a 'mass organisation' rather than a part of government such as the armed forces, their role is also rather different from that of trade unions in most non-socialist societies. The official Soviet view is that in a workers' state, where the means of production are owned and controlled by the workers themselves, there is no need for trade unions to take strike action in defence of their members' interests. (Strikes, as it happens, are in fact perfectly legal.) The proper function of the trade unions, in the Soviet view, is to act (in Lenin's words) as 'schools of socialism', administering a variety of cultural facilities and raising workers' skills, productivity and socio-political awareness rather than promoting antagonisms for which there is no social basis. The usual Western view, at the other extreme, is that Soviet trade unions are no more than an agency of the party for disciplining the workers and compelling them to engage in various forms of unwelcome 'voluntary' activities, and that they are of little value to a worker with a genuine grievance against his management. There is probably some truth in both of these views. Soviet trade unions, in line with the claims of the authorities, are certainly massive organisations with over 136 million members in 1986 (over 98 per cent of the labour force), running extensive cultural and sporting facilities, travel services and holiday homes, administering the state social insurance fund and participating extensively in the running of the enterprise. When conflicts arise between individual employees and the management, however, as they are bound to do in even the most enlightened workers' state over matters such as grading, maternity leave and compulsory overtime, the role of Soviet trade unions is rather closer to the Western stereotype.

Trade unions in the USSR are organised on the industrial principle in 29 separate bodies, each of which is affiliated to the All-Union Central Trade Union Council. The structure of each union is similar to that of the party, with primary organisations in each factory or workplace electing committees which in turn elect to territorial committees and then to central committees elected at congresses or conferences which are held every five years. The All-Union Council is elected at a general Trade Union Congress which is held at similar intervals, and it elects a Presidium and a Secretariat to take charge of its day-to-day activities. The All-Union Council enjoys considerable authority over individual unions and their local organisations through the operation of the principle of democratic centralism, on which the whole trade union structure, like the party, is based. At the national level the All-Union Council is supposed to be consulted by the Soviet government on all labour matters, it enjoys and occasionally exercises the right of legislative initiative, it takes part in the deliberations of the bodies that determine pay and prices, and together with the Council of Ministers and the party Central Committee it periodically issues decrees on matters of interest to its members. The All-Union Council publishes a daily newspaper, *Trud* (Labour), which has a circulation of more than 18 million copies per issue, and which sometimes publishes mildly controversial articles on labour and social questions as well as a regular selection of the half-million or so letters it receives from its readership every year. The All-Union Council is also involved in the formulation of the annual plan and budget, and its chairman is a member of the Presidium of the USSR Supreme Soviet.

Most trade union activity, however, takes place within the unions themselves and at the level of the individual enterprise, and it is probably here that the trade unions have the greatest opportunity to influence decisions in the interests of their members, albeit on relatively small-scale issues. The trade union at each enterprise, for instance, signs a 'collective agreement' with the management every year, covering matters such as welfare and the distribution of bonuses as well as output and productivity; and it must give its approval before any worker is dismissed. Labour disputes are referred in the first instance to a commission within the enterprise itself, composed of managerial and trade union representatives. Most disputes appear to be settled relatively quickly at this level, and as often as not in the worker's favour. If the worker is not satisfied with the commission's decision he can take his grievance to an ordinary court of law, and here again it is not uncommon for his complaint to be upheld (this occurred in about half of the cases studied in a number of recent Western investigations). Soviet trade unions, then, are in the last resort subject to the overriding authority of the party; but if they are to carry at least a minimum of credibility with their members, as the party presumably intends, they must be seen to exert a certain amount of influence in support of the interests of their members and if necessary against the wishes of management. It appears that this influence is used mainly to attempt to secure higher levels of industrial safety, lower wage differentials, greater observance of legislation on the employment of women and young people, and a less arbitrary, more 'collegial' style of government.

The influence of the public

Finally, and by no means least, it should not be thought that the Soviet mass public lack any influence over the resources that are allocated in their name, despite their inability to throw out their government at a general election or to take the kinds of action against it that are possible in a Western liberal democracy. Some of the ways in which the Soviet public can at least attempt to influence the allocation of resources in the economy, as well as other matters, have already been indicated in previous chapters. The electoral process, for instance, provides no choice of candidate, but it does provide the opportunity to write complaints or comments upon one's ballot paper or to threaten not to vote until a particular local grievance has been attended to. It is also possible to write to one's deputy or to the local soviet, or to visit a deputy's surgery or the local soviet offices in person. Party members, a substantial proportion of the adult and particularly of the urban male population, have additional means of obtaining access to political information and of expressing their political opinions (although the influence of rank-and-file party members is generally agreed to be fairly minimal). Individual scholars who are members of influential research organisations, such as the institutes of the Academy of Sciences, have further opportunities to contribute advice and information in their areas of expertise. A substantial proportion of the population, moreover, are themselves part of the state machinery in some sense: more than 2 million citizens are deputies to local soviets, for instance, and more than 30 million serve as members of the various commissions that assist the soviets in their work.

Of particular importance is the ability to write letters to party, state and other bodies, a form of political participation by the mass public to which the authorities have recently been giving a good deal of encouragement. The Central Committee itself established a Letters Department in 1978 to deal with the stream of letters (more than half a million a year) that reach the central party apparatus alone; and similar departments have been established in other institutions. The letters department in the party newspaper, *Pravda*, is in fact the paper's largest. The paper has a daily circulation of over 10 million copies and it receives about 500 000 letters from its readers every year, all of which are sorted into categories and passed on to the appropriate authorities for their consideration. The Soviet national daily press altogether receives a total of between 60 and 70 million letters every year, all of which are supposed to be acknowledged and dealt with within a specified time period. Some, in addition, are taken up by the newspaper's own reporters, who investigate the matter at first hand and in some cases are able to confirm instances of unlawful dismissals, corruption, or victimisation which can then be put right by higher levels of authority. A number of factory managers are reported to have been dismissed as a result of these investigations.

There appears to be some scepticism among the Soviet public as to the effectiveness of political interventions of this kind. A sociological survey in Lithuania in the late 1970s, for instance, found that about 80 per cent of those polled put the trustworthiness of the main Lithuanian daily paper *Tiesa* at 75–100 per cent, 'some' estimated it to be about 50 per cent, and 'a few' reported that they 'did not believe a word of the paper about the economic achievements of the USSR, that there was a lot of boasting but daily life was full of shortcomings and bungling' and so forth. The better educated were particularly likely to take a sceptical attitude towards the newspaper's trustworthiness and to turn to other sources of information for political news, in particular to Western radio broadcasts. The same study found, however, that 88 per cent of those who were polled regularly discussed articles in the newspaper with their family and workmates, 37 per cent regularly cut out articles of particular interest to them, about 25 per cent remembered an occasion when they or their friends had approached the newspaper about a personal matter, and 19 per cent said that the editorial board had helped them. The influence of the popular press on policy is therefore not a factor to be ignored, particularly when local violations of the law, shortages or other problems are involved rather than matters of a national or particularly controversial character. This was especially likely to be true under current policies which, since the mid-1980s, have emphasised the need for greater *glasnost'* or 'openness' in public affairs, notwithstanding the belated reporting of the Chernobyl nuclear explosion in 1986.

It is also possible for the Soviet public to exercise a degree of influence over public policies by various forms of unofficial or indirect action. This can range from, for instance, going slow at their place of work, 'voting with their feet' to change their place of employment or refusing to buy shoddy goods, to protests, demonstrations, black marketeering and strikes. The population of Georgia, for instance, as we have already noted, took to the streets in 1978 when it was rumoured that the constitutional status of their national language was in danger; and in the summer of 1980 some 70 000 workers at the giant Togliatti car works in central Russia went on strike for two days, according to Western press reports, because of poor food supplies. Similar protests have been reported from other parts of the Soviet Union at other times. The political significance of such actions has not been lost upon the party leadership, and Brezhnev devoted a good deal of attention to their implications at the 26th Party Congress in 1981. Matters such as the food supply and the availability of consumer goods and services, he pointed out, were part of the everyday life of millions upon millions of Soviet citizens. People went to shops every day, to canteens, and to laundries. What could they buy? How were they received? How much time did they have to spend upon these and other household chores? 'It is on the strength of how these problems are solved that people largely judge our work,' Brezhnev went on. 'They judge it strictly, exactingly. And this should be remembered, comrades'. It is probably considerations such as these that have kept the price of transport, housing and basic foodstuffs unchanged in the Soviet Union for many years, although the price at which these goods are sold is a small and diminishing proportion of what it actually costs to produce them.

For all its authoritarian features, then, it would be wrong to suggest that the policy process in the USSR, in economic as in other matters, is not influenced to some degree by the pressures, interests and advice of groups, individuals and institutions both within and outside the formal structures of party and state. The management of economic policy, the example we have chosen to consider, is in principle conducted on a 'command' or administered basis, but with considerable 'market' modifications. The central authorities, ultimately, can prevail, but they are not necessarily united upon a common policy position, and in any case they may find that the bodies which are supposedly responsible for implementing their decisions take the side of their own area or institution rather than that of the central party authorities upon the issue in question. Interests within the governmental structure itself, such as the military, must be treated with some consideration; experts must be listened to, since their advice may be expensive to ignore; and major social institutions such as the soviets and the trade unions must be allowed some scope for the exercise of their authority if they are not to be wholly disregarded by the public and if the party itself is not to be swamped by the mass of routine work that they undertake. Nor, as we have seen, is the long-suffering Soviet public entirely without the means of bringing pressure to bear in support of its particular preferences in such matters. The Soviet policy process, at least within the area of economic management, is evidently not a pluralistic one: the powers of the central leadership are far greater than those of Western governments, and the means by which their actions can be opposed or resisted are far fewer. Equally, however, policies in the USSR are not simply promulgated by the party and then implemented; they are the result of a recognisably political process, and the final outcome is a negotiated rather than simply an imposed one.

The politics of agriculture in Eastern Europe

The position of agriculture in communist societies, the second of the policy areas we have chosen to consider in this chapter, is in one very real respect anomalous. The Marxist legacy is quintessentially an urban, industrial one, yet the post-war revolutions that took place in Eastern Europe occurred mostly in overwhelmingly agrarian countries – the Czech lands and what became the GDR were the only exceptions. This anomaly, which has been the subject of a long-running debate since the days of Marx himself, posed a number of dilemmas for East European policymakers. These were, if anything, made even more difficult by the model of revolution imported from the Soviet Union. The dilemmas, very simply, turned on the question of what the role of agriculture in a developing society was to be, how a revolutionary socialist consciousness was to be instilled in the peasantry (it was generally assumed to be lacking), and how the control of the state over the land was to be established and maintained.

The answer to these questions was given at the outset of the communist period by the direct implementation of the Soviet model, in other words collectivisation. But with the growth of differentiation among the East European states after 1956, a variety of agrarian strategies have emerged with very different results. In one respect only was the imposition of the Marxist variant of modernisation decisive and common to all the East European countries: the Marxian model, like the Western model of modernisation, looked to the disappearance of the peasantry, the introduction of industrial methods of production in the countryside and the transformation of the bulk of the population into urban workers. This solution to Eastern Europe's age-old peasant problem was completely at variance with the ideas of pre-war populist reformers.

The strategy adopted at the outset, therefore, had two objectives, one short-term, the other long-term, neither of them, of course, peculiar to the Marxist road to industrialisation. The short-term aim was to generate a surplus of agricultural production with which to pay the price of the investment needed for the first stage of industrialisation. In the longer term, the communists' aim was to create an agricultural system that could feed the urban population. In addition to economic goals communist policy makers had a third, less explicit objective, namely to extend the control of the state over the land.

There were two strands in this thinking. Historically agriculture in Eastern Europe had been largely outside the ambit of politics, and both political and economic objectives demanded that this cease to be the case. Secondly, because the communist parties of the pre-war period had been unable to derive much advantage from peasant radicalism and because after the war they recognised their rather shallow roots in the society, much of the opposition to their assumption of power having come from the peasantry, they saw in the peasant a reservoir of backward, capitalist thought and values which had to be liquidated. It was to reach these goals that the collectivisation drive of the early 1950s was launched and conducted with so much force. The Soviet experience of the 1930s served in this respect as a model for Eastern Europe.

Towards collectivisation

Two stages occurred in the collectivisation drive. The first, during the Stalinist period (1948–53), consisted of the initial push to bring the land under state control, and met with considerable resistance. The second, which was carried out with perhaps greater sophistication (1958–61), was successful in bringing the bulk of agricultural land into the socialist sector. The socialist sector, as in the USSR, consisted of two broad sub-sectors: state farms and collectives. State farms were directly owned by the state and run by the ministries of agriculture, whilst in collectives individual members technically retained their title of ownership and drew profits roughly in proportion to the amount of land that they had taken into the collective. State farms were generally made up of land which had already been owned by the state before the communist period, large estates which had been nationalised after the war and former German property, for example in western Poland, the Sudeten areas of Czechoslovakia and in parts of Hungary.

Within this broad pattern of development certain variations occurred virtually from the outset. In Yugoslavia, the communist authorities pushed towards collectivisation during the Stalinist period (1945–50), but after the break with Stalin in 1948 they reversed this policy and encouraged decollectivisation. The reason for this was largely political. The Yugoslav leadership enjoyed a fair measure of popularity and even legitimacy during and after the war, and much of its success derived from having been able to mobilise the country's peasantry in its support. The policy of collectivisation, however, was deeply unpopular, and once the leadership began to rely fully on domestic sources of support it was discontinued. This had the effect of transforming agriculture into an area of stability in society. The long-term aim of the Yugoslav planners was a gradual modernisation of agriculture through the build-up of industry, a drift off the land and the use of market mechanisms to promote agricultural growth. In the event, Yugoslav agriculture has remained backward in some regions but highly developed and prosperous in others. At the same time, the crucial socio-economic problem associated with backward agriculture – rural overpopulation – was resolved by exporting the country's labour surplus to Western Europe as migrant workers.

In Czechoslovakia the pattern was much closer to the standard one, and by 1968 over 95 per cent of agriculture was in the socialist sector (state farms and co-operatives). The remainder, mostly hill farms in Slovakia which were very difficult to collectivise satisfactorily for technical reasons, were brought into the ambit of state control in the 1970s. It should be noted that Czechoslovakia, being an industrialised country even before the communist capture of power, had only a relatively small agrarian sector. In 1968, only about 15 per cent of the population was engaged in this sector, a figure which has been declining since; these are levels comparable with those in Western industrialised countries. On the whole state control of agriculture has worked well in Czechoslovakia, a proposition borne out by the fact that in 1968, during a period of weak party control, not one collective farm broke up. On the whole the country's agrarian population seem reasonably satisfied with the system as it now stands.

The GDR and Bulgaria, starting from very different base lines, ended up with comparable types of agriculture in the 1970s – essentially, they sought to apply integrated industrial methods to agricultural production. The achieved some success in this, although agricultural produce played a much greater part in Bulgaria's product structure than in the GDR, as might have been expected in the light of the much higher degree of industrialisation in the latter.

One important factor present in all the countries where agriculture was collectivised was the private plot. This was a small area of land, generally half an acre or less, where the individual farmer was free to produce what he wanted without direct supervision. Certain types of agricultural processes, like horticulture, are highly intensive and demand constant and high inputs of either labour or capital. Collectives, where the incentive to work long hours was largely absent, generally handled these areas of production very badly, with the result that the private plot assumed major importance in the feeding of the urban areas. Fruit and vegetables, poultry, eggs and pork were often supplied from the private plot. From the state's point of view this system had major advantages. It engaged the energies of the collective farmer and provided him with a surplus income for his own consumption, and that surplus was in turn devoted to the development of the countryside, a phenomenon particularly striking in the vicinity of large towns. At the same time, because the ownership of a private plot was made contingent on membership of a collective, some state control was retained, although this was often residual.

On the other hand, the existence of the private plot is difficult to reconcile with the official ideology of collectivism, as it encourages entrepreneurial attitudes and the preference of private (family) goals over social ones. That explains why the private plot has been abolished completely in Albania and, at different times, discouraged in Bulgaria, where the state seeks to retain a higher degree of control than elsewhere.

How the various East European parties arrived at these policy outcomes in agriculture is a complex question, demanding a close examination of developments in each country. Traditional attitudes towards the peasants, the self-confidence of the party concerned and the overall economic climate all played a role in policy formation at various times. To look at this process of policy formation more closely, the situation in two countries that have not so far been mentioned, Poland and Hungary, will be examined in detail, both to illustrate the nature of policy formation in the communist states and as paradigmatic cases of two types of agrarian development.

Poland and Hungary: contrasting agrarian policies

What makes the comparison between Poland and Hungary useful is that the two countries, despite differences in size, began from virtually identical positions in 1945. Both had a tradition of large estates which were broken up after the war, both suffered extensive war damage and both had relatively weakly established communist parties which were obliged to contend with considerable peasant resistance. It is true that there are considerable differences in size between the two countries – Poland is 312 500 sq km in total area as compared with Hungary's 93 500 sq km – and likewise in population, with around 37 million Poles compared with 10.7 million Hungarians (see Table 1.1). But in political terms, they started with near identical policies in the late 1940s.

The land reform, involving massive redistribution of land coupled with the creation of state farms, involved the bulk of the peasantry in both countries. Collectivisation began in Poland in 1948 and in Hungary in 1949, in the aftermath of the Soviet–Yugoslav break and the period of the coalition between the communists and non-communist parties. In the new phase, that of monolithic Stalinism, the communist leaderships were determined that no vestige of private economic activity should be allowed to remain on the land. Collectivisation was pressed ahead with great energy, including force and severe discrimination against those who refused to join collectives.

There are indications, however, that even at this very early stage some divergences between Hungarian and Polish policies had begun to emerge. In Hungary, at the height of the collectivisation drive in 1953 some 18.3 per cent of the land was in collective ownership, and a further 36.6 per cent was directly owned by the state. In Poland, on the other hand, the figures were lower: in 1956, 9.2 per cent of the land was collective and 13.5 per cent was held as state farms. The explanation for this divergence is not wholly clear. In the first place, it must be sought in the greater ruthlessness with which the Hungarians pushed on with Stalinisation. The reason for that may be partly sought in history and the psychological legacy of the end of the war. The Poles emerged from the war traumatised by five years of German occupation and the bloodbath of the Warsaw Rising. The Hungarians did not undergo such a traumatisation; rather, there were mixed feelings of guilt at having been Hitler's last satellite and resignation at having become annexed into the Soviet sphere. In any event, both parties pursued policies of extending state control over the land and of using the surplus produced by agriculture to help finance industrialisation.

There was one further parallel between Poland and Hungary in this early period that deserves mention. The leaders of the 1956 anti-Stalinist popular movements, Władysław Gomułka in Poland and Imre Nagy in Hungary, both fell out with their pro-collectivisation factions over agricultural policy. Taking their cue from Stalin, who apparently urged the Hungarians as early as the spring of 1948 to begin collectivisation, the Hungarian and Polish parties (led by Mátyás Rákosi and Bolesław Bierut respectively) forced their pro-peasant factions into the wilderness. Gomułka was purged and Nagy was sent into political obscurity. Their return in 1956 was to a significant extent based on their popularity with the peasantry, who saw them as liberalisers (a misperception in the case of Gomułka). Thus in the first stage the process of decision-making over agriculture proved to be relatively straightforward, with a minimum of debate and rational argument based on the actual situation being subordinated to the transcendental goal of Stalinism transformation.

The second stage of agricultural policy dates from around the beginning of the New Course, the mild relaxation introduced after the death of Stalin in 1953. In both countries this was accompanied by the erosion of collectivisation and the dissolution of collectives from the bottom up – peasants simply opted out and the state apparatus (i.e. the security forces) did not intervene. The thinking of the party leaderships that lay behind this apparent retreat was the acute food shortages that afflicted both countries. Collectivisation and the fear of it among those unaffected resulted in significant falls in food production and the feeding of the urban population became a major problem. The relaxation of collectivisation led to some improvement in agricultural production, and in Poland this had, by 1954, surpassed 1949 levels. In Hungary, where Imre Nagy had been installed as prime minister in 1953 with Soviet backing, there was an attempt to reverse decollectivisation two years later when Nagy fell. This had disastrous consequences for food production as many peasants resorted to passive resistance.

However, it was the eventual outcome of 1956 that produced the really significant divergence between the two countries. In Poland, Gomułka, now party leader, concluded that his position in the country was best served by deferring collectivisation. A relatively conservative peasantry, it was thought, left largely alone by the state, would act as a neutral body in society and gradually industrialisation would liquidate traditional peasant production. There was no question of abandoning the socialisation of the land; rather it was simpler to leave this to some later date and to achieve it by noncoercive methods. In Hungary the situation was completely different. The country's new party leader, János Kádár, enjoyed next to no support, and he concluded that the most effective way of securing his power was by deliberately depressing popular aspirations and suppressing claims for autonomy. After dealing in this fashion with the workers and the intelligentsia, it was the peasants' turn in 1959. A renewed collectivisation drive was launched in 1959 which ended in 1961 with almost all the land inside the state sector.

In the debate in the Hungarian leadership on collectivisation two main arguments were advanced. The first was that peasants could be persuaded to join only if the superiority of collectives made them more attractive than private cultivation. The supporters of this line of thought argued that collectives should be given special incentives, investment and technical assistance. The other faction laid much greater stress on coercion, and its attitudes were permeated by anti-peasant sentiment. In the event, a compromise position was adopted. Thus unlike the previous collectivisation, peasants were allowed to keep any livestock they brought with them, they received a cash payment on joining and were allowed an adequately sized private plot. At the same time, although police measures were not employed on a mass scale – several hundred thousand persons had been condemned in the early 1950s – there was coercion in the villages. Non-joiners were threatened with fines, with having their children expelled from school or university and those with two jobs, i.e. in industry as well, were forced to give one up. This campaign achieved its aims, and by 1962, 75.1 per cent of the land was collectivised, 6.5 per cent remained private and 18.4 per cent was in the hands of the state farms.

At around the same period in Poland, various alternatives were being put forward as to the best way of achieving the gradual socialisation of the land. They all rejected force, having seen it fail in the 1950s. The first of these, which had the backing of Gomułka himself, was to encourage the spread of voluntary co-operatives, known as Agricultural Circles, which were supplied with disproportionate investment funds in an endeavour to promote mechanisation and thus spearhead the socialisation of the countryside. The second current of thought favoured the expansion of contractual deliveries between the farmer and the state as the most effective means of cementing economic and eventually political relations. A vertical integration of the private and socialist manufacturing sectors through contractual deliveries, it was thought, would benefit the farmer and transform him into a kind of industrial worker, for whom land was no longer a semi-mystical cult object but a factor of production like any other. The third school of thought continued to stress collectivisation as the only effective means of achieving the stated aim. Anything else would simply be a veiled form of private production. The last set of ideas, which were to influence thinking in the 1970s, revolved around 'etatisation' (statification), the acquisition of land by the state from elderly or inefficient peasants in return for an annuity. In the event, as the Gomułka regime lost its élan in the 1960s and had other, more pressing problems to deal with, the question of agriculture was shelved and agricultural production tended to stagnate.

In Hungary too the 1960s were a period of stagnation, but unlike in Poland they were not a wholly arid period in terms of debating policy options. One early development was the removal from office of the dogmatic agricultural boss, Imre Dögei, who had been among those insisting on the rapid collectivisation policy. But during the 1960s Kádár and the centrist group around him gained in confidence and began to promote their so-called alliance policy, the acceptance of political neutrality coupled with economic participation as sufficient for 'the construction of socialism'. Gradually, during the 1960s, important changes came to affect the agricultural sector as well as the intelligentsia and the workers. One key development in this respect was the decline of the anti-peasant pressure group in the party and the corresponding rise of an agrarian lobby.

Several factors appeared to have been instrumental in this change. In the first place, the anti-peasant group was associated with the failed economic policies of the early 1960s, which had been the central factor impelling the leadership to prepare the 1968 reforms, the New Economic Mechanism (NEM). The agrarian lobby started from the premise that the existing ownership structure of the land was inviolate, and that to retain ideological legitimacy in the face of the not inconsiderable pro-worker elements in the party it would have to transform Hungarian agriculture on the bases that existed. In essence, the approach they chose was to increase the independence of the collective, to provide it with the greatest possible autonomy in the economic sphere and to create relations with the state that depended on coercion only as a very last resort.

The proportion of the budget devoted to agricultural investment in Hungary rose from about 10–12 per cent to about 18–20 per cent per annum in the late 1960s. Obligatory plan targets in agriculture were scrapped in 1965 and supply quotas went a year later. Subsequently, collective members were given a good deal of freedom to run their own affairs, notably in selecting their own officials, including the president of the collective. This meant that for all practical purposes it was financial success that ensured re-election. Collectives were also given the right to contract independently with manufacturing enterprises (i.e. without the permission of the Ministry), and they were allowed to buy their own machinery and in some instances even to engage directly in foreign trade, something which is normally a strict monopoly of foreign trade enterprises. The net result of this was substantially to increase collective farm members' earnings: between 1966 and 1970, farmer's real wages went up by 41 per cent.

The other main element in Hungarian agrarian policy at this time was the encouragement of collective farm members' private plots. Production in the private plot, as noted earlier, is a key component of agricultural production in certain areas. The policy consists basically of encouraging the farmer to work an extra shift on his own land in exchange for a marked rise in his income and thus consumption levels. Some sociologists have called this an 'amphibious mode of production', in other words a mode of production relying both upon production in the state or collective sector and upon production in the private sector. In Hungary the agrarian lobby was successful in ensuring the economic prosperity of the private plot by relaxing the regulations governing private investment. Farmers were permitted to buy small tractors – up to 15 hp – and were given access to fertilisers and fodder. The net result of this was that in pig breeding, dairy produce, poultry, eggs, fruit and vegetables, the private plot became the primary supplier of the urban areas. And as long as such production was profitable, there was no interruption in supplies.

The agrarian lobby in Hungary

The nature of the agrarian lobby in the Hungarian leadership is not easy to disentangle, but some of the strands are evident. After 1956, as discussed above, the hardline anti-peasant dogmatists were eventually defeated and this allowed the lobby a relatively clear run. Its membership was made up of party leaders of peasant origin, backed by the populist section of the intelligentsia – a powerful current of thought in Hungarian intellectual life since the interwar era – the technical intelligentsia (economists and agronomists), and the most articulate section of the farmers themselves. In the more relaxed political climate of the late 1960s, a period of looser party control, an influential pressure group, the National Council of Co-operatives (*Termelőszővetkezetek Országos Tanácsa*), came to play a political part in articulating the co-operatives' interests, challenging the occasional conservatism of local party and state bodies and establishing the legitimacy of a separate agricultural interest in the political fabric. Finally, mention must be made of the Politburo member in charge of agriculture, Lajos Fehér, who was in many ways the apex of the pyramid, his presence in a position of power guaranteed the continued weight of agriculture in the allocation of resources.

The other source of political power lay in the importance of agricultural production and particularly in its amphibious nature. In 1973–74, the hardline faction of the leadership launched a counter-attack, relying on the dissatisfaction of urban workers as their primary pretext. The chief target of the attack was the growing autonomy of various institutions (see the remarks on 'portfolio chauvinism' in Chapter 3), but the independence of agriculture was something that they regarded as equally reprehensible. Fehér was purged and, more significantly, restrictions were introduced on the private plot. Small-scale production was heavily taxed and the price of agricultural machinery was raised. The result was dramatic: farmers simply refused to produce, on the grounds that it was not worth their while to put in an extra shift, in their spare time, for insufficient profit. The number of beef cattle sold fell by 200 000, pigs by 1.6 million and a shortage of dairy produce replaced the previous glut. Now threatened by a far more serious current of urban dissatisfaction, the authorities retreated and the restrictions were removed or modified. The significance of this episode was to demonstrate that there were clear limits to the party's power, that the agrarian lobby possessed not only resources at the level of policy making but also had the effective support of society itself. These represented, as it were, the outer perimeter within which agrarian policy had to move. From the mid-1970s no further attempts were made to impose restrictions on the autonomy of Hungarian agriculture with any success.

The contrast with Poland could not be clearer. After the removal of Gomułka in 1970, the new party leader Edward Gierek initiated a set of policies which were eventually to culminate in something close to an agricultural catastrophe and his own downfall. Gierek began by making major concessions to the peasantry. He abolished the system of compulsory deliveries at low prices and replaced them with contracts and taxes, the selling of machinery to private peasants was at long last permitted, and the peasant population was included in the health system. The results of this were favourable – there was an increase in agricultural investment and output, something which enabled Gierek to launch his policy of higher food consumption for the urban population. The stability of food prices had become a fixed point in the relationship between rulers and ruled as a result of the riots of December 1970 and the strikes of 1971. In the early years of Gierek's rule the strategy appeared to be working. Agriculture was to have a twofold task: to satisfy domestic consumption and to help defray the country's mounting imports bill. Between 1971 and 1975, the output of Polish agriculture grew by 4.1 per cent per annum, a respectable figure by any standards.

However, in the mid-1970s, from about 1974, the strategy began to fail. The costs of investment rose, partly as a result of higher world prices, and consequently peasant incomes fell, which in turn acted as a disincentive on output. Parallel with this economic trend, at around the same time, the Polish party launched a renewed campaign against private agriculture. This did not take the form of collectivisation but rather the last of the four variants discussed in the Gomułka era, the purchase of agricultural land in exchange for annuities. Had it simply been a straightforward equation of this kind it might have worked, but instead the authorities began a policy of squeezing the peasantry with the objectives of forcing small farmers off the land and promoting the consolidation of small holdings. The net effect of this was to destroy the tentative accommodation between the party and the peasantry of the early Gierek years, to accelerate the flight from the land and to persuade many farmers to cut production for the market.

After the 1976 attempt to raise food prices, announced and rescinded within twenty-four hours after widespread strikes and demonstrations, the Polish party took another look at agriculture. It was decided to increase the level of investment, but the bulk of this was directed into the inefficient state sector. Discrimination against the private sector was not only widespread, but also remarkably petty. By the end of the decade significant sections of the peasantry had become actively opposed to the system.

This was in many respects a most remarkable phenomenon. Peasants tend generally to be quiescent and neutral, to react to a hostile state passively. In Poland, however, activist groups began to campaign for a better deal for farmers, to detail discrimination in *samizdat*, to raise the level of peasant education by running an unofficial peasant university and to mount occasional demonstrations against the state. But the most lethal blow was the withdrawal of statistically large sections of the peasantry from producing for the market. Because the state refused to make fodder available to private farmers who had no supply contract with the purchasing organisation, 28 per cent of farmers withdrew from cattle breeding, 35 per cent from pig breeding and 20 per cent from both, according to 1978 figures. The most striking manifestation of this was that the estimated gap between supply and demand for meat in 1980 was 25 per cent.

The neglect of agriculture in Poland

There is no easy explanation for this neglect of the agrarian sector in Poland by the country's policy makers. One important factor was the erosion of the party's sense of direction and purposiveness, which permitted the strengthening of various interest groups without any adequate balancing or equilibrating mechanism. This allowed industrial lobbies to acquire disproportionate access to investment funds and to starve agriculture. Furthermore, this lack of central control offered local party and state office holders the opportunity to pursue their own policies towards the farmers, and these were generally directed at eliminating private agriculture.

At a deeper level, there must also be an explanation for the absence of any agrarian lobby such as emerged in Hungary. The answer to this does not lie in the existence of a private sector as such, but in the difficulty of fighting for a higher allocation of resources for a private sector in a system where private production is ultimately regarded as illegitimate. This was the case despite the fact that in Poland the leadership repeatedly insisted that the private sector was there to stay for an appreciable period of time. The actions of the highest policy-making levels belied this, in particular the creeping socialisation of the 1970s. The real significance of the private ownership of land was that there was no group within the party that could profit politically from backing the peasants; on the contrary, it was an ideologically weak cause. In consequence agriculture became the orphan child of Polish politics.

A second structural factor influenced this course of development. Whereas, as suggested, the Hungarian party was able to incorporate the populists who provided both political and intellectual backing for a prosperous agriculture – always an uneasy proposition given the anti-agrarian bias in Marxism – this was absent in Poland. Its absence was partly explained by the existence of the façade party, the United Peasant Party, which attracted many who might otherwise have joined the communist party. Hence the nucleus for a potential agrarian lobby could never be formed. The problem was further exacerbated by the interest taken in the Polish peasantry by the powerful Roman Catholic church. For the church, the peasantry was its most loyal reservoir of supporters. This made it doubly difficult for any potential defender of the peasant interest to legitimise his arguments in the eyes of party dogmatists – such arguments could be written off as 'objective' support both for rural capitalism and for the reactionary church.

A third factor inhibiting effective action on agricultural policy was the lack of any economic urgency. Here timing played a fortuitous role. Whilst the Hungarians, having had to face their economic and agrarian crisis in the 1960s, had no option but to rely on domestic production, the Polish leadership discovered an alternative resource – Western injections of capital. The availability of seemingly unlimited funds pressed on Poland by Western bankers allowed policy makers to postpone the mounting crisis of Polish agriculture. By spending loans on current consumption deficits in agricultural production were temporarily made up, whilst the future was all the time being mortgaged. This particular trap snapped shut in 1980–81, when Poland's debt service ratio went over 100 per cent – the country no longer earned enough from exports to finance its debt service charges. Not only could the food gap no longer be closed by imports, but, of course, Polish industry was likewise starved of imported raw materials and components.

These three factors together form the key components in the formation of Poland's agricultural policy in the 1970s. A fourth, somewhat lower-level trend, to which passing reference has been made, was the way in which the behaviour of local officials towards farmers contributed significantly to the crisis. A document circulated in *samizdat* in July 1980, entitled 'Polish Farmers to Workers on Strike', detailed many of these practices. Local party secretaries had virtually uncontrolled powers over farmers:

> At any time, they can take our land and expropriate us, move our children to remote schools, prevent us from finishing the building of a barn or a house, call up our sons for military service and send them to a state farm . . . Often without our permission, they will send combine harvesters into our fields and harvest unripe corn at our expense . . . [If we want to make any purchases] for every single item we have to come with a written application.

The scope of the harassment was very wide and the need for bribing officials universal. Against this background it was hardly surprising that when the power of the party evaporated in 1980–81 there should have been unremitting pressure from farmers for the establishment of an independent trade union, Rural Solidarity. It was noteworthy that the post-

Gierek leadership resisted this as long as it could – anti-peasant attitudes appeared to have been ingrained in the highest levels of the Polish party.

The 1980s saw surprisingly little change in either Polish or Hungarian agricultural policies – earlier policies were continued, often under rather different circumstances. The post-martial law regime in Poland persisted with a strategy of starving agriculture of investment funds, although some of the worst bureaucratic interventions of the 1970s were moderated. The peasantry remained marginalised and the influence of the economic bureaucracy – with its base in heavy industry – on the political leadership ensured that agricultural policies remained strictly minimalist. The countryside was persistently short of agricultural inputs (machinery, fertiliser, construction materials and so forth) and the shortage of manufactured and consumer goods on the market offered little incentives for the peasantry to raise its output significantly. Polish agriculture was expected to produce enough to feed the country, but under no circumstances was a relatively prosperous peasantry to be allowed to emerge. By the same token the Church project for creating an agricultural investment fund, to be financed by sources in the West, remained a dead letter. The authorities did not actually veto the plan, but refused to accept its implementation by using delaying tactics.

In Hungary, the trend towards relying on a combination of collective and private labour continued, even though the agricultural lobby encountered considerable opposition from industrial interests and those in the party who were allied with it. To some extent, however, the patterns found everywhere in Soviet-type systems, with an emphasis upon size rather than flexibility, began to make themselves evident in Hungary as well. Large-scale agriculture for instance, tended increasingly to be favoured over smaller operations. There were indications too that in some areas existing methods had begun to yield diminishing returns, but there was no evidence of serious new thinking on the kind of methods that might replace them. In effect, the agrarian lobby had become a stabilising factor in the political equation and no longer sought significant change, once its own interests had been largely satisfied.

Education and the policy process in China

Given the general absence of private ownership and inherited wealth, education in the communist states is the major factor determining both individuals' careers and also the shaping of society. It is regarded therefore as too important a matter to be left to one specialised department. Thus in China the institutional framework within which educational policy has been formulated is somewhat complex. In the past it has included the Ministry of Education (and, at different times, a separate Ministry of Higher Education); the Ministry of Culture; other ministries which run their own schools and institutes; and separate Academies of Sciences and Social Sciences. The State Planning Commission is heavily involved and so, too, is the Propaganda Department of the Central Committee. In 1985 the Ministry of Education was abolished and replaced with a more powerful body, the State Education Commission. In fact educational policy has been a central concern for China's most senior leaders.

Where China differs significantly from other major communist states is that in education, as in much else, fundamental ideological disagreements persisted long after the party came to power. In so far as ruling communist parties have followed a general pattern of development it has been to lose gradually their commitment to wider revolutionary goals of egalitarianism and the like and to favour increasingly the pursuit of strategies likely to lead to rapid economic development. Mao was unusual as a party leader, however, in that his radicalism increased in the later part of his life. This was especially evident in the Cultural Revolution of 1966–76 when he rounded on the leaders who favoured elitist strategies of modernisation.

There may be room for honest doubt over Mao Zedong's personal role in some of the policy areas associated with the Cultural Revolution, but with regard to education the position is clear. From 1964 onwards he made a number of statements which were highly critical of educational developments up to that time, and he took an impish delight in denigrating the role of intellectuals past and present. In May 1966 his directive calling for the ending of 'bourgeois' domination in education ushered in a period when most schools and universities were simply closed down as teaching institutions and those involved in education, together with 'the masses', were invited to join in a 'great debate' on how education might best be reorganised. As the Cultural Revolution unfolded the Ministry of Education ceased to function (and was not revived until 1975) and many schools and universities became battlegrounds on which Red Guard factions fought each other. According to figures produced during the 'Gang of Four' trial, no fewer than 142 000 teachers and cadres under the Ministry of Education were accused of various 'crimes' and persecuted during this period.

One of their 'crimes' was said to be that they had been training an elite at the expense of the masses. Another was that much of the education provided was deemed to be 'irrelevant'; courses were too dependent on book knowledge and practical subjects of immediate applicability were scorned. Instead of helping to build a more just society, consistent with the goals of Chinese socialism, the system actually contributed to social stratification. And worst of all, education paid insufficient attention to politics. Students 'studied behind closed doors' and were all too willing to share the traditional intellectuals' contempt for manual labour. On graduation they sought comparatively well-paid and secure jobs in the cities and refused to go to the countryside where their skills were supposedly most needed.

Many schools and universities did not re-open in any meaningful sense until 1971. However, in that year a national education conference was held, a loosely organised 'science and education group under the State Council' was established to provide guidance, and a 'revolution in education' was declared to be in progress. The new system was characterised by five features. First it stressed 'universalisation'. Enormous efforts were devoted to increasing primary and secondary school provision (particularly in the countryside) while the tertiary sector was savagely cut back. Further education received considerable official attention also.

Second, there was extensive curricular reform. This included drastically shortening courses at all levels and, it was claimed, making them more practical and relevant to the local economy. It was commonplace for schools to set up their own workshops and experimental farms; workers and peasants entered schools to 'mount the rostrum' to teach practical subjects and pupils were sent to production units for on-the-job training. At the highest levels, researchers in the universities, at the institutes and the Academy of Sciences were 'mobilised' to find solutions to problems submitted by communes and factories. Theoretical and 'esoteric' subjects and long-term research projects were frowned upon and scientific experiments in the 'unreal' atmosphere of the laboratory were played down. The term 'open door schooling' was to be much invoked.

Third, attempts were made to democratise the system by deliberately downgrading the importance of expertise. Professional educators at all levels lost influence. Fourth, the importance of politics was stressed and came to permeate the entire curriculum. Even 'neutral' subjects like mathematics were invested with political content. Finally, methods of selecting students were changed. The higher the level, the more attention was given to admitting people on the basis of 'good' class background and political consciousness.

The 'revolution in education', stripped of its Marxist jargon, contained elements which are part of the conventional wisdom of educational systems elsewhere, such as 'learning by doing', 'intermediate technology' and 'positive discrimination'. In purely quantitative terms the achievements were remarkable, as the following figures indicate. Between 1966 and 1976 the primary school population grew from just over 103 million to 150 million. Junior middle school enrolments rose from 11 million to 43 million and senior middle from 1 370 000 to 14 830 000. In 1965 only 9 per cent of senior secondary students were from rural areas; in 1976 the figure was 62 per cent. Women, too, benefited. In 1976 they filled 33 per cent of university places, a figure which has since declined. In the same year they 'peaked' at primary school level, with 45.5 per cent of the enrolments. National minorities also made important gains.

There was, however, a high price to pay. The radical ideas advanced by Mao and others were seldom implemented with sensitivity or skill and what frequently resulted was the establishment of a crude and corrupt anti-intellectualism. The acquisition of a high degree of skill was seen as a contemptible ambition of 'stinking intellectuals'. Practical work was often elevated to such an extent that it came to replace formal classroom instruction entirely. The involvement of laymen in education, far from leading to 'democratisation', placed many institutions under the control of ignorant louts selected through no discernible democratic process, who relied on intimidation and often encouraged pupils to rebel against their mentors. The attempt to select university students on the basis of non-academic criteria resulted in considerable corruption as cadres used their influence to ensure that their children were admitted by 'the masses'. The emphasis on politics gave students little incentive to study anything else and had a baneful effect on scientific and intellectual creativity. The xenophobia of the left also isolated China from the international academic community.

Tertiary education suffered the worst. Student enrolments, which had numbered 674 436 in 1965, fell to 47 815 in 1970 and slowly rose to 564 715 in 1976. By the most conservative estimate China 'lost' at least one million university graduates in this period, and the quality of those who were produced was often poor. Another serious casualty was the specialised secondary school system, which normally provided China with many of her intermediate-level technicians.

Some Chinese leaders were expressing criticisms of the 'revolution in education' as early as 1972 and in 1975, Zhou Rongxin, the newly-appointed Minister of Education, sought to curtail its excesses. But little headway could be made against the leftists who had seized considerable power in educational circles until, with Mao's death in September 1976, they lost their protector. The inability to put right the damage done to education while Mao was alive is a fitting comment to the aura surrounding the Chairman's name; the speed with which his policies on education were reversed is equally a testimony to the unpopularity they had aroused.

Despite factional differences the post-Mao leadership has been characterised by a desire to pursue modernisation rather than the millennium, and it has attached great importance to the development of an adequate educational infrastructure. Especially since 1980 the educational system has benefited from the general demographic trend which has resulted in the death or retirement of most of the original 'revolutionary generation' at central and provincial level, who had rarely received much formal education themselves and who did not regard it highly. Their successors, increasingly, have been relatively well-educated. A glance at the rising stars of the 1980s reveals that China is now following the example of the USSR in that a university degree is virtually *de rigueur* for advancement. Education in recent years has been controlled by people who have a reasonably clear idea of the issues involved.

The major break with the 'revolution in education' to take place in the late 1970s was the drive to provide 'elevation' in place of the appallingly low standards of the preceding decade. A principal reform here was inevitably the restoration of tertiary education to its 'rightful' place. In part this was simply quantitative. The number of regular universities, for instance, jumped from 404 in 1977 to 704 in 1981, and student enrolments increased from 625 319 to 1 279 427 over the same period. Old scholars, condemned as 'bourgeois authorities', were rehabilitated and less-qualified instructors appointed during the Cultural Revolution were sometimes assigned to less demanding work. Courses were lengthened, political content was judiciously pruned away, and productive labour often came to mean nothing more than carrying out laboratory experiments.

Most importantly, the Chinese university system rejected the selection methods of the Cultural Revolution. In 1977 extremely competitive entrance examinations were restored which tested students' ability across a range of academic subjects. As the system stabilised the better universities, designated as 'key points', recruited the cream of China's youth on a nation-wide basis. Positive discrimination did not disappear entirely but could no longer be a substitute for academic merit. Indeed, the stress on examinations again gave rise to a phenomenon familiar in most educational systems: the children of the well-educated themselves did disproportionately well in the educational arena. As early as 1978 the leadership had to defend itself against the charge that social stratification was once more taking place.

Another feature of elevation which deserves particular mention was 'opening up' to the West and Japan. This broke with the Maoist policy of 'self-reliance' and began as early as 1977 when the Ministry of Education began to collect on a fairly systematic basis foreign textbooks and to expand holdings of scientific periodicals. The most noticeable feature of opening up was, of course, the decision to send academics and students abroad in fairly large numbers.

In the school system, in addition to going back to a more formal curriculum and conservative teaching methods, the 'key point' concept was also applied. Usually at secondary level (but not exclusively), 'key points' were elitist institutions. Their greatest strength was (and is) the quality of teaching staff who are well-educated and, moreover, have been trained to teach. Predictably, the curriculum of 'key points' was almost exclusively academic. 'Key points' also had good equipment and adequate buildings, and received the best students. Practice varied over time and place but generally a 'key point' would accept students from a wide catchment area on the basis of academic performance. And the curriculum taught was narrowly academic.

Ironically this was also the case in the general secondary schools which the bulk of children attended in the late 1970s. For despite the rhetoric of the Cultural Revolution, technical and vocational education had in fact been badly affected. The problem was that the massive secondary school expansion of the 1970s did not particularly stimulate the development of vocational *education* although it did divert students to a good deal of manual labour of little relevance to their studies. With the benefit of hindsight it is difficult to see how things could have been otherwise. This rapid increase in the provision of secondary places was accompanied by a huge rise in the number of teachers. Between 1968 and 1976 the number of full-time junior middle teachers rose from just over 379 000 to over 2 million, and senior middle teachers increased from 77 910 to 694 343. As a result the number of secondary school students per teacher actually decreased.

Most teachers, however, were unqualified, and some had not even been educated up to the level at which they were supposed to be teaching. Few had any qualifications to teach technical subjects. Moreover, even had they been competent to do so they lacked the opportunity, because the expansion of educational provision was not matched by any increase in state expenditure. Indeed it actually declined. Many schools were unable to provide adequate buildings or furniture, let alone equipment. Forbidden to spend much time on 'book knowledge', teachers in the Cultural Revolution led their charges to productive labour with little educational content.

When it became safe to do so a good deal of productive labour was dropped, leaving most secondary school children (except for those in 'key points') receiving a very poor 'academic' education. Moreover, the numbers involved continued to rise. Junior middle school enrolments peaked at about 50 million in 1978 and senior middle at nearly 6 800 000 the year before. The consequence was unsatisfactory both nationally and individually. Most secondary school leavers were ill-equipped to enter the world of work and, in the case of those who had been through senior middle school, often had ambitions to enter universities and pursue high-level careers which could not realistically be met.

The initial response of Chinese leaders to problems of secondary education in the late 1970s was elitist: the weakest schools were to be closed. At junior middle level their number was reduced from 136 365 in 1977 to 87 077 in 1980. The number of students dropped from 49 798 900 to 45 382 900 over the same period. At senior middle school level the cuts were much more savage. There, the number of schools was reduced from 64 903 to only 31 300. Enrolments fell from 18 000 000 to 9 697 000. The burden of cuts fell most heavily on the rural areas where a stock of 50 916 senior middle schools in 1977 was reduced to only 18 475 in 1980. The number of primary schools was also reduced in the late 1970s, dropping from 982 300 to 917 300. But this was not accompanied by any attempt to reduce intake, and the primary school population actually increased marginally between 1977 and 1980.

Since 1980 Chinese leaders have moved to a more balanced

view of educational development. It has been recognised that the tortuous path of education has in part been the result of chronic under-funding of the educational sector. This imposed a series of extreme 'either-or' choices on decision-makers and made the educational arena one of exceptionally high conflict. In theory 'universalisation' and 'elevation' were always supposed to go hand in hand; in practice they did not. It is now realised that the modernisation of China requires university graduates, mid-level technical personnel *and* a literate work-force also.

One of the most important developments of the 1980s has been an increased emphasis by the leadership on professionalism at all levels. It is noteworthy that the people in charge of the educational bureaucracy have increasingly been those who are university graduates and who have usually worked for a considerable time in education before achieving the highest offices. In 1985 the importance of education was recognised with the appointment of Li Peng as its supremo and the reorganisation of the educational establishment. In his late fifties, Li Peng was a political leader of the highest stature. An engineering graduate, educated in the Soviet Union, his rapid rise since 1982 was due to his zealous and efficient support of Deng's reforms and his close relationship with premier Zhao Ziyang, to whom he is widely regarded as a likely successor.

Significantly, Li did not simply become Minister of Education. Over the years the Ministry has been known as one of the weaker branches of the state bureaucracy, mainly because huge areas of educational work and training have been outside its control. This division of labour had created major weaknesses, with considerable inefficiency resulting from over-compartmentalisation. The solution, therefore, was to replace the Ministry of Education with a State Education Commission headed by Li Peng. This, in fact, is a super-ministry charged with co-ordinating China's huge range of educational programmes.

At lower levels of the system the drive for professionalisation has also been pronounced. In universities, for example, a reform drive has devolved decision-making powers to individual institutions. Within institutions academic staff have been given increased powers to elect colleagues to administrative posts and to establish academic and administrative committees similar to those found in the West. Vigorous efforts have also been made to strengthen the university system more generally. The number of regular universities rose to 805 in 1983 and to 1016 in 1985. The student body increased to 1 206 823 in 1983 and to 1 703 100 in 1985. In keeping with the dictates of modernisation the major fields of study are (in rank order) engineering, teacher training, medicine and pharmacy, agriculture and natural sciences. However the new professional approach has caused the leadership to appreciate the value of training a cadre in disciplines relevant to economic management and administration. As of 1983 some 71 100 students were enrolled in finance and economics courses compared with a mere 90 in 1975. Postgraduate students remain a tiny minority of the total, but considerable progress has none the less been made.

The most serious difficulty in Chinese education is the continuing failure to produce enough school-leavers with technical and vocational skills. The inadequacies of massive general middle school provision in the 1970s was, as mentioned above, initially met by the negative policy drastically reducing the numbers involved. Responsibility for giving young workers relevant skills devolved to the units or systems in which they worked. The People's Republic has long had a remarkably extensive programme for non-formal education involving every form of in-service, part-time, day-release, evening classes, and distance learning imaginable, offering everything from courses in how to prepare Peking Duck for trainee chefs to engineering degrees which officially were claimed to be the equivalent of those offered by regular universities. The system could not, however, cope with the failures of the formal institutions, despite an increase in non-formal technical programmes at the secondary level run by various enterprises which raised enrolment from 2 200 000 in 1979 to 3 300 000 in 1982. The expansion of the university sector made the imbalance of qualified manpower particularly acute. In 1982 it was reported that there was one university graduate for every middle-level technician, whereas a ratio of 1 : 3 would have been more appropriate.

By the start of the 1980s the problem was receiving increasing attention, not least because of survey research carried out by educational research institutes. In this instance educational researchers were instrumental in persuading the Ministry of Education that the crisis could not be resolved by simply tinkering with the system; radical transformation was required. It was duly decided that the answer lay in the senior middle schools. By the early 1990s 50 per cent of students at this level are to be receiving technical and vocational, rather than 'general' education. Junior middle schools also were to adopt a more vocational curriculum.

Although the programme of transformation began in 1982 it has encountered great difficulties. One of these is simply the shortage of suitable teachers and equipment. A further problem is that education of this sort is not highly valued by parents or students nor by many education officials and teachers. It is likely that the middle schools being transformed are those with the least clout and in the poorest districts. 'Good' students still attempt to obtain an academic education.

In May 1985 the Central Committee itself addressed this problem in a key Decision on the Reform of China's Educational Structure. This honestly admitted that 'we have failed to make a genuine breakthrough in the development of vocational and technical education, although we have stressed its need for many years'. The reason was that 'the outworn concept of belittling vocational and technical education is deeply rooted'. To overcome this, the Decision stipulated two measures. The first was the need to conduct education in order to foster the concept that it was an honour to work in any trade or profession. The second was more important. Labour and personnel systems were enjoined to bring in relevant rules and regulations to put into effect the principle of 'training before employment'. In effect this means that all units are to give top priority to employing graduates of vocational and technical schools.

The evidence and events of the past decade strongly suggest that the Central Committee's stress on 'educating' the populace to appreciate the benefits of vocational training will not in itself be of any greater significance in reversing traditional attitudes as to what constitutes 'real' education than it was to creating the Chinese version of the 'New Socialist Man'. The new pragmatic emphasis on money, however, is likely to be more attractive. If the Central Committee's insistence on priority career prospects for those with vocational and technical training is properly implemented, and if the remuneration offered to such people is raised to an appropriate level, there is much more chance of China developing the cadre of 10–15 million technical personnel it hopes to produce by the early or mid-1990s. Greater expenditure will also be required on this form of education. The Decision cited above does recognise that general educational expenditure must increase: 'For the foreseeable future, central and local government appropriations for educational purposes will increase at a rate faster than the state's regular revenues, and the average expenditure on education per student will also increase steadily.' Probably the best hope for technical and vocational education is the fact that China remains fundamentally a relatively authoritarian society and that the widespread consensus among the political elite as to the value of this sort of education will be translated into hard cash. Money will also be needed to remedy the problem of teacher quality in general senior middle schools as well as technical and vocational ones.

At primary and junior-middle school level the prospects are more hopeful. The 'right to education' was written into the State Constitution of 1982. In 1984 Jiangsu province became the first in China to introduce compulsory education with fines to be levied on parents who failed to keep their children there. In 1985 the National People's Congress legislated to introduce compulsory primary education on a national basis, beginning with the relatively advanced coastal provinces and moving gradually inland. The Decision of May 1985 stipulates that a nine-year system of primary and junior-middle school compulsory education should encompass most of the country by 1995. Special financial assistance is to be given to areas inhabited by national minorities and economically-underdeveloped areas generally to help them make progress.

At first sight the idea of universalising a nine-year system of basic education appears unrealistic. In the early 1980s Chinese educators regularly referred to the '9–6–3' formula. This meant that nine out of ten children enrolled in the primary school first grade, six completed the five (occasionally six) years, and only three graduated with a satisfactory performance. Similarly, it was regularly reported that many primary school teachers were unqualified: the figure of 50 per cent was regularly given and occasionally higher figures were reported. It was widely noted that basic schooling had been adversely affected by the successful introduction of the 'production responsibility' system in agriculture which gave peasants a strong incentive to keep their children out of school so that they might contribute to household income by carrying out a wide range of simple but valuable agricultural tasks.

It would appear, however, that another official policy, namely the family limitation campaign, has had some compensatory effect. From an all-time high of just over 150 000 000, primary school enrolments dropped to 135 780 000 in 1983 and to 133 700 800 in 1985. The number of teachers showed no corresponding decrease. Thus there are real possibilities for improving teaching either by instituting smaller classes, or providing in-service training, at little or no extra cost. There is also some evidence that where peasant communities have become prosperous as a result of the agricultural reforms, they have a renewed sense of the importance of education and have both ploughed money back into rural schools and encouraged their children to further their education.

The case of education demonstrates that the Chinese policy process has greatly developed since the death of Mao. Those involved in it nowadays possess a greater measure of professional competence than their predecessors. They are more likely to base their decisions on hard evidence rather than ideological desiderata. Leadership is becoming more collective and consensual and change is more incremental and less violent. In this, as in other respects, the Chinese educational system had moved rather closer to the pattern in other communist states by the late 1980s.

Further reading

A considerable literature is now available on groups and the policy-making process in the communist states. The pioneering contributions are those of Gordon Skilling; see particularly Skilling (1966) and (1973). A symposium on the utility of the group approach, 'Pluralism in communist societies: is the emperor naked?', appeared in *Studies in Comparative Communism*, vol. 12 (1979). Two sceptical contributions are Janos (1970) and Odom (1976); see also Skilling's reflections upon the debate (1983) and the discussions on pluralism and the role of groups in policy-making in Solomon (1983). The opportunities for political participation by the mass public are considered on a comparative basis in Schulz and Adams (1981); Holmes (1981b) considers the policy process in communist states with particular reference to industrial policy in the USSR and the GDR.

On the USSR more specifically the most helpful single work, which has considerable relevance for the other communist states, is Skilling and Griffiths (1971). Also useful are Juviler and Morton (1967), for the Khrushchev period, and Smith (1980), for the Brezhnev period. On the development of the Soviet economy see Ellman (1979), Nove (1986) and Gregory and Stuart (1986). On the politics of economic reform, see the chapters on the *apparatchiki*, industrial managers and economists in Skilling and Griffiths (1971); see also Lewin (1975), Hough (1969), Azrael (1966), Andrle (1976) and Rutland (1985). On the role of the military, see particularly Colton (1979), Jones (1986) and the International Institute of Strategic Studies' *Military Balance* (London, annual). On the politics of labour, see Lane and O'Dell (1978), Ruble (1981), and Schapiro and Godson (1984). The role of letters from the mass public is considered in White (1983b), and 'covert political participation' is considered in a stimulating article by DiFranceisco and Gitelman (1985).

On the politics of agriculture in Eastern Europe many of the books listed in previous chapters contain short discussions that are relevant, although no one volume is addressed to an analysis of how the policies concerned were formulated. Specific works on individual countries include chapters on

Poland, Czechoslovakia and Yugoslavia in Karcz (1967), and there are chapters on Poland, Czechoslovakia, Hungary and the GDR in Laird (1977). Lewis (1973) considers the social role of the peasantry in Poland, and Lewis (1979) provides a more general survey of East European peasant politics. Held (1980) deals with the transformation of Hungarian agriculture up to 1975; Narkiewicz (1976) considers the peasantry and Polish populist politics up to 1970. Detailed village-based studies include Salzman and Scheufler (1974) on Czechoslovakia, Halpern and Halpern (1982) on Serbia, Hann (1985) on Poland, and Hann (1980) on Hungary. Swain (1985) deals with the efficiency of collective-farm agriculture in Hungary. Finally, a two-volume survey edited by Ivan Volgyes (1979) contains much information on rural sociology and agricultural policy outcomes.

In addition to the works cited in previous chapters, the policy-making process in China is considered in Oksenberg (1982), which deals with economic policy-making, and Barnett (1985), which deals with the making of foreign policy. On educational policy-making more specifically, see Price (1975), which sets out the basic framework of the educational system. Mao's ideas on education are considered in detail in Hawkins (1974). A specialised study which deals with many of the issues mentioned in this section is Taylor (1981), a study of the politics of university enrolment. The origins of the 'revolution in education' are discussed in Gardner (1971). More recent developments are surveyed in Hayhoe (1984); and currents of opinion among Chinese youth in the 1980s are considered in Rosen (1985).

6

Democracy and Human Rights

Communist states are widely known for their economic and social achievements such as their generally high rates of economic growth, their low levels of unemployment and inflation, their virtual elimination of illiteracy and their comprehensive provision of health care. There are few, however, who would be inclined to argue that they have made a positive contribution of the same kind to the field of politics, or to the enlargement of human liberty in particular. It had been supposed by Marx that, broadly speaking, once capitalism – the last of the class-divided and exploitative societies – had been abolished, there would be no more need for a separate sphere of political administration, and the state (in Engels's celebrated phrase) would 'wither away' or 'die out' (*aussterben*). In the communist states, however, there has been little sign of a process of this kind (some have unkindly suggested that the only thing that has withered away is the *idea* that the state should wither away). The communist states, on the contrary, have generally been large, powerful and authoritarian institutions, in which the rights and liberties of the citizen, at least in Western terms, have been systematically repressed; they are generally regarded, not as having inaugurated a new era of freedom, but as having added a new chapter to the history of dictatorship.

The communist states, however, do not claim to have constructed a form of democracy which conforms to the precepts of Western liberal theory. On the contrary, they have a democratic theory of their own which, in line with Marxist and indeed with some earlier theories of democracy, places more emphasis upon the content of democracy than upon its form, and upon the socio-economic rights of citizens rather than upon their formal independence of state power. In terms of this theory, which cannot simply be ignored, the communist states have constructed a society far more democratic than that of their major Western counterparts. To describe the communist states as uniformly repressive, moreover, is unduly gross, even in terms of Western liberal theory. The degree to which individual rights have been respected has varied from country to country, from period to period and from area to area, and general statements of this kind also obscure the gradual but perceptible development in the communist states of, if not a rule of law, then at least an increased tendency on the part of the authorities to avoid the routine perversion of judicial procedures and the denial of what is called 'socialist legality'. For all the limitations and imperfections of such developments, they deserve at least to be taken into account in any assessment of democracy and human rights in the communist states.

The USSR: democracy, law and dissent

Soviet democratic theory is based upon classical Marxist theory, in terms of which there can be no 'democracy' in the abstract but only particular forms of class democracy depending upon which social group owns the means of production and thereby, it is thought, holds political power in the society. In the Soviet Union, as in the other communist states, the means of production – factories, farms and so forth – belong to the people as a whole, and it is the people, rather than a narrow exploiting group, who control the national resources and supposedly ensure that they are used for the benefit of all members of the society. As the current edition of the *Great Soviet Encyclopedia* puts it, bourgeois democracy, such as exists in Western countries, is a 'form of dictatorship of capitalists over proletarians and other semi-proletarian and non-proletarian toiling classes and strata of the population. It is characterised by a blatant contradiction between the declared "power of the people" and the actual domination of the exploiters'. In a socialist democracy, on the other hand, as in the communist states, there is a 'complete accord between the form and content of democratic institutions, laws etc. and the power of the toilers'. These societies, it is argued, are characterised by real and not fictitious rights for the people as a whole, by an absence of inequalities based upon race, class, religion or sex, and by the broadest possible participation of ordinary people in the administration of cultural and economic as well as political affairs. A democracy of this kind is held to be the 'historically highest type of political democracy' and the 'only possible form of socialist state'.

These principles of socialist democracy, it is argued, are fully applied in the contemporary USSR, as in the other communist-ruled states. All power belongs, according to the Constitution, to the people, who exercise it through the soviets of people's deputies which they elect and which alone have law-making powers. The people, it is pointed out, are themselves well represented in these bodies, in line with the Soviet principle that the people should administer the state directly rather than leave it to a professional class of politicians. The soviets at all levels of the system, as we have seen in Chapter 3, are indeed representative of all sections of the nation, of all its nationalities, age groups, genders and classes (there are more women in the USSR Supreme Soviet than in the British, French, Italian and American legislatures put together, for instance, and ordinary workers and peasants, rather than company directors and lawyers, are in a majority at all levels). It is of course accepted that the communist party, a small minority of the total population, plays a 'leading' or 'guiding' role in the work of such institutions and in political life generally. But, it is pointed out, ordinary workers and peasants constitute a majority of the party's membership, and for them it is an instrument of rule, a means of ensuring that their preferences are reflected in the policies that are pursued by the Soviet government. What, it might be asked, could be more 'democratic' than that?

The Soviet Constitution, it is argued, extends these principles further. Unlike the constitutions of capitalist states, it is pointed out, which do no more than proclaim the rights of citizens in purely abstract terms (the 'right of anyone to dine at the Savoy [a luxury London hotel]', though very few will in practice be able to afford to do so), the Soviet Constitution actually provides the means by which the rights that it proclaims can be enjoyed. The right to education, for instance (Article 45), is 'guaranteed' by the free provision of all forms of education, by the payment of scholarships and grants to students, and in other ways. Similar means are provided by which the other rights mentioned in the Constitution, such as the right to work, to housing, to social security and to health care, can at least ostensibly be made available to all citizens. The Constitution also provides and again nominally guarantees a wide range of civil liberties, such as the right to freedom of scientific, technical and artistic work, the right to take part in the management of state and public affairs, the right to associate in public organisations and the rights of freedom of speech, of the press and of assembly. The last of these, for instance (Article 50), is supposedly guaranteed by 'putting public buildings, streets and squares at the disposal of the working people and their organisations, by broad dissemination of information, and by the opportunity to use the press, television and radio'.

Most of these rights, however, are qualified in various ways. The right of freedom of speech, of the press and of assembly, for instance, is guaranteed only in so far as it is 'in accordance with the interests of the people and in order to strengthen and develop the socialist system'. The rights of freedom of scientific, technical and artistic work and to associate in public organisations (Articles 47 and 51), similarly, are granted only in so far as they are 'in accordance with the aims of building communism'. This means that it is in fact the communist party, as the only legitimate interpreter of the people's best interests and of the requirements of the building of communism, which decides whether these rights are to be enjoyed or not, and they are in practice extended only to approved individuals and organisations such as the trade unions, the Komsomol and the co-operatives. Further more general restrictions are contained in Article 39, which states that citizens' enjoyment of their rights must 'not be to the detriment of the interests of society or of the state', and in Article 59, which states that citizens' performance of their duties and freedoms is 'inseparable from the performance of their duties and obligations', which include the duty to engage in socially useful labour, to protect state property and to bring up their children to be 'worthy members of socialist society'. In any conflict of interpretation, moreover, it will be the party's wishes that prevail, as there are no means of challenging its decisions in the courts or of enforcing the observance of some of the other provisions in the Constitution, such as the right to inviolability of the home and of postal and telegraphic communications (Articles 55 and 56).

Official sources claim, as we have noted, that in making such decisions the party is guided by the interests of the majority of the population, and more particularly of the workers and peasants who make up a majority of its members. This claim would be more convincing were it not for the fact that the party, as we have seen, is a highly centralised, hierarchical institution, and that workers and peasants account for a steadily diminishing proportion of the total as one moves upwards in the hierarchy. Workers and peasants, for instance, accounted for 56.8 per cent of the party's total membership in 1986 (and this figure is itself somewhat suspect because of the continued tendency to report such statistics in terms of social origin or occupation at the time of entry rather than in terms of current occupation, which may often be white-collar). In the Central Committee elected in the same year, however, there were only twenty-three workers or peasants, no more than 7 per cent of the total, and in the Politburo itself there are none at all (though most of its members are admittedly from poor backgrounds). Much the same is true of representation in the soviets as one moves from the local to the national level. The party and state leadership may, for various reasons, promote policies which are in the interests of the mass of the population, or at least enjoy majority support. But there is little guarantee, in terms of social origin, that they will do so, and there are few means of compelling them to do so should they decide otherwise.

Law and the courts

This situation results largely from the fact that in the USSR, unlike the Western liberal democracies, the courts are not independent of the government but form part of the same integrated state system. The Western doctrine of the separation of powers is regarded by Soviet official theorists as a smokescreen for the defence of capitalist interests, whatever the legal textbooks might say. In the USSR, on the other hand, the court system is seen as one which represents and promotes the interests of the majority of the population, and which like all the other parts of the state system is directly or indirectly responsible to the people. All judges in the USSR, for instance, are elected, accountable to their electors, and can be recalled in the same manner as deputies to the soviets. The Soviet court system is organised at three levels: at the local level, where people's courts (the judges in which are elected directly by the population) deal with minor criminal and a large number of civil cases; at the regional level, where regional courts (the judges in which are elected by regional soviets) deal with appeals from the people's courts and with more serious criminal and civil matters; and at the republican level, where supreme courts (the judges in which are elected by republican Supreme Soviets) deal with appeals from the regional courts and with civil and criminal cases of some gravity. At the apex of the system is the Supreme Court of the USSR, elected by the USSR Supreme Soviet, which supervises the administration of justice at lower levels and in addition exercises original jurisdiction over cases of exceptional gravity.

The Constitution prescribes that court proceedings shall be open to the public in all but exceptional circumstances, that the defendant in a criminal trial shall have a right to legal assistance, and that judges and the people's assessors who assist them in their work shall be 'independent and subject only to the law' (Article 155). In practice these guarantees are subject to a number of serious qualifications. In the first place, the election of judges and of people's assessors is controlled by the party through the *nomenklatura* in the same way that elections to all other positions of importance are controlled, and no candidate is likely to be considered, whatever his technical competence, unless he or she is willing to accept the principle of party dominance. Judges are also subject to the authority of higher court officials and of the Procuracy (a mainly supervisory body) in their work, and their decisions may be set aside if they fail to accord with the wishes of those at higher levels of the system. It is clear, moreover, that the party keeps a close watch on the work of the courts and intervenes in detail whenever it considers it necessary to do so, particularly when matters of a politically sensitive nature are involved. The work of the courts is supervised at the highest levels by the Administrative Organs Department, one of the departments of the Central Committee apparatus, and according to *émigré* testimony it is normal practice for legal judgements in particularly controversial cases to be drawn up in this department. In the ordinary run of cases, however, most of which are civil and of little state significance, detailed party intervention of this kind is neither common nor even necessary.

It would be wrong, moreover, to imply that there had been no significant improvement in the administration of Soviet justice over the years. In the Stalin period, for instance, the most elementary legal norms were routinely disregarded. The criminal code of the time, adopted in 1926 and subsequently much amended, contained the notorious Article 58 on 'counter-revolutionary crimes', whose various sections provided severe penalties for any form of real or imagined dissidence. People were arrested and imprisoned, according to Solzhenitsyn, for the most preposterous of 'crimes':

A tailor laying aside his needle stuck it into a newspaper on the wall so it wouldn't get lost and happened to stick it in the eye of a portrait of Kaganovich [at that time a prominent member of the Politburo]. A customer observed this: Article 58 – ten years (terrorism) . . .

A tractor driver of the Znamenka Machinery and Tractor Station lined his thin shoes for warmth with a pamphlet about the candidate for elections to the Supreme Soviet, but a charwoman noticed it was missing (she was responsible for the leaflets) and found out who had it. Counter-revolutionary Agitation – ten years . . .

A *deaf and dumb* carpenter got a term for counter-revolutionary *agitation*. How? He was laying floors in a club. Everything had been removed from the big hall, and there was no nail or hook anywhere. While he was working, he hung his jacket and his service cap on a bust of Lenin. Someone came in and saw it. Article 58 – ten years.

If the court could find no specific offence that the defendant had committed it could sentence him 'by analogy' with some other crime, and sentences could also be passed retrospectively. In addition the NKVD (People's Commissariat of Internal Affairs or security police) administered a separate court system, the Special Board, set up in 1934, which could try a suspect in his absence and impose whatever sentence it wished, including the death penalty. In the later 1930s it appears to have handled hundreds of cases daily.

Following the death of Stalin in 1953 a new emphasis began to be placed upon 'socialist legality', or the proper observance of judicial procedures. The NKVD Special Board was abolished in the same year; large numbers of people were released from prison camps and their sentences investigated and quashed if they were found to lack a proper foundation in law; some of the leading officials of the security police were tried and executed; and most important of all, a new criminal code was adopted which outlawed many of the abuses of legality of the previous period. The new code, adopted in the form of general principles for the USSR as a whole in 1958 and then in the form of more specific codes for each of the union republics in 1960 and 1961, prohibited trial by analogy or retrospective justice; only actions specifically designated as criminal at the time of their commission could be used as the basis of judicial proceedings. An associated Code of Criminal Procedure prohibited night-time interrogation and torture, which had previously been widely practised. The security police (now called the KGB) retained certain powers of arrest and investigation, particularly in the case of 'especially dangerous crimes against the state' such as espionage and treason, but their powers were greatly reduced and their investigations were placed under the supervision of a department in the Procurator General's office. From this time forward, at least in theory, no trial could take place other than in a properly constituted court of law and in accordance with established court procedures.

The present position is that it is unusual (as well as illegal) for people to be arrested simply for their beliefs or their expressions of opinion. They must, as a rule, engage in actions which are specifically designated as criminal at the time of their commission if they are to fall foul of the authorities, and they will be properly tried in open court, with the right to employ a defence counsel, if they do so. Far fewer people, also, are in detention than was the case under Stalin: between 1 and 2 million altogether, it is estimated, of whom perhaps 10–20 000 may be classified as political prisoners in the ordinary meaning of the term, as against the 10 to 15 million who were languishing in the prison camps at the time of Stalin's death in 1953. The individual citizen, however, has no firm guarantee of equitable treatment if the authorities decide to persecute him, and there have been frequent reports of deviations from the established norms in such cases. Some critics have been expelled from the USSR against their wishes, others have been tried in proceedings which were effectively closed to the public by filling the courtroom with specially invited audiences (often secret policemen), and in a small but disturbing number of cases apparently sane dissidents have been accused of having 'delusions of reforming society' and diagnosed as schizophrenics. The Soviet authorities have yet to provide a satisfactory explanation of such cases.

The law as it stands, moreover, is both unusually comprehensive and rather ambiguous in its formulation, lending itself easily to abuse if the authorities decide accordingly. The article under which political dissenters are most frequently sentenced, for instance, is Article 70 of the RSFSR Criminal Code, which deals with 'anti-Soviet agitation and propaganda'. It reads as follows:

Agitation or propaganda carried on for the purpose of subverting or weakening the Soviet regime or of committing particular, especially dangerous crimes against the state, or the circulation, for the same purposes, of slanderous fabrications which defame the Soviet state and social system, or the circulation and preparation and keeping, for the same purposes, of literature of such a content, shall be

punished by deprivation of liberty for a term of six months
to seven years, with or without additional exile for a term
of two to five years, or by exile for a term of two to five
years.

In addition Article 190, which deals with 'crimes against the
system of administration', prohibits the 'systematic circulation in an oral form of fabrications known to be false which
defame the Soviet state and social system' and the 'preparation or circulation in written, printed or other forms of works
of such content', and provides for a prison term of between
three and five years for those who are found guilty of having
violated it. The result is that the authorities have a good deal
of scope in which they can, if they wish, deprive critics of
their liberty or otherwise inconvenience them without necessarily stepping outside the strict letter of the law.

Religion and political dissent

Let us consider these matters a little further by looking more
closely at the two main categories of people involved in cases
of this kind, religious believers and political dissidents. Religion in the USSR is officially speaking a private matter; the
church is separated from the state, citizens are guaranteed the
right to profess any religion and to conduct religious worship,
and incitement of hatred on religious grounds is specifically
prohibited (Article 52 of the Constitution). There is in fact a
very large community of religious believers in the USSR,
much larger than the total membership of the CPSU. About
50 million citizens are estimated to adhere to the Russian
Orthodox Church, the national church of Russia, which is
headed by the Patriarch of Moscow and has jurisdiction over
Orthodox communities abroad as well as over those within
the USSR itself. In addition there are about 30 million
Muslims, mostly in Central Asia; about 5 million Roman
Catholics, mostly in the Ukraine and in Lithuania; about 2
million Jews, mainly in the Ukraine and in Moscow; and
there is a small Buddhist community in the Far East. All of
these groups are registered with the Council for Religious
Affairs, which is attached to the USSR Council for Ministers,

but they administer their own affairs and are exempt from direct taxation and from censorship, since technically speaking they are non-state bodies and therefore not subject to government control. Groups of believers, provided they are at least twenty in number, have the right to seek the use of a church building from a local soviet, free of charge apart from tax and insurance, and the right to train and ordain their priests. More than 20 000 churches and eighteen religious seminaries were reported to be in operation in the USSR in the late 1980s.

Religious believers, these guarantees notwithstanding, are in practice subject to a variety of forms of discrimination or unequal treatment, and they have frequently come into conflict with the authorities over matters which in most Western countries would present no legal difficulties. The Constitution, for instance, provides for the right of anti-religious, but not (as it did until 1929) of religious propaganda; and the rights that it does provide are restricted in a variety of ways – religious instruction, for instance, may not be given to anyone under the age of 18. Two-thirds of the churches which existed in pre-revolutionary Russia have been closed, at the behest of the authorities rather than of the congregations themselves, and various forms of informal discrimination also exist. It is known, for instance, that religious believers will not be appointed to teaching posts or to other positions concerned with the care of the young, and the Jewish community, as in Tsarist times, appears to be subject to a number of further disabilities, such as a limit upon the number of their members who will be admitted to universities and their effective exclusion from the Soviet diplomatic service. A number of mainly Protestant sects which have refused to register with the authorities and are therefore regarded as illegal organisations suffer additional harassment, as do the religious groups whose members refuse, for reasons of conscience, to receive medical treatment or to serve in the armed forces, both of which are regarded as violations of Soviet law. Nor have active religious believers been allowed to acquire positions of any prominence in Soviet public life.

Political, like religious dissenters are a relatively new phenomenon in the USSR, at any rate since the defeat of the left and right oppositionists within the communist party in the 1920s. The dissidents of the present day, who have come to public attention since the early 1960s, are not generally members of the party and are usually more concerned to secure the extensive democratic rights with which all citizens have theoretically been endowed than to change the party's policies from within. The first dissidents to become widely known in the West were the literary critic, Andrei Sinyavsky, and the translator, Yuly Daniel, who were put on trial in 1966 and sentenced to seven and five years' imprisonment respectively for having published works abroad which were held to have 'defamed the Soviet system'. Both Sinyavsky and Daniel denied the charges and had in fact taken no steps themselves to transmit their works abroad, scarcely evidence of an intention to circulate slanderous falsifications as the law required. The court, none the less, found them guilty under Article 70 of the Criminal Code and sentenced them accordingly.

The arrest of Sinyavsky and Daniel was soon followed by similar action against other dissidents. In 1968 Alexander Ginzburg and Yury Galanskov were found guilty of circulating materials on the Sinyavsky–Daniel trial, and Pavel Litvinov and some others were arrested on Red Square for demonstrating against the Warsaw Pact intervention in Czechoslovakia. In 1970 the historian Andrei Amalrik was put on trial and convicted; in 1974 Alexander Solzhenitsyn was arrested and then deported; and in 1976 Amalrik, Leonid Plyushch and Vladimir Bukovsky were encouraged or compelled to follow him into emigration. In 1978 Anatoly Shcharansky was found guilty of treason and Yury Orlov of anti-Soviet agitation and propaganda (in 1986 both of them were permitted to emigrate); and finally in 1980 Academician Andrei Sakharov, one of the few prominent dissidents to have remained in the USSR and at liberty, was sent into internal exile in the city of Gorky, 250 miles east of Moscow and out of bounds to foreigners. The authorities have also made every effort to reduce the flow of *samizdat* or self-published material, such as the unofficial periodical *A Chronicle of Current Events*, and to break up unauthorised groups and organisations, such as the Helsinki Monitoring Group which has tried to keep a record of Soviet violations of the 1975 Final Act of the Helsinki Conference on Peace and Co-operation in Europe.

It is probably fair to say that the dissident movement has placed the Soviet authorities in something of a quandary. It seems to have elicited a fairly limited response from the Soviet public; no more than about 1000 signatories to the various dissident manifestos and appeals have been identified, for instance, and there appears to be a good deal of quite spontaneous hostility towards a group composed mainly of intellectuals who appear in addition to have been engaged in the seriously unpatriotic activity of washing Soviet dirty linen in public, a practice that has been widely deplored since long before the revolution. At the same time it would be an abdication of the party's leading role, as conventionally understood, to allow official policies to be openly challenged, and above all to allow organised groupings and publications to come into existence outside the scope of party control. The dissidents' example might also become infectious. Attempts have been made in recent years, for instance, to establish an independent trade union movement, and the example of events in Poland since 1980 shows the explosive potential that such a movement might have. The authorities appear to have avoided committing themselves to a single policy to deal with these developments, neither opting for a return to wholesale terror nor, at the other extreme, accepting a more pluralistic definition of the party's leading role. They have rather sought to give concessions, particularly economic concessions, wher-ever necessary; they have encouraged the trade unions and other bodies to deal more vigorously with complaints and grievances; they have permitted or compelled irreconcilable opponents of the regime, as well as substantial numbers of Jews, to emigrate; and they have tried to isolate those who remain, such as Academician Sakharov, from the Western press and from other dissidents.

It is probably too early to say how successful these various tactics will be. It would also be wrong to overlook the efforts that the authorities have been making to strengthen the rule of law in less controversial areas, or to imply that the Western liberal democracies, still less the non-communist world as a whole, are entirely above reproach in matters of this kind. In many Western countries, for instance, communists (as well as right-wing extremists) are debarred from a variety of forms of public employment, including not only the police and the diplomatic service but also, in countries such as West Germany, teaching posts within the higher and secondary education systems. The considerable costs of taking legal action, moreover, may make it difficult for many citizens to take advantage of the extensive civil rights with which they have theoretically been endowed, and the class origins and upbringing of judges in many Western countries may give at least the impression that cases involving trade unions or the rights of private property will receive less than an impartial hearing. None the less, as even Soviet sources acknowledge, public pressure over the years has led to a series of concessions to popular demands in many of the capitalist countries, such as extensive civil and trade union rights, a substantial measure of public ownership in the economy and the establishment of comprehensive health and education systems. It would be difficult to give a comparable series of examples of major measures of public policy which have been brought about by public pressure against the wishes of the authorities in the USSR.

Indeed the whole area of popular control over executive action, whether in the party or the state, is one in which the Soviet system is notably deficient. How, for instance, can a legislature which meets for only three or four days a year, none of whose members works full-time at the job, be expected to monitor the stream of decisions that flows every day from the Soviet government and its agencies? How can the Party Congress or the Central Committee be expected to hold the Politburo and Secretariat to account, when they meet so infrequently and have in any case largely been selected by those bodies? And how can the press and the mass media generally, which are controlled by the party and state authorities, be expected to permit regular and serious criticism of their activities? The Soviet population, as we have seen, are not entirely without the means of influencing the government which rules in their name; but they lack the ultimate sanction, a general election at which it could be dismissed from office. The Soviet leaders, for their part, are not simply protected from the whims of the electorate; they also dispose, through their control of the economy and of the legal system, of the means of depriving critics of their jobs and if necessary also of their freedom. In these circumstances it is not perhaps surprising that the Soviet system, its democratic credentials notwithstanding, has tended in practice to operate in an authoritarian and sometimes in a repressive manner.

Eastern Europe: human rights in a changing context

A great deal of what has been written above about the Soviet Union applies to Eastern Europe also, at least in broad outline. Details differ, sometimes significantly. In essence, all the East European countries have accepted the Soviet doctrine, which is inherent in Marxism–Leninism, that the state must make itself responsible for the continuous redistribution of resources, and that the balance between collective consumption and individual consumption must be shifted towards the former. Equally, individual rights are regarded as subordinate to collective rights as interpreted and allocated by the party.

This is not only theory; much of it has been implemented. In a number of important areas, again paralleling Soviet practice, resources have been made available to provide access for the mass of the population to housing, employment, education, transport, health care and related fields (see also Chapter 7). The consequence of this is that individual choice, which is much more highly regarded in the West, tends to be regarded as of lesser importance. This applies above all to the political sphere, where the rights of the individual are very often ignored and made subject to what is regarded as the collective good. It should be noted, as pointed out in Chapter 2, that this model of state and social organisation has its origins in the pre-communist period, and that on the whole the individual's expectations of the state, for historical and other reasons, are often much greater in Eastern Europe than in the West, especially the USA.

However, changes in the field of human rights have taken place in Eastern Europe since the advent of communist power, and the general trend has been towards the recognition of individual rights. Equally, this is something that society itself appears to prefer. Furthermore, it should be noted that in this sphere too, as in the other areas already dealt with, changes regarding human rights depend on the weakness or strength of party control at any one time. Thus during the Stalinist period, to take the extreme end of the spectrum, the state expected the individual not merely to be loyal but to demonstrate his loyalty actively, by participating in enforced rituals, for example. In terms of human rights, the withdrawal of state control over the individual's private life in subsequent years may be seen as a major gain.

One final general point about human rights deserves exploration. If human rights as a principle is fundamentally about the right to choose, the way in which individuals wish to exercise this choice is not something fixed permanently. Rather, it is conditioned by expectations in a given situation and that, in turn, is dependent upon experience – both collective and individual – and the historical context in which a society has developed. This has predictably led to wide variations from country to country. In some countries, Bulgaria for instance, there appears to be very little demand for the extension of individual rights, although that does not in itself preclude future developments in that direction. By contrast, in Poland in 1980 and after there was clear evidence of the opposite trend.

Law and the courts

The Western doctrine of the rule of law, that justice should be administered independently of political considerations and that all citizens should be equal before the law, is rejected in the East European states, as it is in the Soviet Union. Nevertheless, there has been an appreciable trend in the de-Stalinisation period for the slow evolution of a 'depoliticised' system of the law. Communist jurists have come to see that society benefits from the consistent application of rules and that large areas of legal regulation by the courts do not impinge in any serious way upon the principles of Marxism–Leninism. In fact, the stated objective of 'the construction of socialism' can actually derive benefits from reliability and routine in the practice of the courts.

Essentially three areas of conflict regulated by the courts may be distinguished. In cases of one citizen against another, e.g. in defamation cases, the interest of the state is to uphold order. There is no obvious 'class' interest involved. In the second area, where different state institutions are in disagreement, as when one enterprise may sue another for breach of contract, the interest of the state will generally be to determine the overall, societal interest, and in such cases informal intervention in the work of the courts cannot be ruled out. However, it is in the third area, where the state itself is in conflict with a citizen, that the most serious distortions and illegalities can occur. Here again, a distinction must be made between routine cases and what might be termed 'extraordinary' cases. In the normal administration of criminal justice––murder, robbery, rape, arson – there will in fact be little difference between communist and Western procedures, although criminal procedure in the communist world owes much more to the Continental civil law systems than to the Anglo-American tradition. In other possible conflicts between the state and a citizen, such as a compulsory purchase order by a municipality which is contested by a citizen, the courts may well decide to look at the case on its merits and not automatically award it to the state institution concerned. In more controversial cases involving major state or party interests, however, the courts will be most unlikely to find for the individual citizen concerned.

The demand by society for the independence of the law from political considerations was demonstrated very strongly during the Czechoslovak reform movement in 1968. Virtually from the outset demands were made for the full rehabilitation of the victims of Stalinism and the accused in the show trials, and consonant with the traditions of the country's jurisprudence the rehabilitations were carried out according to a clear and prescribed procedure. Sentences were annulled, even posthumously, and were done so after the facts of the case were re-examined.

A similar reliance on the law against the state was to be found in the move by the independent trade union Solidarity in Poland to gain regular legal status by registration as an officially recognised and properly constituted body. Although the political existence of Solidarity had been settled by the Gdańsk agreement of 31 August 1980, its leaders considered it necessary to provide for a proper legal basis for its existence. The fate of this application illustrated the limits of the autonomy of the Polish courts. At the first hearing, the Warsaw District Court insisted on inserting provisions into the statutes of Solidarity that would have subordinated it to the leading role of the party. Solidarity rejected this move, which was self-evidently the result of party interference in the work of the court, and returned to the political arena to validate its claim by threatening a general strike. At that the Polish leadership gave way and Solidarity statutes were registered in unamended form on appeal to the Supreme Court.

This example points to an enduring feature of the East European tradition – legalism. Many, though not all, of the countries concerned had well established traditions of judicial procedures and legal professions in their pre-communist period. This tradition was certainly one of the strands in the emergence of what has come to be known as the human rights opposition in the 1970s. An important instrument in the armoury of the opposition, again paralleling Soviet trends, was to insist that the authorities abide by their own codes of laws. Arbitrary action by the state, on whatever pretext, was rejected as unacceptable, and the opposition demanded conformity and the equality of all, state and individual, before the law.

Charter 77 in Czechoslovakia, for instance, is widely regarded as a political document and its implications are of course political. But its framers devised it deliberately with the aim of keeping within the framework of Czechoslovak legislation and denied its political nature. The opening passage of the Charter attests to this:

Law no. 120, which was enacted on 13 October 1976, incorporates the International Convention on Civil and Political Rights and the International Convention on

Economic, Social and Cultural Rights, both signed on behalf of the Republic in 1968 and confirmed at the Helsinki Conference in 1975, into our legal system. These Conventions came into force in the Republic on 23 March 1976.

There are numerous other instances of this legalistic approach to politics and the question of human rights in the 1970s and 1980s, not only in Czechoslovakia but also in Poland, the GDR, Hungary and even Romania.

From the authorities' point of view these contentions by the opposition are unacceptable, because they strike at one of the fundamentals of the party's political monopoly. There cannot be any independent justice so far as the party is concerned, hence the demands that the law be administered in a 'revolutionary' or 'class' spirit, of which the party is the sole legitimate interpreter. As a result oppositional demands, though couched in legalistic terms, inevitably bring their proponents into the political arena.

The right to free expression

One important branch of human rights is the right of the individual and of groups in society to express their views with reasonable freedom. In this area the communist states have tended to be restrictive. This is explained partly by the myth of unanimity regarded by communist parties as a vital instrument of legitimation, something which is perfectly logical when a political organisation claims to possess a monopoly of truth derived from Marxism–Leninism. The state in Eastern Europe accordingly retains control over newsprint and printing presses, and over the actual content of what is published by censorship. In practice some exceptions are made to this monopoly, and religious organisations, for example, are permitted to issue their own newspapers, journals and books, although under the customary censorship rules. The only major breaches in this system, however, have come about in periods of weak party control.

Censorship is exercised in two broad ways and the two can overlap. In some countries, notably Poland and Czechoslovakia, there is a formally constituted censor's office which inspects all published material, passes it as fit and has the right to insist on deletions. The basis on which the Polish censor exercises his power has become known through the defection of an employee from the local censor's office in Cracow, who took a vast sheaf of instructions with him. These provide a unique insight into the workings of censorship and more broadly into the way in which the party wishes reality to be presented.

The topics regarded by the party as subject to censorship, it was found, included a number of different categories. There were subjects which were taboo and could not be mentioned at all (the Katyń massacre, where 5000 Polish officers were shot by the Soviet secret police in 1940, was an example); subjects which could only be referred to by a set formula; politically sensitive topics, where current events or ideology were involved; and subjects where allusions might evoke undesirable reactions in the reader. The instructions were remarkably detailed in this respect:

> It is necessary to eliminate information about the direct danger to human life and health caused by industry and chemicals used in agriculture;
>
> No information should be published about the disaster at Katowice in which four miners were killed;
>
> In School No. 80 in Gdańsk, a harmful substance emitted by the putty used to seal the windows caused the temporary closure of the school. No information whatsoever should be published;
>
> There should be no mention of Poland's meat exports to the Soviet Union;
>
> No material should be released about the demolition in Wrocław of the St Clara mills, which were of great historic interest.

As part of the Polish renewal of 1980 and after, a new consorship law was worked out with the aim of liberalising the media and permitting greater freedom of information and debate.

In Hungary there is at present no formal censorship as such. Instead a subtle form of self-censorship operates, where newspaper and journal editors, working in collaboration with the appropriate Central Committee department, control what can appear. The system is informal and relies to a large extent on blackmail – an individual might be told that his article was excellent but politically somewhat sensitive, for instance, so that he could surely see that it would be preferable to publish it at some other time. In Czechoslovakia, on the other hand, the post-1969 regime has instituted an extremely strict censorship regime under which books by banned authors are removed from libraries and shops, the authors in question can never be mentioned in print, let alone have their works published, and the degree of variation from paper to paper is fairly minimal.

In Romania and Albania, to give two further examples, the propagandist rather than the informational role of the press has dominated. In the former, it is a rare day when President Ceauşescu does not make the front page of all the papers with a speech or a public appearance. The Albanian press for its part has acquired a reputation for lengthy and often fearsomely polemical articles.

Some differentiation in press policies has taken place in Eastern Europe as a natural consequence of the differing interpretations of the leading role of the party (see Chapter 4). With the exception of the Albanians, East European parties have tended to acquiesce in the proposition that a measure of openness in debating technical subjects is of value. On occasion these technical subjects can have serious political implications, for instance on questions like regional development or housing policy, both of them concerned with the way in which resources are allocated and, therefore, involving conflicting interests. As a general rule, the more obscure a journal is and the smaller its readership, the more easily it can print only minimally censored material. Part of the process of self-censorship and an important feature of political communication in Eastern Europe has been the ability to camouflage material so as to give it an outwardly orthodox appearance. Controversial proposals or arguments can be dressed up in Marxist jargon and published, sometimes with the connivance of the party, and sometimes despite the censor.

A further role played by the press in East European states is what has been called its 'ombudsman' function, the taking up of instances of abuses and giving them publicity. The publicity can then persuade those responsible to introduce a remedy. The emphasis here has been on single instances and individual cases, rather than general criticism of the way in which the system functions. It is very rare for criticism of this kind to go beyond the middle level of the administration – the manager of a large enterprise might be called to account, for instance, but officials in the branch ministry above him would not.

The response on the part of a section of society to this all-persuasive control of the written word by the state has been *samizdat*. It was noteworthy that throughout Eastern Europe, despite traditions of antagonism towards the Soviet Union, it was the Russian word that gained currency. The evolution of *samizdat* in Eastern Europe postdated the Soviet Union by several years; there was virtually none in the 1960s. But by the early 1970s, a small number of Czech opposition activists began to circulate uncensored material in this way. With the launching of Charter 77 in 1977 the activity expanded enormously and, most significantly, it branched out directly into the political field on a large scale. There had, of course, been semi-political, literary, historical and sociological works in circulation before the Charter, but it gave such activities a new focus and a political purposiveness.

This political purpose was to breach the party's monopoly of information and thereby to undermine an important aspect of the leading role of the party by signalling that society had the right to engage in lateral or horizontal communication without direct control from above. By pooling information in this way, the Chartists hoped to strengthen their movement and to raise the awareness of the rest of society about injustices and the nature of the regime. *Samizdat* had another, more ambitious aim. This was to persuade or constrain the authorities to engage in a dialogue with society, in other words to impel the party to redefine its leading role away from monopoly and towards pluralism. In this aim the *samizdat* movements largely failed.

Poland became the centre of extremely extensive unofficial publication of this kind. By 1980, when looser censorship made the need for *samizdat* less pressing, it was estimated that something like forty publications were appearing on a regular basis, weekly or monthly. The editors of one of these *samizdat* journals, *Opinia*, formally announced in the publication that the editorial offices were open at certain times and that the editors would be pleased to receive personal callers at those times. The explosion of *samizdat* activity in Poland in the late 1970s attested to another striking feature of Polish society – the very wide variety of political currents that existed. These spanned the spectrum from left-wing socialists through liberals and Christian democrats to right-wing nationalists. The imposition of martial law in 1981 resulted in a brief initial gap in the output of uncensored material, but over time this increased vigorously and by the mid-1980s a vast number of more or less regular *samizdat* publications, books as well as journals, were in circulation. They represented the very broad spectrum of opinion in the underground.

There has been rather less *samizdat* activity in the GDR and comparatively little of it has been political. Instead, literature has tended to dominate. The directly political material has consisted mainly of rather theoretical analyses of society, like Rudolf Bahro's *The Alternative in Eastern Europe*, published in West Germany in 1977, or the writings of Robert Havemann, a very senior opposition figure, who fell out with the party in the early 1960s over his demands for the introduction of genuine democracy. There are two aspects to East German activity in this area which distinguishes it from other countries. In the first place, because of the accessibility of West German television and radio (three-quarters of the East German population can watch West German television), the need to circulate material unofficially is not so great – it is generally enough to pass it to West German journalists. Secondly, the East German intelligentsia has remained committed to Marxism, even if they reject the version espoused by the party; this has brought dissidents somewhat closer to the party and has tended to inhibit the formation of genuine opposition groups comparable to Charter 77 or its equivalents in Poland.

The Hungarian opposition began to circulate *samizdat* in 1977, but for a while restricted itself to theoretical discussions of possible political alternatives, for the most part of interest only to other nonconformist members of the intelligentsia. However, after martial law in Poland, which came as a severe shock to the Hungarian opposition, a regrouping was launched with a more directly political aim. In 1986, a group centred on the *samizdat* journal *A Demokrata* (The Democrat) went so far as to issue a political programme, thereby directly challenging the party. The quantity of *samizdat* increased steadily at this time and included several regular journals. In Romania *samizdat* has been confined to protests from neo-Protestant groups like the Baptists and to the Hungarian minority seeking to call attention to national discrimination. In Bulgaria, apart from the odd document, much of it originating from national minorities (Turks, Macedonians, or Pomaks – Bulgarian Muslims), there has been little evidence so far of significant activity.

Yugoslavia is a different case mainly because the party has interpreted its monopoly more liberally. For example, while under conditions of normal party rule in Eastern Europe the reporting of stoppages of work, i.e. strikes, is taboo, in Yugoslavia these have regularly been reported from the 1960s onwards; indeed, monographs have been published on the subject. In other words, the party-controlled press has been able to satisfy the aspirations of society sufficiently to pre-empt any large-scale *samizdat* activity. This picture began to change somewhat around 1979–80, when protests against politically motivated discrimination began to surface. The authorities responded to this with greater harshness than might have been expected and strict measures were taken to prevent the spread of regular *samizdat* activity. The attitude of the Yugoslav authorities in this respect appears to be that the state provides sufficient latitude to satisfy the legitimate needs of self-expression and that no challenges to the party's decisions in this and other areas should be permitted. Publications which have questioned the leading role of the party, in particular, have been suppressed: during the 1971 Croatian national upsurge, for instance, the weekly paper of the cultural society Matica Hrvatska called *Hrvatski Tjednik* began to assume the role of an oppositional organ, and was banned along with other manifestations of the national

movement. When the authorities concluded that the philo-
sophical Marxist journal *Praxis* had overstepped the limits of
the permissible, it too was forced to cease publication.

Freedom of association and assembly

The doctrine of the leading role of the party automatically
reserves the right of association to the party. Attempts to
breach this have generally met with the suppression. Indeed,
party officials will often keep a wary eye on regular informal
meetings which begin to acquire the character of a grouping.
All legally recognised organisations, regardless of their aims,
must submit to party control in some form or another. It was
one of the complaints made public during the Prague Spring
that even angling clubs had to be run in accordance with the
party's leading role. Under normal conditions, the party
ensures that all social organisations are inside the framework
of the state, usually ensured by the requirement of registration with the National Front (or its equivalent), and
registration will be denied if there is any reason to suppose
that the organisation in question has aims at variance with
party policy. On the other hand, the range of organisations
which are accepted can often be wide and can provide
genuine facilities for their members. These range from cultural bodies, like the writers' union or musicians' association,
to veterans' organisations and sporting associations.

In periods of weak party control, groups in society will
generally attempt to exercise the right of association and will
seek to do so within the existing legal framework. In Czechoslovakia in 1968, two such groups with semi-political goals
came to the fore and attracted the condemnation of the
Soviet authorities. One of these was K231, the club of those
sentenced during the Stalinist period under Article 231 of the
Criminal Code, which had the aim of protecting the interests
of the victims of Stalinist persecution. Even more controversial was KAN (*Klub Angažovaných Nestraníků*), the Club of
Committed Non-Party People, which aimed to provide an
organisational focus of political activity for individuals who
did not wish to join the communist party. Neither Club was in
fact accepted for registration under the National Front.

An alternative to founding new associations during periods of weak party control was to take over existing bodies and transform them with a new set of aims. This was evidently what happened to the Matica Hrvatska, a venerable cultural institution set up in the nineteenth century. During the Croatian crisis of 1971, as we have noted, the Matica emerged as a strong challenger to the leading role of the Croatian party and something of a threat to its monopoly of power. It was eventually suppressed in the recentralisation of 1972. A parallel case was the use made of the Polish veterans' organisation, known by its Polish acronym of ZBoWiD (*Związek Bojowników o Wolność i Demokracje*), by the nationalist, anti-Semitic Minister of the Interior, Mieczysław Moczar, during the Polish crisis of 1968. ZBoWiD offered Moczar and his faction, known appropriately as the Partisans, a mass base for criticising the existing party leadership and they were able to mount a serious challenge to Gomułka.

Much more publicity has been attracted by the completely unofficial groups that were organised without permission and in direct opposition to the party in Poland, Czechoslovakia and Hungary in the late 1970s and early 1980s. In Poland, a group of intellectuals founded a Committee for the Defence of the Workers, KOR (*Komitet Obrony Robotników*), after the repression that followed the workers' demonstrations in 1976. KOR's initial objective was to collect money for the dependants of arrested workers and to help with legal advice. Subsequently KOR redefined its aims to include the defence of all groups in society threatened by the state. It renamed itself KSS (*Komitet Samoobrony Spolecznej*) and set out to act on a permanent basis. It was joined by numerous other unofficial organisations, notably ROPCiO (*Ruch Obrony Praw Człowieka i Obywatela*), a liberal–democratic Movement for the Defence of Human and Civil Rights, and by the study group known as 'Experience and Future' (DiP – *Doświadczenie i Przysłość*). The interesting feature of DiP was that it began life in 1978 as an informal brains trust under the aegis of the party, but when its advice proved too critical to be acceptable to the party leadership its members moved into the grey area between toleration and illegality to produce a series of analyses of Polish society and of how its ills should be remedied.

Solidarity was, in fact, the most solidly grounded and effective social organisation to emerge in any East European country. Its structure and aims were difficult to interpret by purely Western political criteria, for Solidarity was obviously a child of its own political environment. This was why it was variously described as a social movement, a trade union, a political movement or interest articulation organisation. It was up to a point all of these. Furthermore, Solidarity changed during the 16 months of its existence and underwent a degree of politicisation as both it and the party jockeyed for power. Initially, its objectives were more clearly trade union and welfare goals than the set of ideas that were expressed in the Solidarity programme adopted at its congress in autumn 1981. This particular document was one of the most radical anti-étatist programmes to emerge from post-war Eastern Europe, and envisaged a Poland where the role of the party was reduced to little more than a benign supervisor of politics with the particular role of representing Poland *vis-à-vis* the Soviet Union. The values expressed by Solidarity strongly emphasised democratic election, accountability, equality, authenticity, and openness. Finally, both as an organisation and as the set of ideas underlying it, the strategies of Solidarity were predicated on a high degree of homogeneity – a belief that Polish society was markedly egalitarian in spirit, in structure and in beliefs. Ultimately, in this context, Polish Solidarity appeared to have adopted at least unconsciously the myth of social harmony which characterised the objectives of the communist party to which it was opposed.

In Czechoslovakia a Committee for the Defence of the Unjustly Persecuted (VONS) was created under the auspices of Charter 77 with the aim of chronicling the trials of dissidents, and a rather less well publicised body, the Committee for the Defence of the Legal Rights of the Hungarian Minority, came into existence in Slovakia. In Hungary itself no political group as such had emerged by 1981, but in 1980 a group of sociologists and others decided to establish the Foundation for the Support of the Poor (SzETA – *Szegényeket Támogató Alap*), with the purpose of collecting money for the needy in Hungary and giving legal advice to the socially disadvantaged in their dealings with the state.

It is in the provision of a cradle-to-grave system of social welfare that the communist states in fact claim to have made their greatest contribution to human rights. They have indeed succeeded in raising the living standards of the vast majority of the population above the subsistence level at which they had previously existed; but this does not mean that poverty has been eliminated, and evidence from several of the Eastern European countries shows that a significant proportion of the population have difficulty in providing for their daily needs. In Hungary about 30 per cent of the population is estimated to be in this position – hence the activities of SzETA – and in Poland data released in 1980 indicated that a similar proportion of the population were affected. Variations in social mobility and health care as between different social groups have also persisted into the communist period; so far as social mobility is concerned, in fact, inequalities may have widened during the 1970s and 1980s, as the intelligentsia have been increasingly successful in monopolising opportunities for their own children through education at the expense of children of working-class or peasant origin.

Closely linked with the question of association is the question of the right of assembly. In the Stalinist period the state itself required large numbers of people to take part in regular mass rituals such as the official demonstrations marking 1 May. With the onset of de-Stalinisation this form of mobilisation was abandoned (except in Albania and Romania), and individuals nowadays no longer have to turn out in their thousands on such occasions. However, there have also been several occasions when the initiative for such demonstrations, with a similarly ritualistic quality, has come from below. The funerals of real or supposed opponents of the party have frequently been used in such a way and the role of the crowd in East European politics has more than once served as an indicator of the popular mood. In Hungary, for instance, just before the outbreak of the revolution of 1956 and in an obvious prelude to it, the funeral of László Rajk, the best known victim of the Stalinist terror, attracted a crowd of up to 300 000. And the revolution itself began with a vast demonstration on 23 October 1956 through the streets of Budapest.

Other cases of mass action include the funeral of one of the leaders of the Croatian national movement, Pero Pirker, in 1972 as a silent protest against the recentralisation being pursued by the party in Yugoslavia at that time; the symbolic lighting of candles on the grave of Thomas Masaryk, the Czechoslovak republic's founder-president and venerated by the population as a democrat, after 1969; and the unofficial celebration in 1978 of the founding of the Polish state (not observed by the party because of the anti-Soviet overtones of the rebirth of Poland in 1918). The self-immolation of Jan Palach in January 1969, in protest against the Soviet occupation of Czechoslovakia, was another, ultimate act of political opposition. There have also been occasions when non-political gatherings have been transformed into political protests by inept action on the part of the authorities. In October 1977, for instance, a pop concert in East Berlin turned into a riot when the police intervened to disperse the crowds following an incident; the pop fans misunderstood the situation and turned on the police, chanting anti-state and anti-Russian slogans.

Religion and the churches

The individual's freedom of conscience is technically guaranteed by the constitution in most of the Eastern European states as well as in the USSR, but there are wide variations from country to country. At one end of the spectrum, in Albania, religion is formally banned and individuals are punished for religious observance. There are reports in the Albanian press, none the less, indicating that many individuals continue to practise their religion covertly – one report complained that during Ramadan consumption in factory canteens had dropped as Moslems, about 70 per cent of the Albanian population, had kept the fast. At the other end of the spectrum is Poland where the Roman Catholic church is a national as well as a religious institution. Its organisational strength is considerable – a full hierarchy, a steady number of vocations, religious orders with some vitality, a network of clubs and a publishing house, as well as the ability to attract about three-quarters of the population to mass on a regular basis. One of the provisions of the Gdańsk agreement of August 1980 was to permit the broadcasting of mass on television – a unique dispensation in the communist world. After martial law, the Catholic Church gradually evolved a strategy of mixing accommodation with resistance to the state authorities. At no point did the Church hierarchy seek a direct confrontation and when threatened with this, as it was by the murder of the outspokenly pro-Solidarity priest Fr Jerzy Popiełuszko and the anti-Church campaign during the trial of his killers, it preferred to draw back from the brink. What the Church has achieved had been to create a viable alternative structure of cultural and welfare activities, which the state has tolerated or harassed only marginally. There is no question, however, that the authority of the Church as the authentic institution commanding the loyalty of most Poles has increased greatly.

In between these two extremes the strength of the various churches differs. In the GDR, an overwhelmingly Lutheran society, the church has adopted a position of 'critical solidarity' towards the party and the state, that is to say it accepts that the construction of socialism is a legitimate aim but reserves the right to express criticism of the manner in which the authorities attempt to achieve it. The authorities have generally ignored such criticism. In Czechoslovakia and Hungary, both Roman Catholic countries with strong Protestant minorities, the position of the churches tends to be rather weaker, as a result of official sanctions (in Czechoslovakia especially) and of secularisation. In Yugoslavia the Roman Catholic churches in Croatia and Slovenia have retained their vitality and regularly come into conflict with the authorities; but overall, a somewhat uneasy *modus vivendi* exists. In Eastern Orthodox societies such as Bulgaria the churches have never claimed the same degree of autonomy and by and large they have been integrated into the framework of the state.

As in the Soviet Union, the state in Eastern Europe has the right to promote anti-religious propaganda, whereas the right of the church to carry out religious education is often restricted in practice. As a general rule believers suffer discrimination, and particularly active individuals may be persecuted. There is a general policy throughout Eastern Europe, Poland to some extent excepted, that believers will not be admitted to higher education, and parents are often warned that they may jeopardise their children's chances in life if they insist on their receiving religious instruction.

Socialist legality, dissent and human rights in China

Like the other communist states discussed in this chapter, the People's Republic of China has conceived of human rights in collective rather than individual terms. In so far as the four state constitutions promulgated since 1949 have enshrined the rights enjoyed in 'bourgeois' democracies, these have regularly been negated by other constitutional provisions, by actual practice or, in some instances, by subsequent constitutional amendment. Thus in 1954 the Constitution stated that capitalists were entitled to own the means of production but subsequently asserted that capitalist ownership would 'gradually' be replaced by ownership by the whole people. Two years later the private sector of industry and commerce was nationalised. The 1975 Constitution guaranteed freedom of the press at a time when the leftist 'Gang of Four' had encased the media in an ideological straitjacket that was exceptional even by communist standards. In 1978 a new Constitution gave the Chinese masses the 'four big freedoms': 'speaking out freely, airing views fully, holding great debates and writing big-character posters'. Two years later, as a result of the 'Democracy Wall' phenomenon, it was decreed that this clause should be deleted. The present Constitution, introduced in 1982, stipulates that it is an offence to attempt to 'sabotage' socialism.

The PRC has, in fact, gone to great lengths to restrict personal choice and it is only since Mao's death that attempts to bring about liberalisation and to establish a reasonably effective system of 'socialist legality' have been instituted. Even so, the state still imposes strict limits on what is permissible and, as will be discussed below, treats with great severity those who overstep the mark.

One method of enforcing conformity has been through ideological control. In common with other communist states the PRC created a massive system of censorship and propaganda. The management of news (with the provision of a variety of 'restricted' bulletins and journals for the elite); the re-writing of history; and the doctoring of photographs to remove all evidence that a disgraced leader was even present on a particular occasion are all too reminiscent of George Orwell's *1984*. Much attention has also been devoted to 'ideological reform' and to 'criticism' and 'self-criticism' in group sessions, where psychological techniques are used to break down a transgressor's resistance and so compel him or her to affirm or renew commitment to the party's goals.

The state has also used a considerable amount of coercion. In the early 1950s a series of mass campaigns were used to destroy the power of 'counter-revolutionaries', 'rural despots' and other enemies of society, many of whom were executed. Those who survived were sentenced to 'reform through labour' and, along with their families, were classified as 'bad elements'. Even after their release such individuals were deprived of political rights, confined to menial occupations, remained under what was in effect a system of permanent probation and, at times of mass mobilisation, were likely to be harassed and humiliated as 'negative examples'.

From 1954 to 1966 a legal system of sorts developed and over 1 100 statutes and decrees were promulgated to add to the handful of very wide-ranging, vague, and highly politicised directives of the early years. But, despite valiant attempts by a few party leaders and legal specialists to establish a modicum of 'socialist legality' in the mid-1950s, it was the public security (police) organs which dominated the legal system. They were responsible for the maintenance of public order; the investigation, arrest and detention of suspects; and the administration of the prisons and 'Reform Through Labour' camps. Although prosecution was supposedly the function of separate procuratorial organs, these tended to be subordinate to the police. Similarly the courts were not so much concerned with determining guilt or innocence, but rather 'educational' institutions which publicised the crimes of the guilty as a warning to others. Indeed, the police possessed legal powers in some instances to imprison offenders without the formality of a trial. Moreover, as sentences were virtually open-ended in that they could be shortened or lengthened in the light of a prisoner's willingness to 'reform', the police had considerable discretion to recommend parole or an extension of the sentence.

Furthermore, the police had considerable powers to control the lives of ordinary citizens. Every household was required to keep a registration book of those domiciled within it, travel was difficult without police permission, and itinerants had to register with the local police on arrival at their destination. And while the size of the public security forces was not exceptionally large, they were assisted by a network of semi-official 'informers'. In imperial China there had been an ancient tradition of mutual surveillance and this reappeared in the form of residents' committees, Youth League branches and other mass organisations which, *inter alia*, made it their business to keep a watchful eye on unlawful or unseemly behaviour. The right to privacy was certainly not one which Chinese citizens enjoyed.

Thus Chinese society before the Cultural Revolution was well-policed in the sense that 'deviant' behaviour could be quickly identified and dealt with. Chinese justice was not, however, as arbitrary as this account might suggest for the system did contain a measure of predictability. For example, people of 'bad' class background like ex-landlords and 'counter-revolutionaries' were well aware that they would suffer more for making 'political' criticisms than would poor peasants or workers. Conversely, party cadres knew that their sins would be punished more leniently if they made a full confession, 'achieved merit' by implicating others, or manifested 'repentance'. There is evidence that many policemen took their job seriously, went to considerable pains to collect and sift evidence, and usually only arrested someone after they had built up a solid case.

The Cultural Revolution, however, destroyed these developing conventions. The legal organs themselves were early victims of the Left's determination to drag out 'capitalist roaders'. In 1967 especially Leftist factions 'seized power' by invading and ransacking police stations and court buildings, and by beating, torturing and imprisoning police and legal officials who, by their training, were assumed to be on the side of established authority and were therefore easy targets for the 'rebels'. In one province alone it was later claimed that 281 police stations were sacked, over 100 000 dossiers were stolen, and large quantities of guns and ammunition were seized. Throughout 1967 and 1968 legal institutions virtually ceased to function and mob rule was the order of the day throughout much of urban China. Rival factions battled for supremacy, sought revenge for real or imagined grievances, and acted with massive violence. Hundreds of thousands of cadres, ranging from Liu Shaoqi, Chairman of the People's Republic, down to minor officials, were attacked and many were paraded before kangaroo courts of Red Guard activists where they were abused, tormented and sometimes tortured as a prelude to being thrown into prison or labour camp. There many of them were to remain until the late 1970s. And, for a considerable number, their eventual rehabilitation had to be posthumous.

In some areas factions even set up their own private prisons. At the Tianjin Soda Works, for example, a prison was set up where, it was later claimed, 'ruffians' used torture to extract confessions from 'leading cadres and the broad masses' who were held in illegal custody for long periods. In 1970, when outrage was mounting, the person responsible found a simple but effective means of suppressing it. He issued a directive making it an offence to comment on the prison's existence. In Beijing 56 children of senior government officials were arrested and put in what was euphemistically called a 'study class' but was, in fact, an unofficial prison. Seventy per cent of them were 20, one was only 14, and some were held there for five years. They were worked hard, ill-treated and forced to write lengthy reports on their parents' alleged crimes.

The reaffirmation of socialist legality

Following the death of Mao and the arrest of the 'Gang of Four', China experienced a massive display of revulsion against the anarchism and brutality of the Cultural Revolution period. From the beginning of 1977 the leadership began a lengthy process of investigation which resulted in the reversal of verdicts on literally hundreds of thousands of people who had suffered unjust punishments ranging from death to demotion in that movement. As the horrifying evidence of lawlessness mounted, the leadership began to stress that such injustices must never happen again. Although primarily motivated by a recognition of the human costs of the Cultural Revolution, the leadership was also conscious of the enormous damage it had done to the economy. Hence the need to restore work discipline and managerial authority by the provision of appropriate rules and regulations was a contributory factor in the demands for the creation of an effective legal system. By 1978 discussions were being carried on at the highest levels, and in the summer of 1979 the Second Session of the Fifth National People's Congress approved a series of laws to serve as a basis for a new legality.

The most important of these was a new Criminal Law which came into effect on 1 January 1980. Although a number of its provisions had appeared in earlier legislation this was the first criminal code ever published in the PRC, and its great merit was to bring together in one relatively short document the major categories of criminal offence and the range of penalties they were likely to attract. An offence was broadly defined as 'any action which endangers state sovereignty and territorial integrity, jeopardises the dictatorship of the proletariat, sabotages socialist revolution and socialist construction, disrupts public order, encroaches upon the property of the whole people, the collective or legitimate private property, infringes upon the personal, democratic and other rights of citizens, or any other action which endangers society and is punishable by law'. Punishment could be given to anyone of sixteen or over, and of sound mind.

Offences were categorised under eight headings. Twenty-four articles dealt with 'counter-revolutionary' crimes. These included plotting to overthrow the government, leading armed rebellions and destroying military installations. But it was also an offence to use 'counter revolutionary slogans . . . to spread propaganda inciting the overthrow of the political power of the dictatorship of the proletariat and the socialist system'. A further eleven articles dealt with 'violations of public security' and related primarily to arson and sabotage likely to endanger life and limb and public property. 'Acts against the socialist economic order' were the subject of fifteen articles dealing with smuggling, forgery, profiteering and speculation.

Nineteen articles covered acts against citizens' personal and democratic rights. These included such 'ordinary' crimes as murder, manslaughter, rape, assault and battery, but also made special mention of offences which became common in the Cultural Revolution. Thus penalties were laid down for extracting confessions by torture; gathering a crowd for 'beating, smashing and looting'; bringing false charges; unlawfully incarcerating a person; and 'seriously insulting' a person by any means, including the use of walllposters to spread libels. 'Encroachments on property' were dealt with in seven articles covering the stealing of private or public property, and embezzlement. The Law then gave attention to 'acts against public order', with twenty-two articles covering a splendid diversity of offences. These included obstructing an official in the performance of his duties; impersonating an official; 'practising witchcraft for the purpose of spreading rumours or swindling people'; being a professional gambler or organiser of gambling; selling obscene books or pictures for profit; manufacturing or selling narcotics; and assembling a crowd to disturb public order in such public places as stations, wharfs, airports, stores and parks. Interestingly, illegal emigration (covered in this section) merited only one year's imprisonment and those organising such traffic were to receive no more than five years.

Six articles covered 'acts against marriage and the family'. These included forcing people to marry against their will, committing bigamy and (an interesting footnote on the influence of the People's Liberation Army in Chinese politics) cohabiting with the spouse of a soldier. 'Vile cases' of failing to look after elderly or sick family members were also criminal offences. Finally, the Law laid down penalties for state functionaries who abused their positions by taking bribes, showing favouritism or practising nepotism, as well as those who opened other people's mail 'without permission'.

In all cases the appropriate punishments were stipulated. In order of ascending degrees of unpleasantness these were:

Surveillance – essentially a form of probation, not to exceed two years.
Detention – imprisonment by the local police force for not more than six months, during which time the offender was allowed to return home for two days a month, and was to be paid for work done under police supervision.
Fixed term or life imprisonment – to be served in prison or labour camps.
Death penalty – by firing squad. However, the law followed earlier statutes in insisting that this was only to be used for the most heinous offences and, moreover, that the penalty should often be deferred for two years, during which time the offender would be imprisoned and given the opportunity to show if he or she had 'reformed'. In this case the sentence might be commuted to imprisonment for life or for a shorter period.

The Law also provided for 'supplementary' penalties, the most notable of which were confiscation of property, fines, and deprivation of political rights. It also echoed earlier enactments (and, indeed, ancient Chinese ideas on legal matters) by stressing that mercy should be shown to those who showed contrition. Voluntary surrender, confession and the achievement of merit by implicating fellow offenders were to be rewarded by reduced punishment. And even in gaol not all was lost – 'good behaviour' could result in early parole.

The Law, then, gave the citizen a reasonably clear picture as to what was forbidden, and the penalties the transgressor was likely to incur. On most of the criminal offences of a 'universal' nature (i.e. murder, theft, rape, arson, etc.), it was fairly specific. To be sure, it continued the principle of 'crime by analogy' laid down in earlier enactments in that a person could be punished for an offence not specified in the Law, which 'approximated' to one which was. But in such cases, the Supreme People's Court was to pronounce on the desirability or otherwise of such a move. For the most part, then, it constituted a 'Good Citizen's Guide to Keeping Out of Trouble', and it was reinforced by a Law on Criminal

Procedure, adopted at the same time. Indeed, this second Law was of especial importance in that it made meticulous arrangements for the handling of criminal cases, and carefully defined the rights and responsibilities of the legal organs and those accused.

Thus it distinguished between the functions of the three branches of the legal apparatus. The police were to investigate and detain suspects. The Procuratorate was to approve arrests, check on police investigations and, where appropriate, institute prosecution. The People's Courts were to try cases. 'No other government organ, institution, organisation or person has the right to exercise such powers.' It was laid down that in minor cases, where a private individual filed a suit, a court could handle the matter on its own initiative. In cases of corruption or 'dereliction of duty' the Procuratorate could choose to prosecute independently; otherwise the police should take the initiative. The Law carefully specified the sorts of cases which were to be tried at different levels, and laid down stipulations as to when legal officials should withdraw from a case (if they were interested parties, if their relatives were involved, and so forth).

It also emphasised that the accused was entitled to defence by him or herself, by a lawyer, by someone appointed by a mass organisation or work unit, by a relative or by a guardian. The court might appoint an advocate for someone who had failed to do so himself. The accused or his advocate had the right to see the material pertaining to the case, witnesses had to be available for examination, and no one could be convicted on the basis of a statement unsupported by other evidence. The Law also made careful provision for those who might help the police with their enquiries. Criminals caught in, before or immediately after the act, together with 'major suspects', could be arrested by anyone, as could escaped prisoners and those on 'wanted' lists. Otherwise the police were required to produce a warrant from the Procuratorate. After arrest, a detainee's family was normally to be informed within twenty-four hours. Moreover, the police were to ask the Procuratorate to examine and approve the arrest within three days. The Law also stipulated the time in which the accused should normally be brought to trial, and laid down detailed regulations governing delays in so doing. It also stipulated that trials should be public (except where state secrets were involved or where the innocent might suffer unnecessary embarrassment), and that there were to be proper appeal procedures. Further laws were also enacted in 1979 governing, *inter alia*, the organisation of the courts and the Procuratorate.

In the 1980s, the Chinese leadership has continued to insist on the maintenance and extension of the legal system, including the provision of legal education programmes for those who work in it and the general populace also. There has, however, been a partial move away from what were, by Chinese standards, the remarkably liberal laws outlined above. The hardening of official attitudes was due to increasing concern about the prevalence of 'white collar' crime stimulated partly, it was said, by the 'Open Door' policy, and crimes of violence. In 1983 a major crackdown was introduced and the laws were amended to increase the penalties for serious crime (including the extension of the list of offences meriting capital punishment) and to weaken somewhat the rights of the accused in order to speed up procedures for handling and disposing of serious cases. In the same year policing was reorganised with the creation of a separate Ministry of State Security. A system of identification cards has also been introduced. It was subsequently claimed that between August 1983 and June 1985 the crime rate had dropped by 36.4 per cent compared with the two years before the crackdown. A notable consequence of this harsher attitude has been a significant rise in the number of executions. Where details are officially published these usually indicate crimes of great gravity, as in a case in Shanghai in February 1986 when four men who were the children of senior cadres had engaged in a series of multiple rapes. There is anecdotal evidence of some resurgence of a traditional Chinese preference for order rather than law, which has led to breaches of 'socialist legality', but at the time of writing it is not clear how serious this problem is.

Political dissidence in China

Criticisms of the political system in China have come from the left as well as the right. In the Cultural Revolution various groups of Red Guards and others produced radical critiques of an extreme nature and called for such changes as reorganising China along the lines of the famous Paris Commune of 1871. Although subsequently branded as 'ultra-leftists' it is difficult to characterise such people as 'dissidents' because they were operating in conditions of near-anarchy when leaders and policies changed with dramatic suddenness, and often believed themselves to be 'faithful followers of Chairman Mao' and of those close to him. This section focuses, therefore, on the two major occasions in the history of the PRC when ordinary citizens have pressed for the introduction of freedoms similar to those enjoyed in 'bourgeois' democracies.

The first took place in 1957, during the 'Hundred Flowers' campaign. This occurred in the aftermath of de-Stalinisation in the USSR and the Hungarian revolt of 1956, events which had a profound effect on Mao and which led him to believe that the socialist system could be strengthened by permitting a greater level of public criticism. Initially, he believed that his regime was based on broad popular support, and that calling for the expression of popular opinion would result in a large number of 'constructive' suggestions. In the event the leadership was taken aback by the response.

At a series of forums, intellectuals and members of the 'democratic parties' which had been allowed to exist in a 'united front' with the Chinese Communist Party after 1949 savagely attacked the party's monopoly of power. They demanded, among other things, such major ingredients of 'bourgeois' democracy as competitive elections, a free press, effective trade unions, academic freedom, and an independent judiciary. Badly shocked by this, the party declared that the 'Hundred Flowers' had become 'poisonous weeds' opposed to socialism, and an anti-Rightist campaign was launched which consigned hundreds of thousands to labour camps. Many remained there for ten or more years and, even when released, were badly treated because of their 'bad element' status. It was not until 1978–79 that it was officially admitted that there had been countless miscarriages of justice at this time.

The second major outbreak of dissent began in November

1978 and took its name from 'Democracy Wall' in central Beijing, where people congregated to put up wallposters and to express their grievances. The use of wallposters had, of course, long been common in China and had been particularly prevalent during the Cultural Revolution. In 1978, as we have seen, the writing of wallposters had been enshrined as a constitutional right. What really inspired the protesters, however, was the decision taken in November 1978 to 'rehabilitate' the Tienanmen incident of 5 April 1976. On that day a massive and largely spontaneous riot had taken place in Tienanmen Square in the centre of Beijing. It was sparked off by widespread resentment at the 'Gang of Four's' crude attempts to suppress demonstrations of mourning for Zhou Enlai, and the campaign of vilification they were then directing against Deng Xiaoping. The rioters set fire to a number of vehicles and a security station, and attacked some policemen and militiamen and persons believed to be leftists. For the best part of the day the rioters controlled the square, but they were dispersed in the evening when numerous arrests were made. It was then claimed that Deng Xiaoping had instigated this 'counter-revolutionary' incident and he was dismissed from his posts.

By November 1978, however, the 'Gang of Four' were in prison, Deng was back in power, and it was decreed that the Tienanmen incident (and similar ones which had occurred in other cities) had been 'completely revolutionary'. This was of great symbolic importance for it implied that 'the masses' had the right to make their views known, and to criticise their leaders. 'Democracy Walls' appeared in major cities, meetings were organised at what were actually referred to as 'Speakers' Corners', and various groups began to publish their own journals. Unlike *samizdat* literature these were openly sold and, in some cases, it was actually possible to take out subscriptions.

This phase of dissent differed significantly from dissident movements in the other communist states in that it did not have the support of leading intellectuals. China's greatest scientists and writers had already been recompensed for their suffering in the Cultural Revolution and, as discussed in Chapter 5, were being given exceptional freedom and responsibility in the interests of 'elite modernisation' policies. Nor was there any significant religious or ethnic element in the protests. It was, rather, a movement of 'little people' who had suffered in the Maoist era and who had not had their grievances redressed. A majority of those participating were concerned with single issues. Thus many people sought justice for wrongs done to themselves or their relatives. Groups of peasants travelled to Beijing and other cities to publicise their poverty. 'Educated youths' came to town to demand that they be allowed to return permanently to the cities; some of these 'youths' had actually been in the countryside for twenty years. In Shanghai, in February 1979, they organised a spectacular sit-in at the railway station, bringing the rail system to a halt until forcibly removed by the police.

Among the more 'political' disaffected elements many confined themselves to scribbling anonymous comments, such as 'I see the press is telling lies again', or 'Everyone talks of "democracy", but it just means we all shout our mouths off and nothing changes'. Some asked searching questions about Hua Guofeng's relations with the 'Gang of Four' and his role as Minister of Public Security at the time of the Tienanmen incident. Others unequivocally blamed Mao for the Cultural Revolution: 'Gang of Four or Gang of Five?'. The most detailed and serious criticisms were to be found in the unofficial journals which were generally produced by young people of 'middle class' families whose education had stopped during the Cultural Revolution and who were too old to resume it after Mao's death. Many had participated in the Red Guard movement and had eventually come to realise that their naive idealism had been simply manipulated by the elite. Their cynicism and sense of betrayal was heightened by the fact that they had tended to end up in relatively menial urban jobs with no great prospects for improvement.

Most of the activists who edited and wrote for unofficial journals wanted democratisation within a framework of socialism. They were not opposed to the party as such and, indeed, some were believed to have close ties with leaders like Deng Xiaoping, who initially tolerated 'Democracy Wall' because it suggested that there was considerable support for his faction in its struggle with that of Hua Guofeng which was far more reluctant to reject many aspects of Maoism. Sometimes the activists were simply ahead of their time in that they demanded changes the leadership was later to introduce. For example, the call for the party to reassess the role of Mao and admit his mistakes was answered in June 1981 when the sixth plenum of the Central Committee adopted a lengthy resolution doing just this. Demands for the dismissal of unpopular leaders like Wang Dongxing also found official favour, as did requests that Liu Shaoqi and other victims of the Cultural Revolution be rehabilitated. The numerous articles on the need for 'socialist legality' were also broadly in keeping with the way official thinking was moving.

But some 'Democracy Wall' writers were critical of Deng as well, and found little to praise in the communist system. The most famous of these was Wei Jingsheng. He came to the attention of the Western world as early as December 1978, and was promptly hailed as a 'leader' of the 'democracy movement', an image which probably exaggerated his importance and also suggested that the 'movement' was far more united than was in fact the case. A thirty-year-old electrician at Beijing Zoo, Wei was the son of a party cadre but had made the mistake of joining a Red Guard faction opposed to Jiang Qing, Mao's wife, and had suffered as a result. In 1978 he began to edit a journal called *Exploration*, and between December 1978 and March 1979 he contributed a number of articles of his own to it. These included a piece on conditions in a maximum security prison near Beijing (where allegedly, Mao's widow was confined), an examination of the circumstances surrounding the unlawful arrest and detention of another dissident, and an attack on Deng Xiaoping after the latter had said 'Democracy Wall' was 'going too far'.

His major statement, however, was a long essay which argued that 'Democracy is the Fifth Modernisation'. In this he scathingly attacked Mao and those people who refused to admit his mistakes and, instead, kept 'running to Democracy Wall to pat Mao on the arse'. He was no more sparing of the new leadership who had replaced faith in Mao with the equally superstitious catchphrase of the 'Four Modernisations' as the panacea for China's problems. He attacked Deng Xiaoping for having thanked Mao for restoring him to office in 1973, but for failing to thank the Chinese people whose efforts had brought him back again in 1977. The attention of his readers was drawn to their own poverty and their lack of rights, both of which were contrasted unfavourably with the situation in capitalist countries. He pointed out, for example, that in the latter it was possible to get rid of leaders the people disliked, mentioning former US president Nixon and former Japanese premier Tanaka as examples. He also challenged the official argument that, under socialism, respect for human rights was directed at the elimination of such social evils as poverty, prostitution and unemployment, affirming that all these existed in the PRC. His readers were urged to ignore the blandishments of the 'despots' who had simply replaced Mao, telling them to 'take control of their own lives' and 'ignore the lords in authority'. This, he implied, would mean struggle: 'Democracy has never developed by itself. It will require sacrifice.'

By March 1979 even Deng had become concerned that 'Democracy Wall' was getting out of hand, not least because participants were sometimes only too willing to share their grievances and criticisms with foreign journalists. In that month Wei was arrested and a general crackdown on dissent was instituted. As one directive put it, 'all slogans, posters, books, journals ... and other representations which oppose socialism, the dictatorship of the proletariat, the leadership of the CCP, Marxism–Leninism–Mao Zedong Thought ... are prohibited'. Steps were taken to curb contacts with foreigners. In October 1979, Wei was put on trial and was found guilty of passing 'military secrets' to foreigners (he had talked to journalists about China's invasion of Vietnam) and of spreading 'counter-revolutionary propaganda and agitation'. He defended himself stubbornly and was sentenced to fifteen years' imprisonment with a further three years' deprivation of political rights. It was widely believed that his failure to show contrition was the principal reason for his severe punishment. Thereafter the unofficial journals were suppressed, Beijing's 'Democracy Wall' was scrubbed clean and a small alternative was provided in an enclosed park where poster-pasters could put up their *signed* offerings under the watchful eye of the police. Finally, in February 1980, a party plenum gravely decreed that experience had shown that the 'four big free-doms' had 'never played a positive role in safeguarding the people's democratic rights' and that 'to help eliminate factors causing instability' the relevant article should be deleted from the Constitution.

At its height the 'Democracy Wall' movement probably embraced only two or three hundred activists and since its suppression there has been little indication of serious political dissent. An 'underground' literature is known to exist but appears to be on a very small scale. Also, in the early 1980s, the Chinese press carried occasional articles indicating that in some areas workers had been attracted by the example of 'Solidarity' in Poland and had pressed for the formation of independent trade unions. In late 1985 there were a series of student protests, including public demonstrations, directed against such diverse phenomena as food price rises, nepotism and corruption, and the unwillingness of military units to vacate university premises taken over in the Cultural Revolu-tion. Students also demonstrated against 'Japan's Second Invasion', meaning the influx of Japanese consumer goods and economic influence. Students from Xinjiang also pro-tested publicly about the use of their home area for nuclear testing and the application of strict population control to Muslims.

Such protests, however, have been mainly directed against specific policies rather than the political system itself and have been easily contained. It is possible that certain sections of the population, adversely affected by the reform policies of Deng Xiaoping, might be inclined to express their grievances outside the formal channels in the future. Nevertheless, there is little evidence to date to suggest that the mass of Chinese people conceive of human rights in the Western sense, and political dissenters have not generally played the same role in China that they have played in the other communist states considered in this chapter.

Further reading

There are several worthwhile treatments of the questions of

democracy and human rights with which this chapter is concerned: see for instance Macpherson (1972), Miliband (1977), Lively (1975), Pennock (1979), Macfarlane (1985) and Sartori (1986). On the Soviet theory of democracy more particularly, see Churchward (1975, ch. 17) and Krutogolov (1980). On the Soviet legal system, see Butler (1983a) and also Barry and Berman, 'The jurists', in Skilling and Griffiths (1971), and Barry *et al.* (1977–79). The RSFSR Criminal Code is translated in Berman and Spindler (1972) and is reprinted together with other legal codes and documents in Simons (1980b) and Butler (1983b). On religious and political dissent, see Tőkés (1975), Feldbrugge (1975), Amnesty International (1980), Shatz (1981), Reddaway (1983) and Minority Rights Group (1984).

On human rights in Eastern Europe, two works edited by Rudolf Tőkés are useful general surveys (Tőkés 1978 and 1979). See also Curry (1983), a more recent overview. Opposition movements in the various countries are analysed in Kusin (1978), Riese (1979) and Havel *et al.* (1985), which deal with Czechoslovakia; Woods (1986), which deals with the GDR; Ostoja-Ostaszewski *et al.* (1977) and Lipski (1985), which deal with Poland; and Sher (1977), which deals with Yugoslavia. On Solidarity in Poland, see Staniszkis (1984), an interpretive work by a Polish sociologist, Ash (1985), an account by a well-informed Western journalist, and Ruane (1982), a good general introduction with extensive quotations from contemporary sources. Mason (1985) considers the movement of Polish public opinion during this period. Up to date information may be found in the journals *Labour Focus on Eastern Europe* and *Index on Censorship*, both published in London; the latter is an invaluable source on all questions of censorship, unofficial literature and *samizdat*. See also *East European Reporter* (London), which deals with Poland, Hungary and Czechoslovakia, and *Poland Watch* (Washington, DC), which gives detailed attention to the largest of these countries. On the media and censorship, see Lendvai (1981) and Schöpflin (1983); see also Robinson (1977) on Yugoslavia and Curry (1984), which gives a detailed inside picture of the operation of censorship in Poland. On religion, see Bociurkiw and Strong (1975) and Ramet (1984), and also the periodical

Religion in Communist Lands (London). Adelman (1984) provides a general study of the role of coercion.

A massive study covering major aspects of the legal system in China is Cohen (1968), which may be supplemented by Li (1970) and the same author's study of the police in a Chinese county in Lewis (1971). Ezra Vogel's 'Preserving order in the cities' in the same volume is also useful. Moody (1977) is helpful for the Maoist period. MacFarquhar (1960) covers the views of the 1957 critics, and provides a detailed study of the background to that movement in MacFarquhar (1974). More recent developments are well covered in Goodman (1981), Seymour (1980) and Garside (1981). The question of political 'crime' is considered in Amnesty International (1984). See also Dreyer (1980) and Leng (1981), which deals with criminal justice in the post-Mao period. The uncertain development of human rights and 'socialist democracy' in more recent years is considered in Copper *et al.* (1985), Henkin *et al.* (1986) and Nathan (1986).

7

The Communist States in Comparative Perspective

So far in this book we have been concerned with politics in the sixteen communist-ruled states, and not to any significant extent with politics in the world outside them. As we suggested in the first chapter, however, comparative communism should properly be thought of as a subfield of comparative politics rather than as a substitute for that method of inquiry, and if we are interested in examining the performance of the communist states in relation to that of similar but non-communist states, in other words in the significance of communist rule as such, then it is clearly the comparative approach that we require. When dealing with the communist states we can normally take for granted a good deal in terms of institutional and other similarities, and the group of states to be considered is fairly easily determined. In dealing with a wider range of political systems, however, the choice of units of comparison becomes somewhat more arbitrary. Should we compare the communist states, for instance, with the major capitalist states, which the communist states have pledged themselves to overtake but which are still, by and large, at a more advanced stage of social and economic development? Or should we compare the communist states with states at a similar level of social and economic development, given the very similar constraints that this is likely to impose upon the political leaderships of such countries? Or should we compare the communist states with all of the world's 150 or so states, irrespective of their ideologies and their levels of socio-economic development?

Even when we have chosen the units of comparison, further problems remain. What, for instance, about the factors which are unique or distinctive to a state, such as its historical experience or religion, and which in turn may have a considerable impact upon its politics quite independent of its form of government and level of socio-economic development? Unlike the natural sciences we cannot isolate these various factors and test them separately for their effects, and yet there are good reasons for thinking that each of them – and perhaps others – may provide at least a part of the explanation that we require. To some extent it is possible to allow for unique cultural or historical factors of this kind by taking 'matched pairs' of stakes which share a common background, such as West and East Germany or North and South Korea, on the assumption that the differences between them must be due to factors other than those they share in common. Even here, however, it is impossible to be certain that cultural or historical differences have been excluded entirely, or that there are no other differences, for instance in natural resources, which may render such comparisons invalid. It is an extremely complicated matter, in other words, to isolate the effects of 'communism as such' upon a country's politics, and it is difficult to be sure that the differences we observe are not caused by factors we have not considered or of which we cannot easily take account.

The choice of criteria by which to compare political systems is also a difficult and somewhat arbitrary one, for there are many ways in which such comparisons could be made and little agreement as to which are the most important. Perhaps the most obvious of such disagreements is the different priorities accorded by different people to the value of political liberty, which is arguably better protected in the Western democracies, as compared with that of social equality, in terms of which the communist states could reasonably be said to have made more progress. But what, for instance about the relative priorities to be attached to political and social values, such as liberty and social equality, as compared with economic values, such as full employment, stable prices and a high standard of living, which most of these states have also sought to achieve? And even in the case of a single value, such as social welfare, how should we compare the performance of the communist states, which typically devote a disproportionate share of the resources to the care and upbringing of the young, with that of the liberal democracies, which are relatively more generous towards their aged, and not just because they tend to have more elderly populations? There is in fact no single agreed order of merit in terms of which political systems can be ranked and classified, and in what follows we shall accordingly examine the performance of the communist states in relation to their non-communist counterparts under a number of different headings: their level of political democracy, their economic performance and their level of social welfare. The relative weight to be attached to performance in each of these fields must necessarily remain a matter for individual judgement.

Communist and non-communist states: levels of political democracy

If there is little agreement about the way in which political systems in general are to be ranked, there is even less about the manner in which their level of political democracy should be assessed. The communist states, as we have seen, have their own criteria; and there are many Western scholars who, while not going so far as to say that democracy is simply a matter of socio-economic rights, would none the less accept that inequalities of wealth and social standing must at least be taken into account in any assessment of such matters. It would probably be fair, however, to say that the majority of scholars, at least in the non-communist world, are agreed that a useful definition of democracy, broadly speaking, must relate to the relative degrees of power enjoyed by the mass of the population and by the governing authorities in a society. Power, in this sense, may derive from the ownership of wealth, as the orthodox communist view maintains; but it may also derive from factors such as control of information, the ability to set agendas, the degree of group cohesion and access to skills, to policy-makers or to a natural resource, factors which were generally unforeseen by Marx. There is again no way in which relative degrees of power can be unambiguously quantified. A number of political scientists, however, have attempted to devise measures of this kind which can be applied to the communist and non-communist nations, and we shall consider some of their efforts in what follows. All exercises of this kind, as the authors of these studies have themselves pointed out, are to various degrees arbitrary and approximate, but they help to clarify at least some aspects of the question, and the alternative, to rely entirely upon impression and assertion, is hardly an improvement.

One of the earliest attempts to measure levels of democracy in communist and non-communist nations in this way was by Robert Dahl in his book *Polyarchy*, published in 1971. Dahl defines democracy as 'a political system one of the characteristics of which is the quality of being completely or almost completely responsive to citizens', a state of affairs not necessarily attained in any of the world's existing political systems but at least a yardstick in relation to which they can all be measured. A political system of this kind, Dahl suggests, requires, as a necessary but not sufficient condition, that all citizens have the opportunity to formulate their preferences, to signify their preferences to their fellow citizens and to the government by individual and collective action, and to have their preferences weighed equally in the conduct of the government. The institutional guarantees of democracy, Dahl argues, can be reduced to two principal dimensions, available to a greater or less extent in different regimes at different times: the extent to which public opposition or contestation is permitted, and the extent to which the population as a whole is permitted to engage in such activities. It is these two dimensions, public contestation and the right to participate, which form the basis of Dahl's classification of regimes. In 'polyarchies' (in effect, liberal democracies) both are maximised; in 'closed hegemonies' (in effect, dictatorships) both are minimised; while in 'inclusive hegemonies' (in effect, the communist states) the right to participate is high but the level of contestation is low.

In the remainder of the volume Dahl is primarily concerned with the conditions that favour or hinder polyarchy, such as the dispersion of economic resources and a relatively high level of GNP per head. Dahl himself points out that many of these factors cannot be measured (or at any rate the necessary data are not available), and that no weighting can readily be assigned to them. In an appendix, however, 114 countries are classified by Dahl and two collaborators according to the extent to which they permit popular participation in elections and, somewhat more arbitrarily, the extent to which they permit public contestation, defined as the freedom to form and join organisations, access to alternative sources of information, free and fair elections and so forth (these are in effect the two dimensions of democracy already mentioned). The results obtained, converted into percentage terms, are set out in Table 7.1 (in all of the states considered electoral participation is close to universal and the results therefore represent the relative extent to which public contestation is permitted). For all the reservations that must necessarily attach to precise measurement of such matters, on which Dahl's methodological discussion must be read in full, one result is immediately apparent: the very low levels of political democracy, measured in this way, of the communist states, and the very much higher levels attained by the major Western states, and even by a developing but liberal democratic state such as India.

A more recent analysis along similar lines has been conducted by Kenneth Bollen. Bollen presents a political democracy index based upon separate indicators of political liberties and of popular sovereignty. The indicators of political liberties included in Bollen's calculations are press freedom, the scope for group opposition and governmental sanctions (actions taken by the government which curtail the political activities of one or more groups of the population, such as the banning of a political party). The three measures of popular sovereignty incorporated in the index are the fairness of elections, executive selection (whether the chief executive is elected or not) and legislative selection (whether the legislature is elected and effective). Each of these indicators was given a score for each country considered; these were then

TABLE 7.1

Communist and non-communist states: some indicators of political democracy and human rights (percentages)

	UK	USA	India	USSR	China	GDR	Poland	Yugoslavia
Dahl, c.1969	87	90	77	13	6	6	16	13
Bollen, c.1965	99	92	91	18	16	18	22	51
Humana, c.1986	94	90	60	20	23	33	41	50

Sources: Robert A. Dahl, *Polyarchy* (New Haven, 1971), app. I, adapted; Kenneth A. Bollen, 'Issues in the Comparative Measurement of Political Democracy', *American Sociological Review*, v1 (1980), pp. 370–90; Charles Humana (comp.), *The Economist World Human Rights Guide* (London, 1986), various pages.

converted into percentages and averaged to obtain the final political democracy rating. Bollen points out that the observed scores are not necessarily 'true' scores, and that minor differences should not be overinterpreted. The results, none the less, are again extremely clear in the respect with which we are concerned: all the liberal democracies, even those in developing countries, record high levels of political democracy, while all the communist states, with the partial exception of Yugoslavia, perform very poorly. The same impression emerges from the *World Human Rights Guide*, also reported in Table 7.1, which attempts to assess regimes around the world in terms of their observance of the Universal Declaration of Human Rights and the International Covenants on Civil and Political and on Economic, Social and Cultural Rights, adopted by the United Nations in 1948 and 1976 respectively. In the fourteen NATO countries included in the survey human rights performance was assessed at an average of 90 per cent (Turkey was by far the lowest, at 40 per cent); in the eleven communist-ruled countries included, however, human rights performance was assessed at no more than 29 per cent, well below the world average of 55 per cent.

A further international survey of this kind is the *Comparative Survey of Freedom*, which is published annually by Freedom House of New York. The Survey incorporates separate measures of political rights, such as the right to participate in the political process through competitive elections and in other ways, and of civil liberties, such as the right to take part in demonstrations and to a degree of personal autonomy in such matters as religion, education and travel. Countries are then ranked in terms of their performance on these two dimensions from 1 (the highest level) to 7 (the lowest). There is again a considerable variation in the level of performance, even among the individual communist states. Yugoslavia, for instance, receives credit for its effective federal system, and Hungary, while it remains a 'Communist state under the control of the party hierarchy', receives recognition for having organised parliamentary elections in 1985 in which competition for most posts was required. The candidate selection process was open, some independent candidates were elected, and run-off elections were required to determine the winner in other cases. Although 'real dissidents' were excluded from the process, the Survey concludes, this was still an 'important step' in the direction of political liberty. Poland, Hungary and Yugoslavia all qualify as 'partly free' in terms of the Survey. All the other communist states, however, are classified as 'not free' with very low scores for both political rights and civil liberties, while all of the member countries of NATO (except Turkey) are classified as 'free' and receive maximum or near-maximum marks on both dimensions.

Quantitative surveys of this kind can hardly be taken as conclusive, given the difficulty of attaching unambiguous scores to many of the indicators concerned and the possibility that the choice of indicators in the first place may have reflected the liberal or other biases of those who have proposed them. The *World Human Rights Guide*, for instance, deliberately takes more of its indicators from the International Covenant on Civil and Political Rights than from the International Covenant on Economic, Social and Cultural Rights, on the grounds that the rights embodied in the latter (such as the right to adequate employment, health and education) are 'concerned with broader social and economic questions' and cannot be allowed to take precedence over classic 'individual' rights such as those to freedom of movement, behaviour and self-expression. This is clearly a choice which, however legitimate, largely determines the outcome of the inquiry. The *Comparative Survey of Freedom*, similarly, acknowledges that many of the criteria on which it is based cannot be quantified satisfactorily and necessarily involve an element of personal judgement. Although the Survey claims not to be a 'capitalist undertaking' and takes account of socio-economic circumstances such as infant mortality and GNP per capita, it none the less assumes that political rights are maximised under conditions of multi-party democracy and it regards thoroughgoing socialism, in practice, as incompatible with basic freedoms. For all their individual shortcomings, however, there is a considerable measure of agreement between these various indices, and they largely agree also with more 'qualitative' assessments of democracy and human rights such as those produced annually by the London-based organisation Amnesty International.

Amnesty, a worldwide organisation which claims to be independent of all governments, political groupings, economic interests and religious creeds, deliberately eschews quantitative or more general comparative assessments of human rights in the various countries with which it deals. Its concern is rather to monitor the extent to which, in each of them, the provisions of the Universal Declaration of Human Rights and other international conventions have been observed, particularly the provisions that relate to the treatment of 'prisoners of conscience' (those imprisoned because of their beliefs, colour, sex, ethnic origin, language or religion who have not used or advocated violence). Its reports make clear that the performance of Western governments is by no means beyond reproach in this connection. In the United Kingdom, for instance, recent Amnesty reports have expressed concern about the judicial procedures employed in political cases in Northern Ireland, particularly the 'Diplock courts', which operate without a jury. There were also complaints about the alleged planting of evidence by the police and about the arrest of peaceful or intending picketers during the miners' strike of 1984–85, some of whom had reportedly been ill-treated in police custody and restricted in their subsequent freedom of movement. In the United States Amnesty expressed particular concern about an increase in the number of judicial executions and about allegations of politically or racially motivated prosecutions. In India, a non-communist but developing country, there were complaints about the detention of prisoners of conscience and about large numbers of political detainees (mostly Sikhs) who were being held without trial or who were awaiting trial under special legislation permitting trial *in camera*.

Reported violations of human rights, however, were on the whole much graver in the communist-ruled countries (as well, of course, as in many others). In relatively liberal Yugoslavia, for instance, there were criticisms of the ill-treatment of prisoners in custody and of political proceedings in which the accused had not received a fair trial. Citizens had also been convicted of 'hostile propaganda' for no more than the peaceful expression of dissenting (often nationalist) opinions. In Poland, Amnesty expressed concern about the arrest and detention of hundreds of prisoners of conscience and about allegations of ill-treatment and torture of prisoners while in official custody. In a small but disturbing numbers of cases political activists had died in unexplained circumstances during or shortly after police interrogation. Among the larger communist countries, China was criticised for the large number of public and often summary executions that had taken place in connection with that country's anti-crime campaign, as well as for the arrest of people who had been peacefully exercising their human rights and for trials of political detainees in which (for instance) the accused had been presumed guilty beforehand in the official press. In the USSR, Amnesty expressed concern about the detention of at least 500 people who had simply sought to exercise their human rights, many of whom had been ill-treated in official custody and some of whom had been detained in psychiatric hospitals.

More detailed, qualitative assessments such as these evidently agree closely with the results of more quantitative and directly comparative investigations. Both, moreover, agree closely with the historical record. As Dahl points out, for instance, there have been many cases of mass coercion in hegemonic or communist regimes, such as the forced collectivisation of agriculture in the USSR in the 1930s, the Cultural Revolution in China (in which, according to the Chinese authorities themselves, nearly three-quarters of a million citizens were unjustly persecuted and nearly 35 000 lost their lives), and in more recent years the forced deurbanisation policies followed with great loss of life by Pol Pot in Kampuchea. No repression on a comparable scale has ever occurred in the liberal democracies. Whatever reservations there might be about individual indices or assessments, findings such as those we have considered do at least point to differences in the extent to which communist and non-communist regimes provide formal democratic rights to their respective populations, such as electoral choice, the ability to form interest groups and a relatively unconstrained press. And while there is some point in the orthodox communist response that socio-economic as well as formal democratic rights must be considered, it is clear from the number of cases of the abuse of power in the communist states, many of which have been acknowledged by the authorities themselves, that the content of democracy may prove a rather vulnerable commodity so long as its form has not been assured. In these respects the onus of proof must remain, as it has done until now, upon the communist rather than the liberal-democratic states.

Communist and non-communist states: comparative economic performance

We are concerned in this volume with the politics of the communist states, not with their economic performance as such. None the less, as we have pointed out, the interpenetration of politics and economics in a communist-ruled country is such that the distinction between them is rather less meaningful than it would be in a Western liberal democracy; and even in a Western liberal democracy the state often plays a central role in economic life and political parties base their appeals to the electorate upon the superior economic performance they claim to be able to achieve. The attitudes of mass publics towards their respective regimes, also, may depend to a considerable extent upon their economic performance. The liberal democracies, unlike the communist states, provide a means of legitimating the actions of government through competitive elections in which the people's will is notionally expressed. Even in the liberal democracies, however, some doubts have been expressed as to the extent to which the regimes concerned will be able to survive a prolonged period of relatively poor economic performance, and in the communist states the need to justify the actions of government in terms of what it provides for its population is rather greater. The performance of the economy is therefore a central aspect of politics in both communist and non-communist systems, and the performance of one compared with the other has considerable implications for politicians as well as for economic statisticians in both cases.

Comparisons of communist and non-communist economic performance are unfortunately fraught with a number of serious and intractable difficulties. In the first place, the concepts employed for economic measurements in East and West are often different. The most important of these, gross national product, is normally defined in the West as the total value of all goods and services made available in the economy within a specified period. In the communist countries, however, a different concept, 'net material product', is generally employed; this is similar to gross national product but excludes 'nonproductive' activities such as governmental administration, finance, education, medicine and other professional services, and also capital construction or depreciation. Economic performance in the communist states is not normally reported in sufficient detail to allow an equivalent of GNP in these countries to be reconstructed with total accuracy. Further problems arise when a common expression of value is required. Conversions by means of official exchange rates are generally of little value for this purpose because exchange rates in the communist countries are centrally administered and often artificial (as the thriving black market testifies). Prices which reflect the real resource costs of each product must therefore be calculated in order to derive theoretically accurate measures of the real growth and distribution of GNP, an exercise which is difficult and highly imperfect.

Calculations of this kind may be expressed in either Western prices or in those of the communist countries. Some goods, however, such as foodstuffs and public transport, are cheaper and account for a higher proportion of total output in the communist countries than in the West; conversely, goods such as motor-cars and computers are much cheaper and account for a larger share of total output in the West than in the communist countries. Expressed in Western prices, the GNP of communist countries will appear to be larger; expressed in the prices of the communist countries, on the other hand, it will appear to be smaller. In neither case has 'real' GNP been altered in the slightest. Comparisons of military spending in East and West are particularly susceptible to distortion of this kind depending upon whether 'dollar costing' or 'rouble costing' is employed. Valuing the military effort of the communist countries in terms of what it would cost to provide the same resources in Western countries tends to inflate the apparent level of communist military expenditure, because the communist countries use relatively large quantities of military manpower which is poorly remunerated and relatively low quantities of advanced technology which tends to be very expensive in local prices. Valuations in terms of the prices of the communist countries themselves has the opposite effect. Comparisons of growth rates in communist and Western countries, although not without shortcomings, may avoid some of these difficulties, but the result can at best convey an impression of relative levels of performance and not of absolute differences in living standards. Comparisons in terms of physical units, such as hospital beds, washing machines or potatoes, avoid the distorting effects of comparisons in terms of monetary equivalents but for their part cannot be converted into a single measure of relative levels of prosperity.

In an effort to achieve greater comparability in such matters the United Nations has initiated an International Comparison Project which seeks to develop measures of GNP in various countries using purchasing power parities rather than exchange rates. So far the project covers only a limited number of countries, and serious methodological difficulties remain to be resolved (the World Bank's *World Development Report* acknowledges that perfect cross-country comparability of GNP per capita may in fact be unattainable). At present, recalculated estimates of GNP per capita are available for only three of the sixteen communist nations considered in this volume: China, Hungary and Yugoslavia. In 1983 GNP per capita in these countries was assessed at US $300, 2150 and 2570 respectively, as compared with India, the United Kingdom and the United States at US $260, 9200 and 14 110 respectively. More comprehensive data have, however, been developed by two of the authors associated with the International Comparison Project, Robert Summers and Alan Heston. According to their figures, based upon a measure of world average relative prices, differences in GNP per capita between a number of communist and non-communist countries between 1950 and 1980 were as set out in Table 7.2 (their calculations in full are set out in Summers and Heston, 1984).

TABLE 7.2

Communist and non-communist states: comparative economic performance (real per capita GNP in US dollars)

	1950	1960	1970	1980
India	333	428	450	498
United Kingdom	2700	3388	4216	4990
USA	4550	5195	6629	8089
China	300	505	711	1135
USSR	1373	2084	3142	3943
GDR	1480	3006	4100	5532
Poland	1516	1996	2731	3509
Czechoslovakia	2182	3189	4027	4908
Yugoslavia	769	1256	2027	3318
Communist– non-communist average (%)	50	67	74	82

Source: Robert Summers and Alan Heston, 'Improved International Comparisons of Real Product and its Composition, 1950–80', *Review of Income and Wealth*, xxx (1984), pp. 207–62.

Whatever figures are employed, there is little doubt that the communist nations, taken as a whole, are less prosperous than the major industrialised countries of the capitalist West. There is considerable variation within both groups, however, and on Summers and Heston's figures, at least, some of the more advanced communist nations such as the GDR and Czechoslovakia may now have drawn ahead of major capitalist nations such as the United Kingdom and Italy respectively in their GNP per capita. The communist states, moreover, have by and large been expanding their economies at a more rapid rate than the major capitalist countries (see Table 7.2), although in both cases rates of growth have been showing a tendency to fall in recent years. There is no communist state whose rate of growth since the Second World War has exceeded that of a capitalist state such as Japan, but their rate of growth as a group has exceeded that of the major Western countries as a group, and the fluctuations in their annual rates of growth have also been much less. This relatively rapid rate of economic growth has been in part a product of the fact that the communist states have started

their growth from a lower point than that of the major
Western countries – the phenomenon known as 'catching
up' – but it has also been in part the result of the deliberate
selection of economic growth as a priority by their political
leaderships, and in the case of at least some of the most
developed communist states it has continued after they have
overtaken some of their capitalist competitors.

It is also worthy of note that the communist states, by and
large, have achieved their levels of economic performance
without the levels of inflation and unemployment that have
become an increasingly prominent feature of the major
capitalist economies in the 1970s and 1980s. Unemployment
and inflation have not been entirely eliminated in the communist countries, particularly in those whose economies are not
centrally planned in the orthodox manner, such as China and
Yugoslavia. In Yugoslavia, for instance, the annual rate of
inflation was officially reported to have reached 80 per cent in
1985, the highest in any European country, and its level of
unemployment has also been considerable, despite the fact
that many Yugoslavs have left the country and found employment in Western Europe. The more conventionally centrally planned economies which exist in the other communist
states also permit a measure of inflation, usually by replacing
older and cheaper goods by newer and more expensive ones of
much the same quality, but also by making increases in the
prices set by the state in order to prevent the prices of goods
getting too far out of line with their production costs. There is
also a certain amount of unemployment in these states as a
result of people changing jobs, although officially no unemployment exists and none is recorded in government statistics.
Most estimates of the degree of inflation and unemployment
that result from such factors, however, are extremely low,
usually in the 2–3 per cent range, and in general it is fair to
say that the centrally planned communist economies have
achieved their relatively high levels of economic performance
without sacrificing their other objectives of virtually full
employment and low levels of inflation. It is not surprising
that this model of economic development has been popular in
many other countries, particularly in the Third World.

It is also fair to say that the benefits of economic growth

have as a rule been distributed more equitably in the communist states than in the majority of non-communist states. Calculations of this kind must inevitably rely upon published data on monetary earnings, which may be difficult to compare across systems and may be to various degrees misleading. The existence of the 'second economy' in most of the communist states, for instance, is an important source of bias, as is the existence of administered privilege – the allocation of superior housing, transport and health care facilities to party and government officials, for instance, as well as the opportunity to shop at special closed stores to which the majority of the population are not admitted but in which prices are lower and the range of goods much better than in the ordinary state retail sector. In Western economies, however, a variety of benefits are also extended to senior employees, such as assistance with school fees and rehousing, car allowances, private health insurance and subsidised meals, and in the Western countries there is also a substantial black economy where monetary transactions take place which are not recorded by the income tax authorities. There may be some rough comparability between these two; in any case neither extends over a sufficient number of people to make a significant difference to the national averages in terms of which such comparisons are usually made. At this level it is clear that the communist states, as a rule, distribute their incomes in a more egalitarian manner than most Western countries.

Comparisons of this kind may be expressed in various ways. The ratio between the earnings of the best-paid and worst-paid tenths of the labour force (the 'decile ratio') is one of the most common such summary statistics. The relevant figures for various countries in the late 1960s and early 1970s, according to the best Western estimates, were as follows (these figures are taken from Peter Wiles's *Economic Institutions Compared*, published in 1977): the USA, the least egalitarian, 6.7; Canada, 6.0; Italy, 5.9; Sweden and the USSR, 3.5; United Kingdom, 3.4; Czechoslovakia, 3.1; Hungary, 3.0; and Bulgaria, the most egalitarian, 2.7. It was not the case that all the communist states were more egalitarian in their income distribution than all of the capitalist states considered; but as a group, their distribution of incomes was certainly more egalitarian than that of the capitalist countries also considered as a group. These findings are supported by a comparative study of income distribution in Poland, the USSR, the United Kingdom and the USA, undertaken by Peter Wiles and Stefan Markowski, which found that in all these countries the distribution of income had become more equal over time, but that it was more equal in the two communist states, taken together, than in the two capitalist states, and that there was no equivalent in the communist states of the rich private capitalists that existed in the United Kingdom and the USA. This, the authors found, was the 'most striking difference between the two systems'. Several other studies, although by no means all (see for instance Morrisson, 1984), have come to similar conclusions.

Communist and non-communist states: comparative social welfare

We turn finally to the area of comparative social welfare, that is to say of the social purposes upon which governments spend their revenues in different systems. A variety of indicators could be chosen to illustrate such comparisons. In what follows we have taken what are widely regarded as among the most important areas of social policy, such as housing, education, health care and social security, and looked at the different patterns of spending of different states and at some of the outcomes, such as infant mortality and life expectancy, that are associated with them. Again, there are many problems associated with comparisons of this kind. The data are often unavailable or of doubtful quality; national averages may conceal substantial within-nation differences, particularly in heterogeneous and multi-ethnic states such as the USSR and Yugoslavia; and allowances must be made for factors such as the different levels of socio-economic development of the countries involved in the comparison as these will tend to have a considerable influence upon the countries' levels of performance in such matters quite independent of the efforts of their government. Social indicators of the kind that have been mentioned, however, in many ways provide a better basis upon which to compare the performance of different political regimes than the purely economic statistics considered in the previous section, since they reveal more clearly the various purposes to which different governments attach the most importance. They are, in other words, one of the best ways in which we can examine the difference that is made to national policies if a country is ruled by communists rather than non-communists.

Some of the evidence relevant to a comparison of this kind is set out in Table 7.3. These statistics record the performance of individual nations irrespective of differences in their total economic resources, although clearly more prosperous nations, by and large, will be better able to finance generous social welfare programmes than their less prosperous communist counterparts. The performance of the communist states, taken as a group, none the less compares not unfavourably in many respects with that of the major capitalist countries, particularly in the fields of housing and health care. Indeed in many respects the performance of at least some of the communist states is as good as or better than that of the United Kingdom and the USA, an impressive performance when it is remembered that their levels of GNP per head are generally much lower.

Controlling so far as we can for variations in levels of prosperity (or GNP per head), some interesting comparisons are revealed. In a close analysis of such matters, for instance, A. J. Groth has found that the communist nations, despite their relative poverty, have been distinctive in the proportion of public spending they have devoted to education. Poorer communist states have in fact provided a better educational service than many wealthier but non-communist nations. Albania, for example, has expanded its educational system much faster and enrolled a higher proportion of the relevant age-groups within it than economically comparable nations such as Spain, Portugal and Greece, and the more developed communist nations have also out-performed wealthier non-communist nations such as France, West Germany and the United Kingdom. Educational enrolment ratios in East Germany have also exceeded those in West Germany and those in North Korea have exceeded those in South Korea, although

TABLE 7.3

Communist and non-communist states: selected indicators of social welfare

	Housing units completed per 10 000 population, 1984	Doctors per 10 000 popn, 1984	Hospital beds per 10 000 popn, c. 1984	Infant mortality rate per 1000 births, 1983	Life expectancy at birth, 1983	Adult literacy at (%), 1980	Students in tertiary education per 10 000 popn, 1984/85
United Kingdom	34	18	78	10	74	99	105
USA	59	23	57	11	75	99	268
India	n.a.	4	8	93	55	36	49
USSR	73	41	129	n.a.	69	100	191
China	n.a.	13	21	38	67	69	13
GDR	73	28	102	11	71	n.a.	78
Poland	53	24	70	19	71	98	94
Yugoslavia	61	19	61	32	69	85	170

Source: Cols. 1–3 and 7: *Narodnoe khozyaistvo SSSR v 1984 g.* (Moscow, 1985); Cols. 4–6: *World Development Report 1985* (New York, 1985).

their respective economic resources would have suggested the reverse. In terms of social security benefits, similarly, such as old age, injury and sickness allowances, Groth (1982) found that the communist states, as a rule, provided a range and level of assistance that was generally high and in excess of that provided by non-communist states at a similar level of socio-economic development. Groth and Hunt (1985) also found that communist regimes were distinctive in the share of their resources that they devoted to culture and mass communications, such as theatre performances, museums, books published, public library volumes and circulation of daily newspapers per head of population.

Issues of this kind may be explored further on the basis of internationally comparable data such as those published annually in the World Bank's *World Development Report*. India and China, for instance, are both low income economies in terms of the Bank's classification, with very similar levels of GNP per capita. China, however, has a substantially higher life expectancy at birth, much lower rates of infant mortality and child death, more doctors and nurses per head of population, and enrols a greater proportion of its population in full-time education at primary and secondary (although not at tertiary) levels. Yugoslavia, according to the World Bank an 'upper middle-income economy', is above the average for all states in this category in its life expectancy and has much lower levels of infant and child mortality, many more doctors and nurses per head of population and substantially better standards of nutrition. In educational terms Yugoslavia's performance is also better than the average for its income group, and comparable with or better than that of more prosperous nations such as Greece, Italy and the United Kingdom. Hungary, another communist nation in the 'upper middle-income' category in World Bank terms, has a better level of health and educational provision than other economically comparable nations and indeed improves upon many of the advanced capitalist countries in its provision of medical and nursing care.

There has been a long and fairly inconclusive debate among political scientists about the extent to which 'politics matters' in variations in spending patterns of this kind.

Comparisons between American states and between Western liberal democracies, for instance, have frequently concluded that factors such as the level of social and economic development of the state or nation concerned may be a better predictor of spending patterns than the political orientation of their governments. These findings have not been universally accepted, however, and certainly when comparisons are made between states at approximately the same level of socioeconomic development some significant contrasts emerge. We have seen this to be true of communist and non-communist nations at approximately the same stage of development; and it is also true of comparisons between 'matched pairs' of states, such as West and East Germany or North and South Korea, the differences between which appear largely to be attributable to their different political regimes. We have already mentioned Groth's findings, which deal in part with these two pairs of states. Jaroslav Krejci, in a more extended study of the two Germanys, found many similarities between them in their economic and social structures despite their political differences. The opportunities for social mobility through education, however, were greater in the GDR than in the Federal Republic, as both higher and secondary education were more accessible to ordinary workers, and opportunities for political mobility for ordinary workers were also greater in the GDR than in the Federal Republic. These findings are borne out in the *World Development Report*, which indicates that the Federal Republic has a slightly higher life expectancy and level of medical provision than the GDR but that the GDR, although less prosperous, has almost exactly the same levels of infant and child mortality and a higher level of enrolment in post-primary education. Again, these are differences which appear to be largely attributable to the different political regimes of the two countries concerned.

It does not necessarily follow that the basic social welfare needs are satisfactorily met in all the communist-ruled countries, still less that their performance is always superior to that of states at a similar level of social and economic development. The slowdown in economic growth experienced by most of the communist countries in the 1970s and 1980s has in fact exposed a number of serious shortcomings in social welfare provision in these countries and has contributed to the emergence or re-emergence of social problems of a kind for which there was supposedly no basis under socialist conditions. One of the most striking indicators of this kind is life expectancy. Unlike the major Western countries, where life expectancy has steadily been increasing, in most of the communist countries it has been tending to decline over the past decade or so, quite against the experience of industrially developed nations. This fall has been attributed to a variety of causes including alcohol abuse, poor nutrition and unhealthy patterns of living, especially in urban areas. Still more remarkably, poverty and other forms of social deprivation have re-emerged, particularly in some of the East European countries which have been engaged in the process of economic reform (which usually means higher prices). In Hungary, for instance, at least 10–15 per cent of the population were estimated to suffer in the mid-1980s from 'multiple disadvantages' (the official euphemism for poverty). The poorest of these had a monthly income of less than half the national average, and had a diet seriously deficient in meat, fish, fruit and vegetables. The individuals concerned were disproportionately pensioners, the elderly and those with large families, whose benefits from the state had lagged behind rising prices and who had little opportunity to increase their earnings in the 'second economy'. In Poland in the late 1970s the 'Experience and Future' study group reported similarly that large sections of the population, particularly the working class, lower-level office employees and pensioners, suffered from serious poverty and even malnutrition.

Quantitative data, moreover, however impressive, may often give a misleading impression of the quality of the services that communist states make available to their citizens. Czechoslovakia, for instance, according to official statistics, had the third highest proportion of doctors to population in the world in the mid-1980s, and the fifth highest proportion of hospital beds per head of population. Czech health services, according to press reports, were none the less suffering from serious problems. A high proportion of equipment is obsolete; there is a shortage of hard currency to buy equip-

·ment and medication from abroad; doctors are poorly paid, and bribes and gratuities are often necessary if urgent or specialist treatment is to be obtained. In Hungary, similarly, free health care is available, as a legal entitlement, to every citizen. Hospital buildings, however, are often antiquated; much of the equipment is obsolete or in poor working order; many basic medications are unavailable because of a lack of hard currency to buy them in the West; and overcrowding in hospital wards is commonplace. In Poland, at least 30 per cent of hospitals are reckoned to be unsuitable for use (it is popularly held that one needs to be extremely healthy to dare to register in a Polish hospital). As elsewhere, there are serious shortages of modern equipment and medicines, and short-comings even in basic hygiene (between 5 and 20 per cent of patients are reported to contract a serious infection during their stay, prolonging their treatment and contributing further to already overcrowded conditions). In Romania, similarly, there are acknowledged to be serious gaps in medical provision in rural areas, and hospital patients are sometimes placed two in a bed because of overcrowding.

Many of these problems, admittedly, are not unknown in more prosperous Western countries, and in general it is still true to say that it is in their medical services, as well as their educational and other welfare facilities, that communist regimes compare most favourably with their non-communist counterparts and indeed for which they appear to be most highly valued by their own domestic populations. In a detailed analysis of health care provision in Germany, Britain and Japan as well as the Soviet Union, for instance, Leichter (1979) found that the USSR had been 'enormously successful in providing all [its] citizens with professionally competent, comprehensive, free medical care', and that the health care system had contributed to a substantial improvement in popular health standards despite the existence of a number of distributional problems, themselves 'by no means unique to the Soviet Union'. The main reason for the health care policies promoted in the USSR appeared to be the regime's ideology: in other words, the provision of a highly centralised, free, comprehensive and universal state-run medical care system, with priority given to the proletariat, was essentially an attempt to 'spell out the humanitarian, egalitarian, and collective implications of socialist ideology'. Communist countries were not unique in introducing a comprehensive national system of health care; they were distinctive, however, in the share of spending that they devoted to education and health care as compared with their non-communist counterparts, and in the content, operation and evolution of the health care systems that they maintained. If communist regimes must generally be accounted authoritarian, as we have suggested earlier in this chapter, they may reasonably be regarded also as broadly egalitarian and welfarist in the social and economic policies that they pursue.

Variations of this kind do not necessarily occur without compensating costs in other areas, and a number of writers have pointed out the extent to which a greater degree of social equality of this kind may be obtainable only by sacrificing a degree of personal liberty. Upward political mobility in the GDR, for instance, is greater than in the Federal Republic because of a policy of political recruitment which deliberately discriminates in favour of the lower strata of the population and against white-collar workers. Income differentials in the communist states, similarly, are generally lower than in the major capitalist states at least in part because middle-class pressure groups, such as those formed by doctors and lawyers in the West, are dominated by the communist party authorities and given very little opportunity to organise on behalf of their members. Levels of economic growth are typically somewhat higher than in the capitalist countries because the political authorities maintain a rate of investment in industry at the expense of popular consumption which the population at large might not ordinarily be expected to favour. And levels of crime are relatively low because it is not easy to escape from the country with the proceeds of one's crime or to find anything of value in the shops on which to spend them. In all of these matters a trade-off is apparently occurring, by which a social or economic value is being realised but at the expense of a political value such as individual liberty or the ability to form or join an organisation.

Several writers have suggested that these combinations may not be accidental, that there is, in other words, a logical connection between a relatively egalitarian society whose political system is authoritarian, on the one hand, and a more unequal society whose political system is liberal–democratic, on the other. Frank Parkin, for instance, has argued that the combination of a market economy and political pluralism is 'one which makes the redistribution of advantages between social classes difficult to bring about'. The government in a pluralist system, he suggests, is simply one power among many; any attempt it might make to bring about a relative improvement in the position of the less privileged is likely to be frustrated by the greater organisational and ideological influence of the dominant class. In a command economy, on the other hand, it is much easier for the government to achieve a redistribution of resources of this kind, because privileged groups have no access to a market to sustain their position and little opportunity to organise in defence of their interests. It follows that 'socialist egalitarianism is not readily compatible with a pluralist political order of the classic western type'; egalitarianism seems, on the contrary, to 'require a political system in which the state is able continually to hold in check those social and occupational groups which, by virtue of their skills or education or personal attributes, might otherwise attempt to stake claims to a disproportionate share of society's rewards' (this quotation comes from Parkin's *Class Inequality and Political Order*, published in 1971).

It would be too much to say that the experience of the communist states considered in this volume unambiguously supports such a proposition, and unduly pessimistic to suggest that the future holds out no other potential. It is, however, by and large the case that the periods of communist rule which have permitted the greatest degree of personal liberty, such as the New Economic Policy period in Russia or the Dubček period in Czechoslovakia, have generally been associated with a relative widening of social and economic differentials, and that periods of particularly authoritarian rule, such as in the 1950s in Czechoslovakia or the period of the Cultural Revolution in China, have generally been associated with a narrowing of differentials and a general hostility towards material rather than moral incentives. It is, of course, also possible for a particularly authoritarian communist regime to increase differentials, such as during Stalin's campaign against 'petty bourgeois equalitarianism' in the USSR in the 1930s. The experience of the communist states, however, does suggest that both liberty and equality may be more difficult to combine than had originally been supposed, and none of these states has yet managed to maximise both for an extended period of time any more successfully than any of the major liberal democracies (though there are considerable variations between individual countries in both cases). If politics is about choice, this, it would appear, is one of the most fundamental that rulers and peoples in both East and West have so far had to make about the system of government under which they live.

Further reading

The comparative analysis of political systems in terms of their outputs is considered further in Almond and Powell (1978, part IV); see also Groth (1971) and Pryor (1968), a pioneering study. Related issues of comparative political analysis are considered in Dogan and Pelassy (1984). Useful sources of cross-national data are the *United Nations Statistical Yearbook* (New York, annual), the *UNESCO Statistical Yearbook* (Paris, annual), the World Bank's *World Development Report* (New York, annual), and Ruth Sivard, *World Military and Social Expenditures* (Washington, DC, annual). The need to relate the communist states to broader comparative perspectives of this kind is argued in Kautsky (1973) and in Bunce and Echols (1979).

On comparative levels of political democracy, see Dahl (1971), Bollen (1980) Humana (1986), and the Comparative Survey of Freedom reported in Gastril (1986). Amnesty International publishes an *Annual Report* on the observance of human rights on a global basis, and has also produced more detailed surveys of human rights and the treatment of prisoners of conscience in the USSR (1980), China (1984) and Yugoslavia (1985). A somewhat more partisan report is produced by the United States Department of State: *Country Reports on Human Rights* (Washington, DC, annually since

1977). Wider comparative issues of human rights in East and West are considered in Lane (1984) and Szymanski (1984).

Comparative economic performance is reviewed in Wiles (1977), Ellman (1979, ch. 10), and Gregory and Stuart (1985). The difficulties of comparing performance and measuring living standards in East and West are considered in US Congress Joint Economic Committee (1982), Summers and Heston (1984) and Marer (1985). On income differentials, see Wiles and Markowski (1971) and Morrisson (1984). Comparative surveys of social welfare include Groth (1971) and (1982), Krejci (1976), Connor (1979), Leichter (1979), Madison (1980) and Echols (1981). The research reports produced regularly by Radio Free Europe and Radio Liberty provide abundant and up-to-date information on social conditions in the USSR and Eastern Europe.

On the association between socio-economic and political systems more generally, see Parkin (1971), Brus (1975), Lindblom (1977) and Selucky (1979). On the rather wider question of socialism and the experience of the communist states, see Kolakowski and Hampshire (1974), Bellis (1979), Bahro (1981), Lane (1982), Nove (1982), and Fehér, Heller and Márkus (1983). Matters of this kind are also reviewed in periodicals such as *Monthly Review* (New York, monthly), *New Left Review* (London, bimonthly) and *Critique* (Glasgow, biannually). *World Marxist Review* (Prague, monthly), the English edition of *Problems of Peace and Socialism*, gives the point of view of the communist regimes themselves.

Bibliography

Adelman, Jonathan (ed.) (1984) *Terror and Communist Politics* (Boulder, Col.: Westview).

Akiner, Shirin (1985) *The Islamic Peoples of the Soviet Union* (London: Kogan Paul International).

Almond, Gabriel and Powell, G. Bingham, Jr. (1978) *Comparative Politics: System, Process and Policy*, 2nd ed. (Boston: Little, Brown).

Amnesty International (1980) *Prisoners of Conscience in the USSR*, 2nd ed. (London: Quatermaine House).

Amnesty International (1984) *China: Violations of Human Rights* (London: Amnesty International).

Amnesty International (1985) *Yugoslavia: Prisoners of Conscience* (London: Amnesty International).

Andrle, Vladimir (1976) *Managerial Power in the Soviet Union* (Aldershot: Saxon House).

Armstrong, John A. (1965) 'Sources of Administrative Behavior: some Soviet and Western European Comparisons', *American Political Science Review*, vol. 59, no. 3 (September), pp. 643–55.

Ash, Timothy Garton (1985) *The Polish Revolution: Solidarity* (London: Coronet).

Azrael, Jeremy (1966) *Managerial Power and Soviet Politics* (Cambridge, Mass.: Harvard University Press).

Bahro, Rudolf (1981) *The Alternative in Eastern Europe* (London: Verso).

Bartke, Wolfgang and Schier, Peter (1985) *China's New Party Leadership* (London: Macmillan).

Barnett, A. Doak (1967) *Cadres, Bureaucracy and Political Power in Communist China* (New York: Columbia University Press).

Barnett, A. Doak (1985) *The Making of Foreign Policy in China* (London: I. B. Tauris).

Barry, Donald D. *et al.* (eds) (1977–79) *Soviet Law since Stalin*, 3 vols (Leyden: Sijthoff).

Bell, John D. (1986) *The Bulgarian Communist Party from Blagoev to Zhivkov* (Stanford, Calif.: Hoover Institution Press).

Bellis, Paul (1979) *Marxism and the USSR* (London: Macmillan).

Berman, Harold J. and Spindler, John W. (eds) (1972) *Soviet Criminal Laws and Procedures: the RSFR Codes*, 2nd ed. (Cambridge, Mass.: Harvard University Press).

Beyme, Klaus von (1982) *Economics and Politics within Socialist Systems* (New York: Praeger).

Bialer, Seweryn (1980) *Stalin's Successors* (New York: Cambridge University Press).

Bociurkiw, Bohdan and Strong, John W. (eds) (1975) *Religion and Atheism in the USSR and Eastern Europe* (London: Macmillan).

Bollen, Kenneth (1980) 'Issues in the Comparative Analysis of Political Democracy', *American Sociological Review*, vol. 45, no. 3 (June), pp. 370–90.

Brandys, Kazimierz (1981) *A Question of Reality* (London: Blond & Briggs).

Brown, A. H. (1974) *Soviet Politics and Political Science* (London: Macmillan).

Brown, Archie (1980) 'The Power of the General Secretary of the CPSU'. In Rigby (1980), pp. 135–57.

Brown, Archie (ed.) (1984) *Political Culture and Communist Studies* (London: Macmillan).

Brown, Archie and Gray, Jack (eds) (1979) *Political Culture and Political Change in Communist States*, 2nd ed. (London: Macmillan).

Brugger, Bill (ed.) (1985) *Chinese Marxism in Flux, 1978–84* (London: Croom Helm).

Brus, Wlodzimierz (1975) *Social Ownership and Political Systems* (London: Routledge).

Brzezinski, Zbigniew K. (1967) *The Soviet Bloc: Unity and Conflict*, rev. ed. (Cambridge, Mass.: Harvard University Press).

Bunce, Valerie and Echols, John M. (1979) 'From Soviet Studies to Comparative Politics: the Unfinished Revolution', *Soviet Studies*, vol. 31, no. 1 (January), pp. 43–55.

Bunce, Valerie and Echols, John M. (1980) 'Soviet Politics in the Brezhnev Era: "Pluralism" or "Corporatism"?'. In Kelley (1980), pp. 1–26.

Butler, W. E. (1983a) *Soviet Law*. (London: Butterworths).

Butler, W. E. (ed.) (1983b) *Basic Documents on the Soviet Legal System* (New York: Oceana).

Carrère d'Encausse, Hélène (1979) *An Empire in Decline* (New York: Newsweek).

Chang, Parris H. (1978) *Power and Policy in China* (University Park: Pennsylvania State University Press).

Chen, Jerome (1968) *The Criminal Process in Contemporary China* (Cambridge, Mass.: Harvard University Press).

Churchward, Lloyd G. (1975) *Contemporary Soviet Government*, 2nd ed. (London: Routledge).

Cohen, Jerome (1968) *The Criminal Process in Communist China* (Cambridge, Mass.: Harvard University Press).

Cohen, Lenard and Shapiro, Jane (eds) (1974) *Communist Systems in Comparative Perspective* (New York: Anchor).

Cohen, Stephen F. (1985) *Rethinking the Soviet Experience* (New York: Oxford University Press).

Colton, Timothy J. (1979) *Commissars, Commanders and Civilian Authority* (Cambridge, Mass.: Harvard University Press).

Connor, Walker (1984) *The National Question in Marxist–Leninist Theory and Strategy* (Princeton, NJ: Princeton University Press).

Connor, Walter D. (1979) *Socialism, Politics, and Equality* (New York: Columbia University Press).

Copper, John *et al.* (1985) *Human Rights in Post-Mao China* (Boulder, Col.: Westview).

Curry, Jane L. (ed.) (1983) *Dissent in Eastern Europe* (New York: Praeger).

Curry, Jane L. (ed.) (1984) *The Black Book of Polish Censorship* (New York: Random House).

Curtis, Michael (ed.) (1979) *Totalitarianism* (New Brunswick, NJ: Transaction Books).

Dahl, Robert A. (1971) *Polyarchy* (New Haven, Conn.: Yale University Press).

Dahl, Robert A. (ed.) (1973) *Regime and Oppositions* (New Haven: Yale University Press).

Dawisha, Karen L. (1980) 'The Limits of the Bureaucratic Politics Model: some Observations on the Soviet Case', *Studies in Comparative Communism*, vol. 13, no. 4 (Winter), pp. 300–26.

Deakin, William, Shukman, Harry and Willetts, Harry (1975) *A History of World Communism* (London: Weidenfeld & Nicolson).

Deng Xiaoping (1984) *Speeches and Writings*, ed. Robert Maxwell (Oxford: Pergamon Press).

DiFranceisco, Wayne and Gitelman, Zvi (1985) 'Soviet Political Culture and "Covert Participation" in Policy Implementation', *American Political Science Review*, vol. 78, no. 3 (September), pp. 603–21.

Doder, Dusko (1978) *The Yugoslavs.* (New York: Random House).

Dogan, Mattei and Pelassy, Dominique (1984) *How to Compare Nations. Strategies in Comparative Politics* (Chatham, NJ: Chatham House).

Dreyer, June (1980) 'Limits of the Permissible in China', *Problems of Communism*, vol. 29, no. 6 (November–December), pp. 48–65.

Dunlop, John B. (1983) *The Faces of Contemporary Russian Nationalism* (Princeton, NJ: Princeton University Press).

Dunlop, John B. (1985) *The New Russian Nationalism* (New York: Praeger).

Echols, John M. (1981) 'Does Socialism mean Greater Equality? A Comparison of East and West Along Several Major Dimensions', *American Journal of Political Science*, vol. 25, no. 1 (February), pp. 1–31.

Ellis, Jane (1986) *The Russian Orthodox Church* (London: Croom Helm).

Ellman, Michael (1979) *Socialist Planning* (Cambridge: Cambridge University Press).

Etkind, Efim (1978) *Notes of a Non-Conspirator* (Oxford: Oxford University Press).

Fehér, Ferenc, Heller, Agnes and Márkus, György (1983) *Dictatorship over Needs. An Analysis of Soviet Societies* (Oxford: Blackwell).

Feldbrugge, F. J. M. (1975) *Samizdat and Political Dissent in the Soviet Union* (Leyden: Sijthoff).

Feldbrugge, F. J. M. (ed.) (1979) *The Constitution of the USSR and the Union Republics* (Alphen aan den Rijn: Sijthoff and Noordhoff).

Fetjö, Francois (1974) *A History of the People's Democracies*, rev. ed. (Harmondsworth, Mx.: Penguin Books).

Fischer-Galati, Stephen (ed.) (1979) *The Communist Parties of Eastern Central Europe* (New York: Columbia University Press).

Fleron, Frederick J., Jr. (ed.) (1969) *Communist Studies and the Social Sciences* (Chicago: Rand McNally).

Friedgut, Theodore H. (1979) *Political Participation in the USSR* (Princeton, NJ: Princeton University Press).

Friedrich, Carl J. (ed.) (1969) *Totalitarianism in Perspective* (New York: Praeger).

Friedrich, Carl J. and Brzezinski, Zbigniew K. (1965) *Totalitarian Dictatorship and Autocracy*, 2nd ed. (Cambridge, Mass.: Harvard University Press).

Furtak, Robert K. (1986) *The Political Systems of the Socialist States: An Introduction to Marxist–Leninist Regimes* (Brighton: Wheatsheaf).

Gardner, John (1971) 'Educated Youth and Urban-rural Inequalities'. In Lewis (1971), pp. 235–86.

Garside, Roger (1981) *Coming Alive* (London: Deutsch).

Gasper, Donald (1982) 'The Chinese National People's Congress'. In Nelson and White (1982), pp. 160–90.

Gastril, Raymond D. (1986) 'The Comparative Survey of Freedom 1986', *Freedom at Issue*, no. 88 (January–February), pp. 3–17.

Gill, Graeme (1986) 'The Future of the General Secretary', *Political Studies*, vol. 34, no. 2 (June), pp. 223–35.

Ginzburg, Evgeniya (1967) *Into the Whirlwind* (London: Collins).

Ginzburg, Evgeniya (1981) *Within the Whirlwind* (London: Collins).

Gitelman, Zvi (1977) 'Soviet Political Culture: Insights from Jewish Emigres', *Soviet Studies*, vol. 29, no. 4 (October), pp. 543–64.

Glazov, Yuri (1985) *The Russian Mind since Stalin's Death* (Dordrecht: Reidel).

Golan, Galia (1973) *Reform Rule in Czechoslovakia, 1968–1969* (Cambridge: Cambridge University Press).

Gold, Thomas B. (1985) 'After Comradeship: Personal Relations in China Since the Cultural Revolution', *China Quarterly*, no. 104 (December), pp. 656–75.

Goodman, David S. G. (1981) *Beijing Street Voices* (London: Boyars).

Goodman, David S. G. (ed.) (1984) *Groups and Politics in the People's Republic of China* (Cardiff: University College of Cardiff Press).

Goodman, David S. G. (1985) 'The Chinese Political Order after Mao: "Socialist Democracy" and the Exercise of State Power', *Political Studies*, vol. 33, no. 2 (June), pp. 218–35.

Gregory, Paul R. and Stuart, Robert C. (1985) *Comparative Economic Systems*, 2nd edn. (Boston: Houghton Mifflin).

Gregory Paul R. and Stuart Robert C. (1986) *Soviet Economic Structure and Performance*, 3rd ed. (New York: Harper and Row).

Groth, Alexander J. (1971) *Comparative Politics: A Distributive Approach* (New York: Macmillan).

Groth, Alexander J. (1982) 'Worker Welfare Systems in Marxist–Leninist States: a Comparative Analysis', *Coexistence*, vol. 19, no. 1 (April), pp. 33–50.

Groth, Alexander J. and Hunt, William R. (1985) 'Marxist–Leninist Communication Systems in Comparative Perspective', *Coexistence*, vol. 22, no. 2 (July), pp. 123–38.

Gureyev, P. P. and Segudin, P. I. (1977) *Legislation in the USSR* (Moscow: Progress).

Halpern, Joel and Kerewsky Halpern, Barbara (1982) *A Serbian Village in Historical Perspective*, new ed. (New York: Irvington Publishers).

Hammond, Thomas T. (ed.) (1975) *The Anatomy of Communist Takeovers* (New Haven, Conn.: Yale University Press).

Hann, C. M. (1980) *Tázlár: A Village in Hungary* (Cambridge: Cambridge University Press).

Hann, C. M. (1985) *A Village without Solidarity* (New Haven, Conn.: Yale University Press).

Harasymiw, Bohdan (1969) '*Nomenklatura*: the Soviet Communist Party's Leadership Recruitment System', *Canadian Journal of Political Science*, vol. 2, no. 4 (December), pp. 493–512.

Harasymiw, Bohdan (1984) *Political Elite Recruitment in the Soviet Union* (London: Macmillan).

Harding, Harry (1981) *Organising China: the Problem of Bureaucracy, 1949–1976* (Stanford, Calif.: Stanford University Press).

Harding, Neil (1977, 1981) *Lenin's Political Thought*, 2 vols (London: Macmillan).

Harding, Neil (ed.) (1984) *The State in Socialist Society* (London: Macmillan).

Havel, Vaclav *et al.* (1985) *Power of the Powerless* (London: Hutchinson).

Hawkins, John (1974) *Mao Tse-Tung and Education* (Hamden, Conn. Shoe String).

Hayhoe, Ruth (ed.) (1984) *Contemporary Chinese Education.* (London: Croom Helm).

Heinrich, Hans-Georg (1986) *Hungary: Politics, Economics and Society* (London: Pinter)

Held, Joseph (ed.) (1980) *The Modernization of Agriculture: Rural Transformation in Hungary, 1848–1975* (New York: Columbia University Press).

Henkin, Louis *et al.* (1986) *Human Rights in Contemporary China* (New York: Columbia University Press).

Hill, Ronald J. (1980) *Soviet Politics, Political Science and Reform* (Oxford: Martin Robertson).

Hill, Ronald J. and Frank, Peter (1986) *The Soviet Communist Party*, 3rd ed. (London: Allen & Unwin).

Hirsowicz, Maria (1986) *Coercion and Control in Communist Societies* (Brighton: Harvester).

Holmes, Leslie T. (ed.) (1981a) *The Withering Away of the State?* (London: Sage).

Holmes, Leslie T. (1981b) *The Policy Process in Communist States* (London: Sage).

Holmes, Leslie T. (1986) *Politics in the Communist World* (Oxford: Oxford University Press).

Hosking, Geoffrey (1985) *A History of the Soviet Union* (London: Fontana).

Hough, Jerry F. (1969) *The Soviet Prefects* (Cambridge, Mass.: Harvard University Press).

Hough, Jerry F. (1977) *The Soviet Union and Social Science Theory* (Cambridge, Mass.: Harvard University Press).

Hough, Jerry F. and Fainsod, Merle (1979) *How the Soviet Union is Governed* (Cambridge, Mass.: Harvard University Press).

Humana, Charles (comp.) (1986) *The Economist World Human Rights Guide* (London: Hodder & Stoughton).

Huntington, Samuel P. and Moore, Clement H. (eds) (1970) *Authoritarian Politics in Modern Society* (New York: Basic Books).

Illyés, Gyula (1967) *People of the Puszta* (Budapest: Corvina Press).

Inkeles, Alex and Bauer, Raymond A. (1959) *The Soviet Citizen* (Cambridge, Mass.: Harvard University Press).

Ionescu, Ghiţa (1972) *Comparative Communist Politics* (London: Macmillan).

Jacobs, Everett M. (ed.) (1983) *Soviet Local Politics and Government* (London: Allen & Unwin).

Janos, Andrew (1970) 'Group Politics in Communist Societies: a Second Look at the Pluralistic Model'. In Huntington and Moore (1970), pp. 437–50.

Johnson, Chalmers (ed.) (1970) *Change in Communist Systems* (Stanford, Calif.: Stanford University Press).

Jones, Ellen (1986) *Red Army and Society. A Sociology of the Soviet Military*, paperback ed. (London: Allen & Unwin).

Jowitt, Kenneth (1971) *Revolutionary Breakthroughs and National Development: the Case of Romania, 1944–1965* (Berkeley: University of California Press).

Juviler, Peter H. and Morton, Henry W. (eds) (1967) *Soviet Policy-Making* (London: Pall Mall).

Kanet, Roger (ed.) (1971) *The Behavioral Revolution and Communist Studies* (New York: Free Press).

Karcz, Jerzy (ed.) (1967) *Soviet and East European Agriculture* (Berkeley: University of California Press).

Karklins, Rasma (1986) *Ethnic Relations in the USSR* (London: Allen & Unwin).

Katz, Zev (ed.) (1975) *A Handbook of Major Soviet Nationalities* (New York: Free Press).

Kautsky, John H. (1973) 'Comparative Communism Versus Comparative Politics', *Studies in Comparative Communism*, vol. 6, nos 1–2 (Spring–Summer), pp. 135–70.

Kavanagh, Dennis (1972) *Political Culture* (London: Macmillan).

Kelley, Donald R. (ed.) (1980) *Soviet Politics in the Brezhnev Era* (New York: Praeger).

Khrushchev, N. K. (1971, 1974) *Khrushchev Remembers*, 2 vols (London: Deutsch).

King, Robert R. (1980) *A History of the Romanian Communist Party* (Stanford, Calif.: Hoover Institution Press).

Klein, Donald W. (1970) 'The State Council and the Cultural Revolution', in Lewis (1970), pp. 351–72.

Kohout, Pavel (1972) *From the Diary of a Counter-Revolutionary* (New York: McGraw-Hill).

Kolakowski, Lezlek (1978) *Main Currents of Marxism*, 3 vols (Oxford: Oxford University Press).

Kolakowski, Lezlek and Hampshire, Stuart (eds) (1974) *The Socialist Idea* (London: Weidenfeld & Nicolson).

Kovrig, Bennet (1979) *Communism in Hungary* (Stanford, Calif.: Hoover Institution Press).

Krejci, Jaroslav (1976) *Social Structure in Divided Germany* (London: Croom Helm).

Krutoglov, M. A. (1980) *Talks on Soviet Democracy* (Moscow: Progress).

Kusin, Vladimir V. (1978) *From Dubček to Charter 77* (Edinburgh: Q Press).

Laird, Roy *et al.* (eds) (1977) *The Future of Agriculture in the Soviet Union and Eastern Europe* (Boulder, Col.: Westview).

Lane, David (1981) *Leninism: A Sociological Interpretation* (Cambridge: Cambridge University Press).

Lane, David (1982) *The End of Social Inequality? Class, Status and Power under State Socialism* (London: Allen & Unwin).

Lane, David (1984) 'Human Rights under State Socialism', *Political Studies*, vol. 32, no. 3 (September), pp. 349–68.

Lane, David (1985) *Soviet Economy and Society* (Oxford: Blackwell).

Lane, David and Kolankiewicz, George (eds) (1973) *Social Groups in Polish Society* (London: Macmillan).

Lane, David and O'Dell, Felicity (1978) *The Soviet Industrial Worker* (Oxford: Martin Robertson).

Lapidus, Gail W. (1984) 'Ethnonationalism and Political Stability: the Soviet Case', *World Politics*, vol. 36, no. 4 (July), pp. 555–80.

Leichter, Howard M. (1979) *A Comparative Approach to Policy Analysis: Health Care in Four Nations* (New York: Cambridge University Press).

Lendvai, Paul (1981) *The Bureaucracy of Truth: How Communist Governments Manage the News* (London: Burnett Books).

Leng, Shao-chuan (1981) 'Criminal Justice in Post-Mao China', *China Quarterly*, no. 87 (September), pp. 440–69.

Leslie, R. F. *et al.* (1980) *A History of Poland since 1863* (Cambridge: Cambridge University Press).

Lewin, Moshe (1975) *Political Undercurrents in Soviet Economic Debates* (London: Pluto).

Lewis, John W. (ed.) (1970) *Party Leadership and Revolutionary Power in China* (London: Cambridge University Press).

Lewis, John W. (ed.) (1971) *The City in Communist China* (Stanford, Calif.: Stanford University Press).

Lewis, Paul G. (1973) 'The Peasantry'. In Lane and Kolankiewicz (1973), pp. 29–87.

Lewis, Paul G. (1979) 'Potential Sources of Opposition in the East European Peasantry'. In Tőkés (1979), pp. 263–91.

Li, Victor (1970) 'The Role of Law in Contemporary China', *China Quarterly*, no. 44 (October–December), pp. 66–111.

Lindblom, Charles E. (1977) *Politics and Markets* (New York: Basic Books).

Lipski, Jan J. (1985) *KOR: Workers' Defense Committee in Poland, 1976–81* (Berkeley: University of California Press).

Liu, Alan P. (1976) *Political Culture and Group Conflict in Communist China* (Santa Barbara, Calif.: Clio Books).

Lively, Jack (1975) *Democracy* (Oxford: Blackwell).

Löwenhardt, John (1982) *The Soviet Politburo* (Edinburgh: Canongate).

Lowit, Thomas (1979) 'Y a-t-il des états en Europe de l'Est?', *Revue Française de Sociologie*, vol. 20, no. 2 (June), pp. 431–66.

McCauley, Martin (ed.) (1977) *Communist Power in Europe, 1944–49* (London: Macmillan).

McCauley, Martin (ed.) (1979) *Marxism–Leninism in the GDR* (London: Macmillan).

McCauley, Martin and Carter, Stephen (eds) (1986) *Leadership and Succession in the Soviet Union, Eastern Europe and China.* (London: Macmillan).

Macfarlane, L. J. (1985) *The Theory and Practice of Human Rights* (London: Gower).

MacFarquhar, Roderick (1960) *The Hundred Flowers* (London: Stevens).

MacFarquhar, Roderick (1974) *The Origins of the Cultural Revolution* (London: Oxford University Press).

McLellan, David (1979) *Marxism after Marx* (London: Macmillan).

McLellan, David (ed.) (1983) *Marx: The First Hundred Years* (Glasgow: Collins).

Macpherson, C. B. (1972) *The Real World of Democracy* (New York: Oxford University Press).

Madison, Bernice Q. (1980) *The Meaning of Social Policy* (London: Croom Helm).

Manion, Melanie (1985) 'The Cadre Management System, Post-Mao: the Appointment, Promotion, Transfer and Removal of Party and State Leaders', *China Quarterly*, no. 102 (June), pp. 203–33.

Marer, Paul (1985) *Dollar GNPs of the USSR and Eastern Europe* (Baltimore, Md.: Johns Hopkins University Press).

Mason, David S. (1985) *Public Opinion and Political Change in Poland, 1980–1982* (Cambridge: Cambridge University Press).

Maxwell, Neville and McFarlane, Bruce (eds) (1984) *China's Changed Road to Development* (Oxford: Pergamon).

Meyer, Alfred G. (1957) *Leninism* (Cambridge, Mass.: Harvard University Press).

Meyer, Alfred G. (1961) 'USSR, Incorporated', *Slavic Review*, vol. 20, no. 3 (October), pp. 369–76.

Meyer, Alfred G. (1965) *The Soviet Political System: An Interpretation* (New York: Random House).

Mićunović, Veljko (1980) *Moscow Diary* (London: Chatto & Windus).

Miliband, Ralph (1977) *Marxism and Politics* (Oxford: Oxford University Press).

Minority Rights Group (1984) *Religious Minorities in the Soviet Union*, 4th ed. (London: Minority Rights Group).

Mlynář, Zdeněk (1980) *Night Frost in Prague* (London: Hurst).

Moody, Peter R. (1977) *Opposition and Dissent in Contemporary China* (Stanford, Calif.: Hoover Institution Press).

Morrisson, Christian (1984) 'Income Distribution in East European and Western Countries', *Journal of Comparative Economics*, vol. 8, no. 2 (June), pp. 121–38.

Narkiewicz, Olga (1976) *The Green Flag: Polish Populist Politics 1867–1970* (London: Croom Helm).

Narkiewicz, Olga (1981) *Marxism and the Reality of Power* (London: Croom Helm).

Nathan, Andrew (1986) *Chinese Democracy* (London: I. B. Tauris).

Nelson, Daniel N. (1977) 'Socioeconomic and Political Change in Communist Europe', *International Studies Quarterly*, vol. 21, no. 2 (June), pp. 359–88.

Nelson, Daniel N. (1978) 'Political Convergence: an Empirical Assessment', *World Politics*, vol. 30, no. 3 (April), pp. 411–32.

Nelson, Daniel N. and White, Stephen (eds) (1982) *Communist Legislatures in Comparative Perspective* (London: Macmillan and New York: SUNY at Albany Press).

Nove, Alec (1975) 'Is there a Ruling Class in the USSR?', *Soviet Studies*, vol. 27, no. 4 (October), pp. 615–38.

Nove, Alec (1982) *The Economics of Feasible Socialism* (London: Allen & Unwin).

Nove, Alec (1983) 'The Class Nature of the Soviet Union Revisited', *Soviet Studies*, vol. 35, no. 3 (July), pp. 298–312.

Nove, Alec (1986) *The Soviet Economic System*, 3rd ed. (London: Allen & Unwin).

Nuti, Domenico Mario (1979) 'The Contradictions of Socialist Economies: a Marxian Interpretation', *The Socialist Register 1979* (London: Merlin Press), pp. 228–73.

Odom, William (1976) 'A Dissenting View on the Group Approach to Soviet Politics', *World Politics*, vol. 28, no. 4 (July), pp. 542–67.

Oksenberg, Michel (1982) 'Economic Policy-making in China', *The China Quarterly*, no. 90 (June), pp. 165–94.

Oren, Nissan (1973) *Revolution Administered: Agrarianism and Communism in Bulgaria* (Baltimore, Md.: Johns Hopkins University Press).

Ostoja-Ostaszewski, A. *et al.* (1977) *Dissent in Poland* (London: Association of Polish Students and Graduates in Exile).

Parkin, Frank (1971) *Class Inequality and Political Order* (New York: Praeger).

Pavlowitch, Stefan (1971) *Yugoslavia* (London: Benn).

Pennock, J. Roland (1979) *Democratic Political Theory* (Princeton, NJ: Princeton University Press).

Pravda, Alex (1986) 'Elections in Communist Party States'. In White and Nelson (1986), pp. 27–54.

Price, R. F. (1975) *Education in Communist China* (London: Routledge).

Prifti, Peter (1978) *Socialist Albania since 1944* (Cambridge, Mass.: MIT Press).

Prybyla, Jan (1986) 'China's Economic Experiment: from Mao to Market', *Problems of Communism*, vol. 35, no. 1 (January–February), pp. 21–38.

Pryor, Frederick L. (1968) *Public Expenditures in Communist and Capitalist Nations* (London: Allen & Unwin).

Pye, Lucian and Verba, Sydney (eds) (1965) *Political Culture and Political Development* (Princeton, NJ: Princeton University Press).

Racz, Barnabas (1987) 'Political Participation and Developed Socialism: the Hungarian Elections of 1985', *Soviet Studies*, vol. 39, no. 1 (January), pp. 40–62.

Rakowska-Harmstone, Teresa (ed.) (1984) *Communism in Eastern Europe,* 2nd ed. (Bloomington: Indiana University Press).

Ramet, Pedro (1984) *Nationalism and Federalism in Yugoslavia, 1963–1983* (Bloomington: Indiana University Press).

Ramet, Pedro (ed.) (1984) *Religion and Nationalism in Soviet and East European Politics* (Durham, NC: Duke University Press).

Reddaway, Peter (1983) 'Dissent in the USSR', *Problems of Communism,* vol. 32, no. 6 (November–December), pp. 1–15.

Riese, Peter (ed.) (1979) *Since the Prague Spring* (New York: Random House).

Rigby, T. H. (1968) *Communist Party Membership in the USSR, 1917–1967* (Princeton, NJ: Princeton University Press).

Rigby, T. H. (1976) 'Soviet Communist Party Membership Under Brezhnev', *Soviet Studies,* vol. 28, no. 3 (July), pp. 317–37.

Rigby, T. H. *et al.* (eds) (1980) *Authority, Power and Policy in the USSR. Essays dedicated to Leonard Schapiro* (London: Macmillan).

Robinson, Gertrude J. (1977) *Tito's Maverick Media: the Politics of Mass Communication in Yugoslavia* (Urbana: University of Illinois Press).

Robinson, W. F. (1973) *The Pattern of Reform in Hungary* (New York: Praeger).

Rosen, Stanley (1985) 'Prosperity, Privatization and China's Youth', *Problems of Communism,* vol. 34, no. 2 (March–April), pp. 1–28.

Rosenbaum, Walter A. (1975) *Political Culture* (London: Nelson).

Rothschild, Joseph (1974) *East Central Europe between the Two World Wars* (Seattle and London: University of Washington Press).

Ruane, Kevin (1982) *The Polish Challenge* (London: British Broadcasting Corporation).

Ruble, Blair A. (1981) *Soviet Trade Unions: Their Development in the 1970s* (Cambridge: Cambridge University Press).

Rusinow, Dennison (1977) *The Yugoslav Experiment, 1948–1974* (London: Hurst).

Rutland, Peter (1985) *The Cult of the Plan* (London: Hutchinson).

Saich, Tony (1984) 'Party-building Since Mao: a Question of Style?' In Maxwell and McFarlane (1984), pp. 149–67.

Salzman, Zdenek and Scheufler, Vladimir (1974) *Komárov: a Czech Farming Village* (New York: Rinehart and Winston).

Sartori, Giovanni (1986) *Theories of Democracy Revisited,* 2 vols (Chatham, NJ: Chatham House).

Schapiro, Leonard B. (1970) *The Communist Party of the Soviet Union,* 2nd ed. (London: Eyre & Spottiswoode).

Schapiro, Leonard B. (1972) *Totalitarianism* (London: Pall Mall).

Schapiro, Leonard and Godson, Joseph (eds) *The Soviet Worker: From Lenin to Andropov,* 2nd ed. (London: Macmillan).

Schell, Orville (1986) *To Get Rich is Glorious* (New York: Mentor).

Schöpflin, George (1983) *Censorship and Political Communication in Eastern Europe* (London: Pinter and New York: St Martin's).

Schöpflin, George (ed.) (1986) *The Soviet Union and Eastern Europe: A Handbook* (New York: Facts on File).

Schram, Stuart R. (1969) *The Political Thought of Mao Tse-Tung* (New York: Praeger).

Schram, Stuart R. (1970) *Mao Tse-Tung* (Harmondsworth: Penguin Books).

Schram, Stuart R. (ed.) (1973) *Authority, Participation and Cultural Change in China* (London: Cambridge University Press).

Schram, Stuart R. (ed.) (1974) *Mao Tse-Tung Unrehearsed* (Harmondsworth: Penguin Books).

Schram, Stuart R. (1981) 'To Utopia and Back: a Cycle in the History of the Chinese Communist Party', *China Quarterly*, no. 87 (September), pp. 407–39.

Schram, Stuart R. (1984) *Ideology and Policy in China since the Third Plenum, 1978–84* (London: School of Oriental and African Studies).

Shulz, Donald E. and Adams, Jan S. (eds) (1981) *Political Participation in Communist Systems* (New York: Pergamon).

Schurmann, Franz (1968) *Ideology and Organization in Communist China*, 2nd ed. (Berkeley: University of California Press).

Selucky, Radoslav (1979) *Marxism, Socialism, Freedom* (London: Macmillan).

Seton-Watson, Hugh (1960) *The Pattern of Communist Revolution*, rev. ed. (London: Methuen).

Seton-Watson, Hugh (1980) *The Imperialist Revolutionaries: World Communism in the 1960s and 1970s*, rev. ed. (London: Hutchinson).

Seton-Watson, Hugh (1985) *The East European Revolution*, rev. ed. (Boulder, Col.: Westview).

Seton-Watson, Hugh (1986) *Eastern Europe between the Wars, 1918–1941*, new ed. (Boulder, Col.: Westview).

Seymour, James D. (1980) *The Fifth Modernization* (New York: E. M. Coleman).

Shafir, Michael (1985) *Romania: Politics, Economics and Society* (London: Pinter).

Sharlet, Robert (1978) *The New Soviet Constitution of 1977* (Brunswick, Ohio: King's Court).

Shatz, Marshall S. (1981) *Soviet Dissent in Historical Perspective* (Cambridge: Cambridge University Press).

Sher, Gerson (1977) *Praxis: Marxist Criticism and Dissent in Socialist Yugoslavia* (Bloomington: Indiana University Press).

Shoup, Paul S. (comp.) (1981) *The Eastern European and Soviet Data Handbook: Political, Social and Developmental Indicators, 1945–1975* (New York: Columbia University Press).

Simes, Dmitri K. (1975) 'The Soviet Invasion of Czechoslovakia and the Limits of Kremlinology', *Studies in Comparative Communism*, vol. 8, nos 1–2 (Spring–Summer), pp. 174–80.

Simons, William B. (ed.) (1980a) *The Constitutions of the Communist World* (Alphen aan den Rijn: Sijthoff and Noordhoff).

Simons, William B. (ed.) (1980b) *The Soviet Codes of Law* (Alphen aan den Rijn: Sijthoff and Noordhoff).

Simons, William B. and White, Stephen (eds) (1984) *The Party Statutes of the Communist World* (The Hague: Martinus Nijhoff).

Singleton, Fred (1976) *Twentieth Century Yugoslavia* (London: Macmillan).

Skilling, H. Gordon (1966) 'Interest Groups and Communist Politics', *World Politics*, vol. 18, no. 3 (April), pp. 435–51.

Skilling, H. Gordon (1973) 'Opposition in Communist East Europe'. In Dahl (1973), pp. 89–120.

Skilling, H. Gordon (1976) *Czechoslovakia's Interrupted Revolution* (Princeton, NJ: Princeton University Press).

Skilling, H. Gordon (1983) 'Interest Groups and Communist Politics Revisited', *World Politics*, vol. 36, no. 1 (October), pp. 1–27.

Skilling, H. Gordon and Griffiths, Franklyn (eds) (1971) *Interest Groups in Soviet Politics* (Princeton, NJ: Princeton University Press).

Smith, Gordon B. (ed.) (1980) *Public Policy and Administration in the Soviet Union* (New York: Praeger).

Solomon, Richard H. (1971) *Mao's Revolution and the Chinese Political Culture* (Berkeley: University of California Press).

Solomon, Susan G. (ed.) (1983) *Pluralism in the Soviet Union. Essays in Honour of H. Gordon Skilling* (London: Macmillan).

Staniszkis, Jadwiga (1984) *Poland's Self-Limiting Revolution* (Princeton, NJ: Princeton University Press).

Starr, John B. (1979) *Continuing the Revolution: the Political Thought of Mao Tse-Tung* (Princeton, NJ: Princeton University Press).

Suda, Zdenek L. (1980) *Zealots and Rebels: A History of the Communist Party of Czechoslovakia* (Stanford, Calif.: Hoover Institution Press).

Summers, Robert and Heston, Alan (1984) 'Improved International Comparisons of Real Product and its Composition, 1950–1980', *Review of Income and Wealth*, vol. 30, no. 2 (June), pp. 207–62.

Swain, Geoffrey (1985) *Collective Farms which Work?* (Cambridge: Cambridge University Press).

Szajkowski, Bogdan (ed.) (1981) *Marxist Governments: A World Survey*, 3 vols (London: Macmillan).

Szajkowski, Bogdan (1982) *The Evolution of Communist Regimes*. London: Butterworths.

Szajkowski, Bogdan (ed.) (1985ff) *Marxist Regimes*, 36 vols (London: Pinter).

Szymanski, Albert (1984) *Human Rights in the Soviet Union* (London: Zed Press).

Tarschys, Daniel (1977) 'The Soviet Political System: Three Models', *European Journal of Political Research*, vol. 5, no. 3 (September), pp. 287–320.

Taylor, Robert (1981) *China's Intellectual Dilemma: the Politics of University Enrolment* (Vancouver: University of British Columbia Press).

Teiwes, Frederick C. (1979) *Politics and Purges in China: Rectification and the Decline of Party Norms, 1950–1965* (White Plains, NY: M. E. Sharpe).

Tőkés, Rudolf L. (ed.) (1975) *Dissent in the USSR* (Baltimore, Md.: Johns Hopkins University Press).

Tőkés, Rudolf L. (ed.) (1978) *Eurocommunism and Detente* (New York University Press).

Tőkés, Rudolf L. (ed.) (1979) *Opposition in Eastern Europe* (London: Macmillan).

Toma, Peter and Volgyes, Ivan (1977) *Politics in Hungary* (San Francisco: W. H. Freeman).

Tucker, Robert C. (ed.) (1977) *Stalinism* (New York: Norton).

Ulč, Otto (1974) *Politics in Czechoslovakia* (San Francisco: W. H. Freeman).

Unger, Aryeh L. (1977–78) 'Images of the CPSU', *Survey*, vol. 23, no. 4 (Autumn), pp. 23–34.

Unger, Aryeh L. (1981a) *Constitutional Development in the USSR* (London: Methuen).

Unger, Aryeh L. (1981b) 'Political Participation in the USSR: YCL and CPSU', *Soviet Studies*, vol. 33, no. 1 (January), pp. 107–24.

US Congress Economic Committee (1982) *USSR: Measures of Economic Growth and Development, 1950–1980* (Washington, DC: US Government Publishing Office).

Vanneman, Peter (1977) *The Supreme Soviet* (Durham, NC: Duke University Press).

Volgyes, Ivan (ed.) (1979) *The Peasantry of Eastern Europe*, 2 vols (New York: Pergamon).

Volgyes, Ivan (1986) *Politics in Eastern Europe* (Homewood, Ill.: Dorsey).

Voslensky, Michael (1984) *Nomenklatura. Anatomy of the Soviet Ruling Class* (London: Bodley Head).

Waller, Michael and Szajkowski, Bogdan (1981) 'The Communist Movement: from Monolith to Polymorph'. In Szajkowski (1981), vol. 1, pp. 1–19.

Watson, James L. (ed.) (1984) *Class and Stratification in Post-Revolutionary China* (Cambridge: Cambridge University Press).

Westoby, Adam (1983) *Communism since World War II* (Brighton: Harvester).

Weydenthal, Jan de (1986) *The Communists of Poland*, rev. ed. (Stanford, Calif.: Hoover Institution Press).

White, Stephen (1978a) 'Communist Systems and the "Iron Law of Pluralism" ', *British Journal of Political Science*, vol. 8, no. 1 (January), pp. 101–17.

White, Stephen (1978b) 'Continuity and Change in Soviet Political Culture: an Emigre Study', *Comparative Political Studies*, vol. 11, no. 3 (October), pp. 381–95.

White, Stephen (1979) *Political Culture and Soviet Politics* (London: Macmillan).

White, Stephen (1982a) 'The USSR Supreme Soviet: a Developmental Perspective'. In Nelson and White (1982), pp. 125–59.

White, Stephen (1982b) 'The Supreme Soviet and Budgetary Politics in the USSR', *British Journal of Political Science*, vol. 12, no. 1 (January), pp. 75–94.

White, Stephen (1983a) 'What is a Communist System?', *Studies in Comparative Communism*, vol. 16, no. 4 (Winter), pp. 247–63.

White, Stephen (1983b) 'Political Communications in the USSR: Letters to Party, State and the Press', *Political Studies*, vol. 31, no. 1 (January), pp. 43–60.

White, Stephen (1985) 'Propagating Communist Values in the USSR', *Problems of Communism*, vol. 34, no. 6 (November–December), pp. 1–17.

White, Stephen and Nelson, Daniel N. (eds) (1986) *Communist Politics: A Reader* (London: Macmillan and New York: New York University Press).

White, Stephen and Pravda, Alex (eds) (1987) *Ideology and Soviet Politics* (London: Macmillan).

Wiles, Peter (1977) *Economic Institutions Compared* (Oxford: Blackwell).

Wiles, Peter (ed.) (1983) *The New Communist Third World* (London: Croom Helm).

Wiles, Peter and Markowski, Stefan (1971) 'Income Distribution under Communism and Capitalism', *Soviet Studies*, vol. 22, nos 3 and 4 (January and April), pp. 344–69 and 487–511.

Woods, Roger (1986) *Opposition in the GDR under Honecker* (London: Macmillan).

Yevtushenko, Yevgeny (1963) *A Precocious Autobiography* (London: Collins).

Zaslavsky, Victor and Brym, Robert J. (1978) 'The Functions of Elections in the USSR', *Soviet Studies*, vol. 30, no. 3 (July), pp. 362–71.

Zukin, Sharon (1975) *Beyond Marx and Tito* (New York: Cambridge University Press).

Index